Seeds from the Wild Verge

Myth, Nature, and Theology
in the Border Stream of Celtic Wisdom

Brendan Ellis Williams

ISBN: 978-1-951029-14-2

Printed in the United States of America.

Published by Ancient Oak Ritual Arts, in collaboration with Wandering Words Media, Colorado Springs, Colorado, USA

Cover Design by 100Covers.com
Interior Design by FormattedBooks.com

For the Ancestors.

Better far than praise of men
'tis to sit with book and pen…
—*Anonymous, ninth-century Irish*

No ancient lore has perished.
Earth retains for herself and her children
what her children might in passion have destroyed,
and it is still in the realm of the Ever Living
to be seen by the mystic adventurer.
—*A.E., George William Russell*

Contents

Acknowledgements

S pecial thanks to the wonderful folks at Wandering Words Media, for all their guidance in bringing this work to fruition. To Patrick Dobbins for being willing to accompany me on the spiritual and intellective journey that helped form the book's Epilogue; to Sharon Paice MacLeod, an excellent dialogue partner in all things Celtic; and to Kyra O'Keeffe, who gave such helpful feedback as this project was taking shape.

Many heartfelt thanks to Charles Garcia, Matthew Wood, and Seán Pádraig Donahue, who have taught me a great deal about what it means to be a healer and a seer. To Brenda Hillman, Michael Palmer, and Graham Foust, who have taught me a great deal about what it means to be a poet. To Louis Weil, Carol Neel, and Marc Andrus, who have taught me a great deal about what it means to be a scholar, a teacher, and a theologian.

To all my students, and to everyone who has been open, gracious, and courageous enough to entrust to me their education, spiritual care, and formation. There is no other confidence I hold more sacred.

And my deepest gratitude to Adam Kinghorn, David Pearl, Emily Cowan, Justin Cannon, Tonja Reichley, Robin Landers, Kathleen Dragoon, Jack Stull, Nils Hansen, India Wise, Rose Marie Johnson, Colleen Cahill, Eckhart Camden, Miriam-Matta Ghaly, Aidan Schutz, Bill Page, Michael Flynn, Benn Mac Stiofán, Jeremiah Williamson, and all the other dear friends and soul companions—in this life and beyond—who have been truly present with me along the journey, who have supported, encouraged, and believed in me and my vocation, who have lovingly listened and spoken into the development of many of the concepts and insights expressed in this book. 'There is nothing on this earth more to be prized than true friendship.' —*Thomas Aquinas*

Ancestral Streams

I n the dark, enclosing mantle of this storm (too broad in berth of its longing) are questions no narrative, ritual, or custom we presently carry could begin to answer. Stories we once knew for navigation now lost to us, we stumble on in the desert dark, obscured from ourselves, our longings and mistakes. In the strange, formless night, the unanswerable roam like hungry ghosts.

I want to know what haunts you most. I want to know the end of all your cold, inherited aims, your unconsidered prayers, your greatest wagers of imagined worth—: the ones with no root, no ground in Nature's bright, arresting immanence, so long disconnected from the great communion.

In subterrane of our beleaguered dreaming, I want to know once more the primal words—and speak them. I want to know the advent and the end of language. And this—yes, most importantly this—that we are betrayed of our own accord: victims under sword of our confusion, of the madness of our nearest forebears, who sold us, soul and body, into cruel ignominy, down stream on the treacherous currents of religious and material enslavement.

Old Ones: Help us to learn the depth of our sickness, and to speak it. This stark severity can no longer be drowned. Your tongues, still recalling the truths of a living Land, before the time of our severance, are quickly dimming in the Western seas.

A ghostly and courageous injunction, somewhere caught amid yellowing leaves, both appears and disappears: *Light the tall, proud fires of remem-*

bering. Tell these songs from ear to ear, blood to blood, eye to eye—quietly or fiercely, as you wish, but weave again the elder threads—for this storm will leave no forest unfelled, and the season left for grasping now is thin.

To find the work that is truly ours—to find our home once more in firelight, in leaf and loam, in breath and sinew, in river, fern, antler, and bone, in story and song, hymn and prayer of our ancient grandmothers, who yet embrace us, in spite of our apostasy—: this is for us the heart of all possible hopes.

The stories now await our recollection: bodies to re-limb. May those fragile gifts, like ceaseless streams—like Fintan in the cave of primordial waters, womb-bound and shielded, transformed and birthed again—be reborn to us now, and endure through every age, through every time and every world—: all radiance; all pregnant question; all trial and returning dawn; all becoming; all spirit; all gift.

Subversive Orienteering: Map-Talking the Mapless and the Map-Resistant

Wading the border stream, one walks the pregnant waters of liminality, and thus is bound to cross landscapes foreign, strange, oracular, and visionary—: wayfarer on the dynamic, flashing threadways of an *aisling*.[1] This book, as a product of such navigations, will no doubt seem to most an unusual creation—in part because it deliberately defies formal convention, seeking to dissolve long-established cultural and religious boundaries normally maintained as sacrosanct, to dig a fresh soil-bed for new and ancient seedlings: to nourish the root of a sacred tree that has long lain dormant in the pillaged field of so-called Western civilization. Likewise, because the telling of such a walkabout demands the eschewing of expected boundaries in style and genre.

This is a work for which the defiance of formal convention seems indispensable. Given its aims, I suppose it couldn't be otherwise. It is, at one level, a hybrid collection of lyric essays, articles, and meditations, each standing on its own, related to but certainly not dependent on the others. Taken as a whole, the book is part cultural and theological manifesto, part love poem

---

[1] In Gaelic tradition, a 'dream-vision' or poetically rendered sojourn into other worlds or dreamscapes of non-ordinary perception.

to Nature, part communal reform theory, part native Gaelic wisdom, part rewilding, part academia, and part esoterica—part Earth, part Sky, and part Sea. Ultimately, this is a project of wildcrafting for deep spiritual medicines beyond the vale (and the veil), in the dark-webbed misty thicket of forgotten memories: memories of our natural and ancestral origins.

I've come to think of these essays as small pieces of a larger poetic map— one that precludes linear travel: a patchwork quilt of reflective objects, landscapes, and tales simultaneously within and outside of ordinary time. In some ways they are also protest: an ancestral hand-grenade in the machinery of the socio-cultural nightmare we're all presently trapped in: my response to the violent and horrific world that reductionistic materialism, Christian fundamentalism, and other misguided ideologies of the modern West have molded; a critical and poetic sword aimed at the heart of dominator culture.

If nothing else, dear reader, consider this satchel of textual objects an introduction and a prayer: a vessel of sharing for this particular moment in the journey, a collection of kaleidoscopic refractions on one possible vision for a more whole and connected future.

The ossified and institutionalized habits of the male dominator culture of materialism, egoism, and reductionistic rationalism that surrounds and too often constitutes us—socio-politically, academically, and religiously—are inextricably tied to the degenerate ideational and mythic structures that produced them. Those cultural habits, along with the institutions that have enshrined and preserved them, and the life-negating narratives that have long been used to justify them, must be systematically undermined, subverted, defied. Our most pressing task now in the West as I see it is to creatively and unapologetically replace these dominant ideological systems and their associated behaviors not merely with alternative ideas, but with those elements of the human experience that possess real power to unravel the oppressive stranglehold dominator values and agendas presently have on us: real power to enrich and deepen our souls, to transform our hearts and our communities.

The wild, the poetic, the mythic, the multivalently symbolic: these are the tools to which we are now called to return, and they constitute, in essence, all that which is authentically spiritual and truly religious. Devoid of these, we are incapable of glimpsing—let alone entering into conscious relationship and alignment with—the Ground of Being and Her *telos*.

My friend Seán Donahue once said, 'The literal is one of many colonizing narratives that's been enforced upon the world.' In my thinking, 'the literal' here implies the reductionistic, the mechanistic, the rationally and textually obsessed, the anti-mythic, and the anti-poetic. These are merely different angles on one monstrous, dehumanizing, and fundamentalist worldview—one which is sadly pervasive, and touches nearly all dimensions of Western life.

A somewhat less accessible—and, for some, undoubtedly less palatable—notion I wish to convey is that anything born from the aforementioned worldview cannot be utilized to successfully dismantle it. In my opinion, the failure to grasp this is one of the chief failings of the discipline of critical theory. This failure is due to the fact that most of academia has continued to play the same games within the same arena that the dominator culture has established, while ironically decrying both structure and method. Given this, even if the process of disassembly were satisfactorily accomplished, it would leave nothing of value in place of the former structures.

How might these subtle pitfalls be overcome? My intuition says strongly that the answer lies, firstly, in the realm of the mythic. For that reason I have leaned heavily throughout this work on the ancient pillars of myth and folktale, which I feel speak powerfully in different ways to our current cultural state by inviting us into an archaic mode of awareness—by inviting us to step into mythic time. I have tried to avoid overt exegesis of any such narrative, principally because I am wary of treading disruptively on the wild, sacred ground of myth and folk story by subjecting it to rational analysis—one of the chief modern and postmodern instincts that must be shed if we wish to return to the mythic landscape that can heal our hearts, souls, and minds. I am also resistant to imposing too much of my own interpretive lens on something so ancient, which is more than capable of speaking powerfully for itself. Ancient tales of this kind are, as Martin Shaw has wisely pointed out, containers for great psychic potency, each of which holds some portion of 'the soul-story of the tribe.' And that is 'too much weight for anyone's shoulders.'[2]

The needful process of cultural-religious deconstruction requires, in my view, the balm of 're-humation', of return to an adequately deep, properly framed, and reciprocal relationship with the living Earth, and with the whole of Nature. This cultural healing balm, which could be summarized as a return to an animistic worldview, to animistic myth, ritual, and lifeways, could also be approached as a kind of 're-membrance': a reuniting of the severed members of the body. This means not only the re-enfranchising of non-human life on the Earth, but also of our own bodies, souls, and psyches; it means reclamation, rewilding, and restoration to that which is truly and foundationally human, beautiful, untamed by false constructs, dynamic, and life giving. The mythic is, it seems to me, the primary ground on which both deconstruction and reclamation must take place. Such work must be, above all, about reclaiming our indigenous soul, along with its attendant qualities, skills, and wisdoms. Any critical methodology still functioning solely within the bounds of rationalistic rhetorical systems and devices is therefore at some level inherently antithetical to the most needful work at hand.

The stalking devil of anthropocentrism prowls in the darkened hallways of our collective psychic landscape, a child of our disastrous love affair in the Western world with excessive ego and domination, and the foreign mythic narratives that have encouraged and reinforced them. Every crevice of our collective and individual endeavors is haunted by this demonic shadow—even the endeavors intended to be 'spiritual' and to free us from the confines of our sweltering and life-negating prison. We must, as it were, be always on the watch for that roaming lion.

---

2   Martin Shaw, *Snowy Tower: Parzival and the Wet, Black Branch of Language* (Ashland, OR: White Cloud Press, 2014), xvii.

Audre Lorde once asked of an audience of academics: 'What does it mean when the tools of a racist patriarchy are used to examine the fruits of that same patriarchy? It means that only the most narrow perimeters of change are possible and allowable....For the master's tools will never dismantle the master's house. They may allow us temporarily to beat him at his own game, but they will never enable us to bring about genuine change.'[3] This sentiment, of course, applies not only to racist patriarchy, but equally to the horrific ecological injustices of our time, to the cancers of religious and scientistic fundamentalism, and to any other element of the dominator culture that holds us in its oppressive, dehumanizing talons. These things demand to be overturned for the sake of Beauty, for the sake of Life. And such work will require a different sort of focus than the modes we are accustomed to: an untamed nuance grounded in soul and soil, a deep inner rootedness, a mythic reformation and reclamation, a gradual but totalizing and sustainable rewiring of cultural consciousness.

If we follow the lead line of that invitation, we will find ourselves eventually in the deep, dark underworld of mythopoetic awareness, in the place where Cerridwen waits with her cauldron to enlist us in the agonizing, ego-shattering work of spiritual initiation, and in the chthonic excavation of our foolishly cast-off ancestral inheritance.

On an intellectual level, and particularly with regard to the literary, we can begin by intelligently problematizing and actively undermining those structures of dehumanization that colonize the indigenous soul. I hope the present work reflects one considered approach to that task, and inspires some further expressions of it. Such an undertaking requires that methodological normativity, as understood within the safe, domesticated, and sanctioned paradigm of the present dominator culture, is eschewed as no longer useful—or perhaps outright corrosive. This applies to form as well as content.

---

[3]   Audre Lorde, 'The Master's Tools Will Never Dismantle the Master's House', in *Feminist Postcolonial Theory: A Reader*, Ed. Reina Lewis and Sara Mills (New York: Routledge, 2003), 25, 27.

One of the things implied in this process is an active resistance to what in literary theory is referred to as 'formal closure'—and, by extension, the cultivation of liberatory breath in form; in other words, an active courting of the poetic. There is thus a bit of cultivated parataxis afoot here. A bit of the pregnant anarchy of the wild, mythic wood.

All critical devices will inevitably echo, to one degree or another, the methodologies of the established intellectual style and culture that birthed them: provisionally useful, perhaps, but like the proverbial raft of Buddhist folk tradition, to be left behind on the other shore. Ultimately, we must turn to and learn to embody an entirely different set of tools for our collective atonement: mythic and folkloric tools, metaphoric and poetic tools, archaic and animistic tools, which cannot be contained or even fully grasped by the normative frameworks of rationalist intellection.

These threads of what we might broadly call 'indigenous thinking' are like lights in the deep Earth: signs of our truest hope, calling out to us from a long rejected past. They reflect a state of being in archaic time when, to quote again from Martin Shaw, 'our innate capacity to consume—lovers, forests, oceans, animals, ideas—was drawn into the immense thinking of the Earth itself, what Aboriginal teachers call Wild Land Dreaming.'[4] To dream once more with the Land is indeed among the most needful of redemptive possibilities that now lie before us. And we should mark here the crucial difference between dreaming *of* the Land and dreaming *with* the Land—or allowing her powers to dream in us.

Intertwined with this Wild Land Dreaming is the need to dream again with—and be dreamt *by*—the folkloric wisdom of our archaic Ancestors. These two veins through which our true lifeblood unconsciously flows highlight much of what I mean when I use the word 'indigenous'—a word that has in recent years become popular in certain subcultural circles and a source of contention in others. In the most basic sense, 'indigenous' simply implies something particular to a given cultural group, associated over long

[4]   Martin Shaw, 'Small Gods', in *Dark Mountain, no. 7* (Reydon, Southwold: Dark Mountain Project, 2015), 26.

periods of time with a specific natural landscape. Generally one's indigenous land(s) would be the land(s) where the bones of one's Ancestors have been buried for many generations—regardless of whether one was born on that land or not. For example, I would consider my indigenous lands to be the Celtic nations of Ireland, Scotland, and Wales, though I was born in North America. But 'indigenous' can also be used in a broader and more philosophical sense to indicate a particular kind of worldview, namely, one that understands life and the human person in a deeply relational way, and sees the human experience as interdependent with all other aspects of Nature. The foundation of such a worldview might be described as an holistic (and generally animistic) metaphysic, framed and expressed in intimate, interdependent orientation to localized landscape. Throughout these essays I will use the word 'indigenous' in both senses, though primarily in the former sense, to indicate a cultural element or tradition that has originated in a particular landscape; in this sense I will consider it interchangeable with the term 'native'. Most especially I will use these terms to reference native European traditions, which have been systematically marginalized for centuries in Western societies. Some contemporary thinkers have even attempted to make these very terms, 'indigenous' and 'native', taboo for Westerners to use, purporting that their usage necessarily indicates an appropriation or denigration of living, non-Western indigenous cultures. I not only disagree with this repressed and self-debasing approach, but I see it as a sign of the profound depth of cultural and spiritual sickness that most of us in the Western world have tragically inherited and are now spreading like a pathogen to the rest of the world.

All of us have an indigenous past, an indigenous heart and soul, and are capable of restoration to that way of viewing and being in the world, along with whatever cultural nuances and specificities that way of seeing imply for each individual. For most Westerners, those deep human elements in ourselves, along with the worldview they carry—what I would call our 'indigenous inheritance'—are thoroughly buried under generations of repression, self-hatred, cultural effacement, unprocessed grief, materialism, dehumanizing, de-naturalizing, and life negating ideologies.

The systematic burial of our deepest roots has yielded the kind of cultural climate in which so-called spiritual teachers can confidently assert that the aim of spiritual discipline is to make us 'indifferent to created things', and their hearers in turn imagine such statements to be wise.[5] European-descended people groups (and, increasingly, non-European peoples living in the Western world) have now had so many generations of reinforced world-denying ideologies—derived from Judaeo-Christian text and dogma, from faulty exegesis of the same (especially as expressed in literalism and the historicizing of myth), and/or from Cartesian-Newtonian materialism and its reductionistic legacy—that we've lost even the basic memory that we have an indigenous past at all, let alone an indigenous memory or an indigenous knowing in us. This has meant a veritable gutting of our ancestral inheritances in the West. Combined with Western colonialism, it has put the entire planet in peril and led us down a dark garden path which can only terminate in existential vacancy, dis-ease, ecological disaster, and dissolution.

In my estimation, an indigenously informed way of understanding and dwelling in the world is the only thing that might yet save the vast ship of Western human cultures from going under and taking much of the rest

---

[5]   This particular phrase derives from Ignatius of Loyola's *Spiritual Exercises*. Contemporary theologians have attempted to rationalize such statements by stating that their real meaning lies in what one presumably moves *toward* when moving away from care about created things—namely, God, who loves Creation so that human beings don't have to. This is obviously absurd if one perceives God's love and holiness to be revealed in Creation itself, as an ever unfolding theophany: in the wild Beauty of Nature, from which we are inseparable. Very little reflection is required to notice the kinds of horrific, immoral actions that have been—and continue to be—conveniently justified with such cancerous pseudo-theology, whether consciously or unconsciously. As much as one might wish to explain away the obvious contradiction between the crypto-Gnostic worldview of normative Western Christianity and a legitimately incarnational, Creation-focused worldview, the fact remains that they are mutually exclusive; they simply cannot be reconciled. At the end of the day, our preference and focus must rest with one or the other. This applies not just to Christians and Christian religion, but to Westerners and their worldviews more generally.

of the natural world on this planet with us. The archaic tale of the Fox Woman—the Fox spirit who takes on human form as a beautiful woman and marries a hunter, only to be rejected by him because of the wild scent she gives off in the house—instructs us rather precisely, if we have ears to hear, about the nature of what we've done to ourselves.[6] The Fox pelt of the shapeshifter woman, which once hung inside our psychic and cultural doorway, its wild and Otherworldly scent now long rejected by us, might well be the supernal mythic symbol of our possible redemption. Our *possible*—and certainly not given—redemption. The choice is ours to make. We are, to be sure, until a time of real restoration when we welcome the Fox Woman back into our collective and individual houses, a people broken and bereft.

I have strived to allow the wild, Earth-centered, and mythopoetic agenda of this work—which is the central thrust of my vocation: the archaic, animistic work of poesy, Otherworld dreaming, healing, and storytelling—to shine through and dissolve the edges of some of the more didactic elements. I hope this effort has succeeded; it is, and probably always will be, an ongoing dance. Still, some portion of the critical and didactic seems needful, partly in concession to the demands of the rational mind, but moreover to lay bare the objects of my deconstructive efforts in a state of disassemblage—and hopefully to articulate a bit more clearly the permeable rails of a new road, to suggest some tangible tools for the new and ancient work at hand. I ask the patience of the reader wherever the latter approach seemed to demand being elevated to prominence.

Since the essays and articles brought together in this work were each written as independent documents addressing—often to different audiences—a set of common themes within a defined window of time, it is perhaps inevitable that, when brought together in collection, they will contain some instances of overlap in reference, and occasionally in explication. In the final analysis, maintaining the original shape and integrity of each piece seemed

---

[6]   cf. *Chapter 2: Fox Spirit Woman and the Sterile Scent of Alienation*

to me the best approach. While I have attempted to avoid any overt repetition, I again ask the forbearance of the reader with regard to this matter, and humbly invoke a recollection of the formal conceits of the work and their intended purpose, as well as an approach in the reading which affords each document the freedom to stand on its own as a distinct object of transmission and reflection.

In selecting these documents, I have intentionally sought to present what might seem an eclectic admixture of styles: scholastic, poetic, mythic, and aphoristic, to name a few. As I understand it, such an admixture is at least broadly reflective of the ancient bardic-druidic tradition of my Celtic Ancestors. Perhaps there is something here of the *berla filidh*, the veiled or esoteric language of the bards and poet-seers, intended to convey knowledge that cannot be conveyed in bare rational terms or in ordinary language of any type. Particularly in the realm of metaphysics, poetry and metaphor are the language of necessity. To whatever extent such expression is found to break through here, or anywhere in my work, I attribute its presence not to my own ingenuity, but to the grace and will of the Ancestors.

As Peter O'Connor points out, the ancient Celtic mythic and poetic tradition inherently resists linearity: it resists the Graeco-Roman concept of *logos* as reason, logic, linear structure of thought, rational mentation. This is because the Celtic way of seeing is firmly rooted in the living Land, in the plurality of spirit (i.e., in a richly textured animistic experience of reality), and in the divine feminine, all of which constitute its ultimate source and lifeblood. Another way of expressing this is to say that native Celtic thinking, as evinced in the mythic and folkloric material of all the ancient Celtic cultures, is inherently *wild*, in the deepest sense of the word: it is shaped and informed firstly by the dynamics of Nature, the sensuous, the felt presence of bodily experience, rather than the machinations of the rational human mind. In the Celtic myths, O'Connor writes, 'There is a sense of connectedness and interconnectedness, not Logos and separateness.'[7] This points to

---

[7]   Peter O'Connor, *Beyond the Mist: What Irish Mythology Can Teach Us about Ourselves* (London: Orion Books, 2000), 20.

the experiential landscape of what I call, 'conscious interbeing'. Such will be the wild, holistic, and indigenous terms under which we here proceed.

I contend that this archaic approach to the human experience may be profoundly effective, if not absolutely needful, in dismantling the reductionistic thought of our present social and temporal locality, because it can act as a meaningful challenge to the expected (and now tired) forms, categories, genres, and analytical frames that have been sanctioned by the dominator culture. The core, underlying assumption of these latter cultural styles is the conceit that all things either have been or can be rendered quantifiable, measurable, and transparent to the powers of rational human cognition. This Newtonian and Cartesian assumption has produced for us a world de-wilded, de-souled, 'secure', isolated, sterilized, controlled, utterly tedious, and devoid of transformative spiritual capacity. Such ideology is extraordinarily dangerous because it strips us of all that we most crave as human beings, and separates us exponentially from the interior tools we most need to reverse the disastrous course our reductionistic thinking has set us on.

This should go some distance toward answering the question: why this pressing need to dismantle the machine and seek the far green valleys of rewilding? Our inherited socio-cultural assumptions and the mechanistic structures of thought and practice that house them are Life-corroding. They are cancerous to the project of Life itself, and, as we'll discuss, to the 'Great Work' of human awakening and transformation. In short, the dominant (and *dominator*) paradigm, along with its institutions, is gradually killing the heart and soul of humanity—and, by extension, is gradually killing the many diverse creatures who inhabit this planet alongside us.[8]

---

[8]   The concept of 'dominator culture' is an anthropological observation based on the study of relational social dynamics. In the work of Riane Eisler, who first popularized the idea, it refers to a grouping of social organization and cultural dynamics characterized by 'an authoritarian social and family structure, rigid male-dominance, a high level of fear and built-in violence and abuse (from child and wife beating to chronic warfare), and a system of beliefs, including beliefs about human nature, that make this kind of structure seem normal and right.

As we stand now on the edge of hitherto unimagined and ethically uncharted technological developments (e.g., artificial super-intelligence and neurotechnic computing interfaces), of irreversible climatological disaster, of massive overpopulation and the possibility of leaving the Earth to colonize other planets, the lens through which we look—our worldview foundation, which is necessarily our starting point for all attempts to meet these unprecedented challenges—is absolutely critical. If that starting point continues to be mechanistic, reductionistic, and anthropocentric, then it seems to me we will continue to be greatly diminished in our ability to adequately

---

Difference, beginning with the fundamental difference between the female and male halves of humanity, is equated with superiority or inferiority.' 'Difference' here includes the role not only of women or other non-dominant gender identifications in a given cultural milieu, but also the role of non-dominant sexual orientations, non-dominant racial groups, etc. In short, dominator cultural norms—and the mental orientation that feeds them—thrive on emphasizing difference or 'otherness' and marginalizing or scapegoating those creatures (whether human or otherwise) who in some way occupy the category of 'other', which in a dominator context is equivalent to 'lesser'. Dominator cultures stand in contradistinction to partnership cultures, which, by contrast, exhibit 'a more democratic and egalitarian family and social structure, gender equality, a lower level of institutionalized violence and abuse (as there is no need for fear and force to maintain rigid rankings of domination), and a system of beliefs, stories, and values that supports and validates this kind of structure as normal and right.' It is important to note, as Eisler points out, that 'no culture orients completely to either model. But the degree to which it does profoundly affects beliefs, institutions, and relationships—from intimate to international.' Other thinkers, like Terence McKenna and bell hooks, have further developed the concept to include a broader range of socio-cultural features such as a given culture's view and treatment of the Earth and non-human creatures, its view of mind-altering natural substances, its relationship to religious texts, and its potential or actual use of world-denying ideologies. All of these factors are relevant to the present inquiry. McKenna sums up the matter well in stating that 'the overexpression of the dominator model [is] responsible for our alienation from nature, from ourselves, and from each other.' cf. Riane Eisler, 'The Battle Over Human Possibilities: Women, Men, and Cultural Transformation', in *Societies of Peace* (October 2005: www.second-congress-matriarchal-studies.com/eisler.html), accessed October 2018; and Terence McKenna, *Food of the Gods: The Search for the Original Tree of Knowledge* (New York: Bantam Books, 1992), xx.

address such crises at all. The proposition for radical change in the way we see ourselves and the world is therefore nothing less than a life-or-death proposition.

❦

One of the many inspirations for this collection has been my experience in sacerdotal or professional religious life, which has shown me first-hand how deficient our ideologies—especially religious thought and practice—have become in the Western world: inadequately developed, lethargic, sometimes outright apathetic, often largely or completely disconnected from any and all deep roots, and from the rest of Nature, unable to foundationally transform human persons and therefore unable to respond adequately to the ills of the human-made world. So many modes (or shall we say, 'brands'?) of spirituality on offer today are weak, ineffectual, and rootless—not only metaphysically, but intellectually and culturally as well. This is because in most cases they were long ago severed from any legitimate, experiential understanding of: (a) the authentic power of myth, (b) the wisdom of oral traditions, (c) a pre-materialistic, pre-reductionistic holism, and (d) the archaic initiatory technologies that hold the power to actually effect foundational human transformation.

We might rightly say that most spirituality—and institutional religion especially—has become too pedestrian to be useful: overly domesticated, divorced from the authenticity of Nature, neutered, fearful about its relationship to the world, and, in the case of Western Christianity, fearful about its own lack of relevance and its apparently imminent institutional demise.

This corrosion of religiosity has come about not only because of the rise of literalist and reductionistic thinking, and the effective dissolution of real human community and living oral traditions, but also because in the realm of religion there has been a pervasive failure to acknowledge or accept the challenging reality that radical problems call for radical solutions. So far as I can determine, this failure derives from deep-seated institutional self-interest, from a thoroughly engrained fear of change, and a fear of that which is difficult or demanding. This latter element is to some extent constituted by—and certainly exacerbated by—the present 'culture of convenience', which has bred in most Western societies a thoroughgoing fear of existential challenge and an allergy to purposeful suffering.

Most contemporary religion thus remains trapped in a safe, insular, and largely ineffectual bubble. In large-scale, institutionalized religious structures, there is typically more concern with towing normative political lines and preserving careers than with actually changing the world. And in the pews there is generally more interest in comfort, entertainment, and appeasement than in anything remotely resembling real interior transformation. These abortive institutionalized models carry no capacity for effecting actual change, and nothing of the real wildness of divinity, or of the sanctity of Creation. And that, it turns out, is a lethal deficiency—not just for the institutions themselves, but for the larger society, and indeed for the whole of humanity.

It feels more and more apparent that there are far too many people in Western societies who, in spite of the advanced stage of crisis that characterizes their environment, remain unrealistically comfortable and disconcertingly oblivious. It's too easy for such individuals, immune to the toxic content of the dominant culture, to either outright ignore or rationalize away the reality of the crisis, and/or to attribute it to a singular political or economic issue, to something that's easily quantifiable. Unfortunately, the sickness runs remarkably deep and cannot be attributed to one or even several single issues. Dominant culture in the West has become cancerous and, carried abroad through commerce, its contagious socio-economic agendas and the spread of its technologies, is consuming other cultures at an exponential rate. Oddly enough, this dominant Western culture is less a *culture* in the traditional sense and more a collection of shared materialistic ideologies. I sometimes feel it might be more accurate and illustrative to refer to it as a 'non-culture'.

The totality of this situation is something I would submit can only be shifted by the most radical transformation, both personal and collective. No public policy change, no shift of political leadership, no small-scale communal or religious reform, or anything else of that nature can possibly cure it. What is required is nothing less than a total transmutation of thought, worldview, and cultural dynamics. Such a foundational change can only come through an experiential and totalizing breakthrough in perception; it will never come through mere ideation.

As long as folks remain basically comfortable in their external lives, medicated by foolish distractions, cheap entertainment (whether secular or religious), and whatever else numbs them enough to cause them to over-look the fact that they have been robbed of their most essential birthright, they will never even consider making such radical shifts. What does that birthright consist of? In essence, it consists of the experience of being truly, freely, and naturally human, in deeply felt interconnection with the whole of Nature, supported continuously by the diverse voices of a living world, and the cultural expressions of Earth-rooted folktale and myth. It is the archaic and perennial wisdom of our indigenous inheritance—: an inher-itance that belongs to each and every one of us, regardless of our cultural backgrounds or social settings.

Human beings—at least in our world—tend to be naturally resistant to change. Once lulled into a rhythm that pretends or functions as normalcy, even the most critical need seems hardly capable of shifting us out of our ossified behavioral patterns. This is a troubling situation, particularly now as we face an ever more alarming set of outward circumstances on the Earth.

It seems needful to recall that the critical circumstances—ecological, cultural, ideological, communal, technological—now overtaking us in an exponential way are only symptoms of the real root of a more totalizing crisis: a crisis which is fundamentally psycho-spiritual in nature. The tools we've inherited to grapple with that crisis, insofar as they come to us from the systems that have engendered and sustain it, are irrelevant and must be cast away in favor of more efficacious means. In my feeling, those more effi-cacious means must be fresh but firmly rooted in ancient ancestral wisdoms.

The choices that now lie before us are stark. We will have to be willing to do whatever is needful, to sacrifice whatever we must in order to truly transform ourselves, our lives, and our communities, or otherwise go down with the sinking ship. If we relent, then we will hand on to our children and grandchildren little more than an increasingly unbearable nightmare, a truly appalling and unprecedented set of socio-cultural, moral, and ecological crises.

My aim, my hope, my fervent prayer, is to help inspire a better way forward—one that is concrete and actionable; to hand on some tangible and meaningful tools, sourced from and supported by the wisdom of my ancient Ancestors, in order that we and those who come after us might build a life that is more healthful, more humane, more natural, and more true—: a life of authenticity, wholeness, and conscious interbeing.

I hope you'll join me in that work. This book stands as an invitation not only to reflection, but, more importantly, to action.

Since the principal crisis of our times is a spiritual and existential one, any possible solution must begin at that level: at the deepest layer of being. This is the level at which religion, in its purest forms, proposes to operate. The issue is that most of what constitutes spirituality and religion today is simply ineffectual, as we've already observed: reduced to a now largely unexamined collection of rote, repetitive linguistic structures and fallow routines. This means, in short, that religion is now in desperate need of a serious and pervasive transmutation.

Language without relevant, attendant action is ultimately of no value. Even more worthless, however, is talk with no stakes and no soul, which is meant only to placate, and/or to advance a concealed egoic agenda. This is the kind of game that mainstream religion has been engaged in for far too long. Language—particularly 'sanctioned' or 'authorized' language, which plays by and advances the rules and agendas of the dominant culture—may be utilized cleverly to win over those few financially capable parties who will continue to prop up the ivory towers that perpetuate the way of dominance and stagnation, but the glaring paucity of real 'edge' and legitimately transformative action will ultimately betray the underlying agendas of those constructs.

Perhaps a bit of subversive language and symbol, understood through the lens of an ancient wisdom and an ancient hope, along with some empowering, practical resources for cultural reclamation and spiritual formation, might help along the needful process of the demise of such constructs, and of the corrosive lifeways they perpetuate. The way of stagnation is inevitably the way of death. And only the values of Life have any legitimate claim to wisdom or authority.

Any construct that is unwilling or unable to risk real vulnerability and thus real encounter with the Other, with 'Divine Ground', has no capacity for facilitating meaningful change. And most of what we're taught and conditioned to in Western cultures and religions risks nothing. Radical change is prerequisite to breaking the walls of dominator culture that keep us constrained in a seemingly endless cycle of absurd and destructive behaviors, both collectively and individually. Without facilitating such needful risk and transformative action, religion becomes a charade: just one more form of entertainment in a non-culture made of endless placatory and distracting trivialities, endless addictions to infantilizing diversions that promise to fill the 'quick-fix' need of a society oversaturated with consumerism, repression, and existential denial.

Thoughtful, independent, and determined individuals who value and seek to align with the *telos* of Nature, of Life, must struggle to find where legitimate hope can be found in the face of the insanity that now pervasively haunts our inherited socio-cultural and religious structures.

The mechanistic, rationalist approach cannot provide us with meaningful answers; neither can the anti-evidentiary approach of the New Age or the myopic, avoidant approach of religious fundamentalism. Something which breaks completely outside the boundaries of all these commonplace strategies and defies their forms has now become utterly needful.

So far as I can determine, it is only the wild, the poetic, the deeply symbolic, the indigenous, and the mythic that can fill this need and redeem the current course of things, having been authentically reclaimed and brought to bear on the pressing question of our collective future on this planet. And it is only an approach to religion and spirituality that's rooted deeply in direct, personal, and legitimately transformative *experience* that can ultimately be categorized as useful and effective.

Hope will only be uncovered and sustained in the place that is pregnant with possible action. And not only possible action, but meaningful and transformative action. (In particularly desperate outward situations, such action might be found only in the interior landscape, but that should not be seen as resignation, for the interior is the only true birthing-ground of legitimate transmutation.) To frame this in Christian theological terms: the only legitimate eschatology is a participatory one.[9] In the realm of outward experience, people will eventually need to stand up and intelligently name the norms of the dominator culture for what they are: a vast betrayal, which has for centuries been eroding our souls and destroying the life of the planet.

At one level, the younger generations are beginning to see through the veneer of the old inherited structures and are rightly rejecting the guilty parties and their institutions. Still, there is little if anything in their sphere of awareness to adequately replace those structures, and so the alternative, by default, seems to be more consumerism, more technology, more trivial and distracting entertainment—or otherwise an unhealthy focus on reactionary rhetoric and a confused obsession with language and ideology that actually erodes productive discourse. I offer this observation more as invitation than critique.

Where generations of habitual idiocy and grotesque materialism are revealed as fraudulent, a cultural and psychological void will inevitably open, and it will need to be filled with something genuine, something meaningful, deep-rooted, and psycho-spiritually transformative. As I see it, there has not yet been a substantive development of something that can truly fill that space: something that can take the place of dominator structures without repeating the same sinful patterns of negligence and abuse—something that can provide the true depth those structures could never provide.

---

[9]   A 'participatory eschatology' means, in summary, an expectation that a redeemed world—that is, a world in which God's 'Kingdom' or Nature's vision of wholeness, peace, and atonement has been thoroughly actualized and expressed—can only come about by means of legitimate and committed human effort, in partnership with divine providence.

These essays are intended as one contribution to that most needful project of co-birthing a legitimate solution: one possible (and necessarily nonlinear) vision, rendered through one particular set of cultural and linguistic lenses. My aim here is to constructively critique—from within—the largely unexamined assumptions of Western culture and religion as they presently stand, and to add something meaningful to the conversation about what might come to birth in their place, what might be more life giving, more resonant with the truths of Nature, more human, more real.

In spite of the advanced state of cultural disrepair and decay in the West, we have an abundance of useful tools within reach, and a majority of human beings alive in the Western world at this moment are blessed with free and open access to those tools. In other words, we have everything we need to make a better world. There is really no excuse for failing to do so. Nature awaits our shaking loose of the bonds of apathy, cultural idiocy, and alienation. She awaits our return to the mythic Garden.

That return will not be easy. The journey of spiritual re-membrance is necessarily a harrowing endeavor. When nothing is risked, nothing substantive can be gained. This truth seems bound to become particularly poignant when the structures one serves, however consciously or unconsciously, are the very same structures perpetuating the problems one is aiming to expose and resolve. But I cannot personally conceive of a convincing argument for continuing in the same rote way of being, safely housed in familiar structures, when that way—and those structures—have been shown to be utterly bankrupt. The need for foundational change is obvious and impresses itself upon us regardless of the sacrifices or discomforts that may be necessary to bring it about.

If the sanctioned, so-called authoritative, institutionalized norms of language, religion, economy, and governance were in the business of creating effective solutions rather than perpetuating problems, then we would not have the disastrous world in which we now find ourselves unhappily embedded. We've had more than enough of business as usual. In fact, too much more of it seems almost sure to put an end to *all* business, whether usual or not.

And yet, speaking metaphysically for a moment, what could we ever really say is 'usual' about the human experience? Life lived in this form is, from the start, impossibly surreal. For one called to conscious connection with Mystery, the journey becomes stranger and stranger. And the fully engaged pilgrim soul who seeks out real transformation becomes ever more alien in the world of mundane concerns. This is the lot of the true spiritual seeker in contemporary Western cultures. Such seekers are, unfortunately, extraordinarily rare in this world of mechanized, surface-oriented distraction—and they are also profoundly needed, perhaps now more than ever in the history of human life on this planet.

This collection of meditative reflections is rooted in the lived pursuit of Mystery. I hope it will strengthen—through recognition, inspiration, and invitation—other souls along the wayside, who, whether they realize it or not, have the power to shift the cultural contexts in which they are situated.

A foundational premise here is that real change must unfold from the inside out. This applies to systemic or institutional change, and environmental or ecologic change, as well as to personal change. The latter, of course, is completely requisite for there to be any real possibility of the former. Thomas Merton spoke well to this when he wrote, '[Those] who attempt to act and do things for others or for the world without deepening [their] own self-understanding, freedom, integrity and capacity to love, will not have anything to give others.... [and] will communicate to them nothing but the contagion of [their] own obsessions, [their] aggressiveness, [their] ego-centered ambitions, [their] delusions about ends and means, [their] doctrinaire prejudices and ideas.'[10]

Our journey must be, first and foremost, a journey in pursuit of profound interior transformation: a journey beyond the verge of what is sanctioned, safe, and acceptable—beyond the boundaries of the dominant culture. May that journey be richly and abundantly blessed.

---

[10]   Thomas Merton, *Contemplation in a World of Action* (Garden City, NY: Doubleday, 1971), 164.

Fox Spirit Woman and the Sterile Scent of Alienation

The languages of the dying suns / are themselves dying, / but even the word for this has been forgotten. / The mouth against skin, vivid and fading, / can no longer speak both cherishing and farewell. / It is now only a mouth, only skin. / There is no more longing. // Translation was never possible. / Instead there was always only / conquest, the influx / of the language of hard nouns, / the language of metal, / the language of either/or, / the one language that has eaten all the others.

—*Margaret Atwood*

Somewhere back down the line, the West woke up to the fox woman gone. And when she left she took many stories with her. And, when the day is dimming and our great successes have been bragged to exhaustion, the West sits, lonely in its whole body for her.

—*Martin Shaw*

Therewas once a hunter who lived by himself in a small hut, deep in the forest. Scarcely had he seen another human soul in many long years. His custom was to go out early each morning to hunt and trap, and not to return until dusk. One evening as he made his way back through the forest pathways toward home, he noticed a very curious thing: a lively plume of smoke was rising from the chimney of his hut. He had not left a fire to burn in the fireplace before setting out, and he knew there were no other human people in the forest—indeed, for a great many miles around it—so this was curious, to say the least.

Slowly and cautiously, with a hunter's silent skill, he made his way to the front door to investigate. He quietly pushed open the door and saw that there was indeed a bright fire burning at the hearth. He also saw that his dirty hunter's clothes from the previous days had been washed and hung neatly on a line near the hearth to dry. Furthermore, there was a nice warm meal prepared for him, set out on the little wooden table where he was accustomed to eat. But there was no one apart from himself to be seen. At length, though he was very puzzled by the circumstances, he resolved to accept and enjoy the mysterious gifts.

Next morning he set out again at dawn, as was his custom. Upon returning that evening from the hunt, he discovered precisely the same things: a fire burned bright in the fireplace, a warm meal was set out for him, and there was no one apart from himself to be found.

On the third day, he decided he would attempt to discover the identity of the mysterious visitor. At dawn he set out as usual, but only pretended to enter the depths of the forest, and after a short while looped back around to hide in some thick brush where he could watch the front of the hut and see any who might enter.

He waited there for many hours and spied nothing. Finally, late in the afternoon, he saw a Fox come trotting up to the hut, push the front door open with a paw, and enter. This was a strange occurrence, to be sure. Very slowly, with a hunter's silent skill, the hunter made his way to the front door of the house and quietly opened it. What he saw then was the most surprising thing yet: a tall, slender, and beautiful young woman with flowing red hair stood there at the hearth, tending to a fresh fire. Moreover, on a wooden peg where he sometimes hung a cloak or hat, there hung now a beautiful red Fox pelt.

After a few long moments of disbelief, the hunter finally gathered his courage and spoke: 'Are you the one who is responsible for the kindling of the fire these past days, for the washing of clothes and the cooking of meals?' 'I am', replied the woman with gentle confidence, 'and I have come to be the mistress of this house. I have come to be your wife.'

The hunter was dismayed by this circumstance, but the woman was so beautiful and exuded such a contagious charm that he, knowing a good thing when he saw it, said, 'Yes, I think that would be quite agreeable.'

So it came to pass that they began to live as husband and wife—and they were quite happy, indeed. The Fox Woman proved to be an idyllic partner, and they fell quickly in love.

It happened, however, that after some months—when the Foxes' mating season was upon them—that the Fox pelt, which still hung on the peg near the front door, began to emit a very pungent odor, which the hunter found quite disagreeable. For fear of offending his wife, he said nothing of it for some time. But finally the scent grew so intolerable to him that he could no longer bear it, and he confronted her about it as gently as he could. 'My darling', said he, 'would it not be possible, just for this season, to store your beloved Fox pelt outside of the hut—perhaps in a carefully crafted wooden box, to keep it safe?'

Though somewhat irritated by the comment, his wife replied with as much compassion as she could muster: 'No, my dear, I'm sorry but it would not be possible for me to be so far apart from my pelt. It is only for a short season that it may displease you—and I trust that in time you will adapt to it, and perhaps even learn to love it as part of my nature.'

This was not the answer that the hunter wished to hear. He suppressed his frustration as much as he could, but by the day he grew more and more irritable, more and more angry. It was clear that a rift was growing between them. He began to sleep in a small storage room at the back of the hut, to get as far away as he could from the scent of the pelt. Finally one evening he could no longer tolerate it and burst out in anger at his wife: 'For the love of all that's sacred, could you not do this one simple thing for me? Can you not see how I am suffering? If you truly love me, you will take this pelt from my house!'

Visibly devastated, the Fox Woman, his beloved wife, went silently toward the door where the pelt was hanging. She said nothing more to him, but with a look of sorrow that stung the depths of his soul she took down the pelt from its hook, draped it over her shoulders, returned once more to the form of a Fox, pushed open the door and departed, never to be seen or heard from again.

I was first introduced to this wonderful and deceptively simple story by the great Irish philosopher and poet-seer, John Moriarty. He was fond of telling it in order to highlight the radical, artificial, and disastrous chasm Western societies have created between the human person and the wildness of Nature—: our alienation from the wild depths of Beauty in ourselves and in the natural world around us.

The story in this particular iteration comes to us from Inuit folk tradition, though versions of the same basic motif are also found in Celtic and Scandinavian cultures, among others. No one can say for certain where the story's origin lies, though I imagine it to be somewhere deep in the mists of early agricultural society. The motif of an animal that temporarily takes the form of a human woman and marries a man is certainly widespread and very ancient. We might say that the genesis of the story's core motif is untraceable, as all true mythic threads are and must be.

I have sometimes wondered if the central elements of the tale could point back to a kind of Eurasian 'Eden Myth', in part lamenting the beginnings of humanity's separation from the rest of Nature, perhaps reflecting deep-seated anxieties around the transition from hunter-gatherer societies to husbandry and agriculture. At any rate, whatever its shrouded origins might be, this story sings to us now with a powerful resonance we cannot afford to ignore. It is a story that all of us and our children should hear again and again. And not just hear in an outward sense, but embody, deeply absorb, be spoken into by, shattered by, dreamt by, pulled by into the wild mythic landscapes where our deepest memory tells us we truly belong.

While I am inherently resistant to the excessive interpretation or rationalistic analysis of any mythic gift such as this one (really we should allow the story to come alive in our hearts, our breath, our blood, and our dreams, and begin to teach us, in its own time, the secrets of the deep mythic wilderness it inhabits), in a sense all that follows here is commentary on this one short tale. And I have often thought, since first hearing this tale, that all the teaching and writing I've done to this point in my life could be seen as unintended exegesis on this singular and deceptively simple narrative.

Mythologist Martin Shaw has given the story of the Fox Woman a brief closing flourish based on what the story has breathed in him—as all good storytellers are wont to do: 'It is said that to this day the hunter waits by the door of his hut, gazing over snow, longing for the fox woman.'[11] The tale has breathed a similar breath in my soul as well.

All of us in the Western world are that lonesome, dejected hunter, remiss for having exiled the Fox Woman from our midst. We have forsaken the profound Beauty and the gratuitous gift of her wildness, both this-worldly and Otherworldly. We have forsaken those things in ourselves and in the world around us—: those elements which are in fact among the most core, the most central to our authentic humanness. 'The smell of the pelt is the price of real relationship to wild nature: its sharp, regal, undomesticated scent. While that scent is in our hut there can be no Hadrian's Wall between us and the living world.'[12]

But the West has opted instead for the sterility of a domesticated, de-wilded, rationalized, and neurotically controlled environment—: a vapid dwelling. The way an increasing number of our elders die today in postin-

---

[11] Martin Shaw, 'Small Gods', in *Dark Mountain, no. 7* (Reydon, Southwold: Dark Mountain Project, 2015), 32.

[12] ibid.

dustrial Western societies is a perfect icon of our collective alienation: in a barren, white-washed institution, fearful, abandoned and unseen, without real spiritual guidance, without meaningful story or ritual, without recourse to community, to a collective wisdom regarding life and death and what they mean, without connection to the living Earth in which the remains of their chemically saturated bodies will be cast in an unnatural vessel of factory metals, epoxy, and fiberglass.

The severity of devastation we've inflicted on our own alienated souls, on the living Earth, on the ancestral traditions we've rejected, and on the indigenous birthrights of other cultures we've pillaged and destroyed is only just beginning to dawn in our benighted field of perception. Perhaps it's dawning now in the heart and in the sinews of the body, in the intuitive parts of our being; the mind has yet to catch up. It's living in our blood and bones, in our epigenetic memory, in our dreams, in our art. It's showing itself as unprocessed grief—something all of us in the West carry a huge amount of. And that unprocessed grief is in turn creating ever more toxic cultural habits, manifesting as profound discontent, as reactionary political divisions, as reckless materialism, as deepening obsession with the false god of technological progress, as the breakdown of our communities, and the colonialist fetishization of other cultures who seem to retain at least a trace of the sort of deep-rooted sacral connection we intuitively long for but long ago severed from ourselves.

The time for real *metanoia*—for a complete turn in our way of being in the world—is now. In fact, it is long overdue. An archaic transverberation awaits us in the midst of the darkened forest, beyond the concrete wall of our neurotic fears, our addictions, our backwards ideologies, our materialism.

Many of us feel in our bones that something is desperately wrong with the way we're collectively living, with the way we're walking on the Earth. There is a great, painful void in the center of our culture—and in the center of our hearts. We long to fill it, but have no idea how. We are so far from the light of our own indigenous homing star, from our own native wisdoms which carry the practical knowledge that could remedy our present soul-sickness, that we don't consciously recall such a light ever existed for us.

We're caught instead in the dizzying, reflexive nausea of materiality, the fever of techno-egoism, of reductionistic blindness.

The Faustian deal we long ago made was to sacrifice our own true inheritance for the shiny, gold-plated promise of endless material progress and prosperity—the most disgraceful transaction a human community could endeavor to make. That deal has naturally left us miserable, hollow to the core, standing bloody-handed and bereft outside the mythic Garden that we, like foolish children, have half-unwittingly reduced to ruins.

Amazingly, throughout this process we've managed not only to violently colonize all the cultures we feared as Other, but also to colonize our own ancient traditions and our own indigenous souls. In fact, it seems to me that the latter was a large part of the trauma that inspired the former—and the former no doubt evoked in our unconscious all that we had forsaken in our own deep cultural streams. The heartbreak of this reality is too immense to be articulated in words: it is a grief that cannot be captured in the sly nets of textuality.

In the middle of the nineteenth century, an old woman of the Hebrides in Scotland said in an ethnographic interview, given in secret for fear of persecution: 'I remember well the ways of the old people. Then came notice of eviction, and burning, and emigration, and the people were scattered and sundered over the world, and the old ways disappeared with the old people. Oh, they disappeared indeed, and nothing so good is come in their stead—naught so good is come, my beloved one, nor ever will come.'[13]

This Grandmother spoke of a time in her memory when people 'had runes [sacred songs] which they sang to the spirits dwelling in the sea and in the mountain, in the wind and in the whirlwind, in the lightning, and in the thunder, in the sun and in the moon and in the stars of heaven.'[14] This was a time when the people were still connected to the living, dynamic world

---

[13]   This secret lament was spoken to Alexander Carmichael sometime in the middle of the 19th century, during his ethnographic study which culminated in the publication of *Carmina Gadelica*. cf. Alexander Carmichael, *Carmina Gadelica* (Edinburgh: Floris Books, 1992), 281.

[14]   ibid.

of Nature, with all its miracles, both seen and unseen; when they still knew the old songs, passed down through countless generations, for honoring the spirits of Sun, Moon, and River, for blessing and protecting the animals, for planting the seeds, for kindling and smooring the hearth fire, for gathering wild herbs, for healing soul and body, for cleansing and blessing the home—a home in which the Fox pelt still hung, and the fire of an animistic worldview still burned.

The question we stand with now, here on the precipice of irreversible ecological and cultural catastrophe, is this: How can we find our way back to the home-fire, to the hearth of our ancient Grandmothers, their languages, their wisdoms, and their magic; to the warm embrace of real community; to the Salmon stream of initiatory transformation; to the shattering truth, the impossibly deep-rooted numinosity of the primordial Well of Wisdom?

The only pathway leading back to that Well, which is found at the foot of the Tree of Life, is the proverbial path through the forest—not just the symbolic forest of our own unconscious, but the actual, living forests of the sacred and beleaguered Earth, of the mythic treasures buried in our forgotten stories: that way which leads us through the trials of initiation, returns us to the loam-born wisdom of our archaic Ancestors—: the way of our own indigenous inheritance.

Along that path the old Initiatrix, the trickster wise woman of the wood, waits to guide us. She waits patiently for us to find once more the deep courage and clarity of heart to approach her with openness and wonder and an ear that truly listens. She waits to whisper in the ear of our heart the sacred and mysterious instruction that will help to guide us, through needful trials and sacrifices, back toward the firelight: back toward the living spirit of the Fox Woman.

Let's lean our heads in deeply now, in awe, humility, and surrender, toward the bright dark of the ancient, myth-haunted forest, to catch the undying, untamable scent of her radiantly wild soul.

The Long-Lived Ancestors

The Eagle of Gwernabwy had long been married to his female, and had by her many children. She died, and he continued a long time a widower; but at length he proposed a marriage with the Owl of Cwm Cwmlwyd; but afraid of her being young, so as to have children by her and thereby degrade his own family, he first of all went to inquire about her age amongst the elders of the world. Accordingly he applied to the Stag of Rhedynfre, whom he found lying close to the trunk of an old Oak, and requested to know the Owl's age.

'I have seen this Oak as an acorn', said the Stag, 'which is now fallen to the ground through age, without either bark or leaves, and never suffered any hurt or strain except from my rubbing myself against it once a day, after getting up on my legs, but I never remember seeing the Owl any younger than she seems to be at this day. But there is one older than I am, and that is the Salmon of Glynllifon.'

The Eagle then applied to the Salmon for the age of the Owl. The Salmon answered, 'I am as many years old as there are scales upon my skin, and particles of spawn within my belly; yet I never saw the Owl other than she now appears. Though there is one older than I am, and that is the Blackbird of Cilgwri.'

The Eagle next repaired to the Blackbird of Cilgwri, whom he found perched upon a small stone, and enquired of him the Owl's age.

'Do you see this stone upon which I sit', said the Blackbird, 'which is now no bigger than what a man can carry in his hand? I have seen this very stone of such weight as to be a sufficient load for a hundred oxen to draw, which has suffered neither rubbing nor wearing, save that I rub my bill on it once every evening, and touch the tips of my wings on it every morning, when I expand them to fly; yet I have not seen the Owl either older or younger than she appears to be at this day. But there is one older than I am, and that is the Frog of Mochno Bog, and if he does not know her age, there is not a creature living that does know it.'

The Eagle went last of all to the Frog and desired to know the Owl's age. He answered, 'I never ate anything but the dust from the spot which I inhabit, and that very sparingly, and do you see these great hills that surround and overawe this bog where I lie? They are formed only of the excrements from my body since I have inhabited this place; yet I never remember to have seen the Owl but an old hag, making that terrifying noise, *Too, hoo, hoo*! always frightening the children of the village.'

So the Eagle of Gwernabwy, the Stag of Rhedynfre, the Salmon of Glynllifon, the Blackbird of Cilgwri, the Frog of Mochno Bog, and the Owl of Cwm Cwmlwyd are the oldest creatures in the whole of the world.[15]

---

[15]   As collected by P. H. Emerson, in *Welsh Fairy-Tales and Other Stories* (London: D. Nutt, 1894); adapted by the author.

Stars in the Soil,
Old Woman in the Land

T
he fire that burns on Beltaine at Uisneach is the fire of Macha. The fire that burns on Beltaine at Uisneach is the restorative fire of rewilding, of ancestral reclamation. The fire that burns on Beltaine at Uisneach is Brigid's fire, the undying flame of Wisdom that flashes in the depths of Connla's Well, that wills to impregnate this visible world with magic, depth, animistic theophany, atoning grace.

This Beltaine fire is the fire of resistance to conformity, to patriarchal oppression and dominator culture; it's the ancestral signal fire of deep-rooted and purposeful rebellion, kindled against the ever marshaling forces of mechanistic, materialistic, reductionistic, and authoritarian powers—whether of church or state or any combination of the two. It's the light of sovereignty that burns in defiant opposition to the fire of Patrick, kindled on another distant hill.

Patrick's fire is the fire of domination, subjugation, dehumanization, exploitation, and isolation, of the desacralizing of Nature and indigenous lifeways—: the fire that negates and destroys the values of Life. It is the fire that sets in motion a gradual, systematic disconnection from Otherworld realities, a denial of the inherent sanctity of Creation, an amnesia regarding its ensoulment, its manifold sacralities, its endless spiritual grace.

The Beltaine fire is the scandalous and rebellious fire of wild Beauty, of fertility, freedom, wholeness, reciprocity, and interconnection—: the fire that feeds the values of Life. It is the fire of restoration to ancient mythic origins, to relationship with the poetic, to the great plurality of divinity, to a vision that sees beyond the material, into the vast ocean of Otherworld numinosity and the soul's eternal sojourn. May *this* fire boldly burn forever.

Just as the Fox Woman suddenly appeared in the house of the lonely hunter, Macha, the Horse goddess, Mother of Sovereignty, appeared one night, a beautiful woman, at the house of Crunniuc. She did not reveal her name or nature; she simply stated she had come to be his wife. Her presence there in Crunniuc's household caused him to flourish, to accrue abundance in all aspects of life. As part of their agreement, he was to keep silent about her powers, her unprecedented gifts, divine strength, and grace. But, as so often happens with people lacking vision and respect for Otherworld realities, the old fool couldn't help himself, and at an assembly with the king of Ulster he boasted so brashly about his new wife's strength that the king was insulted and provoked. So offended was the king by Crunniuc's impertinent and outlandish boasting that he forced Macha, then nine months pregnant with Crunniuc's twin children, to race against the royal Horses. It was this, said the king, or Crunniuc's life was forfeit. Macha won the race to save Crunniuc, but the twins died in childbirth at the conclusion of the race. Macha then pronounced a curse on Ulster: that from thenceforth, through nine generations, in the hour of their greatest need the men of Ulster would lose all strength, and instead for nine nights feel the full intensity of Macha's labor pains. She then took up the dead twins in her arms and leapt away through the air, over the heads of the cursed men of Ulster, never to be seen there again.

There are echoes of this story in the Welsh tale of Pwyll and Rhiannon, though the manner in which Rhiannon, also clearly a Horse goddess, appears to Pwyll and makes clear her intentions, is quite different. Like

Macha and the Fox Spirit Woman, Rhiannon is the decider—she informs the witless man of her decision to marry him and inhabit his house—but the man she has chosen, Pwyll, must chase her down on horseback in order to win her hand.

The same basic motif of the Horse spirit, Mother of Sovereignty, expressed in these two mythic figures is also found in the Gallic figure of Epona, and further illumined by the Irish sacral kings' symbolic mating with a Mare in the ritual of coronation, as reported by Gerald of Wales.

Finn, the great warrior-poet, invites Sadb, a spirit inhabiting the form of a Doe, into his lodge. She transforms into a beautiful woman, and becomes his wife. When Finn returns to roaming with his warrior band, Sadb, like the Fox Woman, shapeshifts back into the form of a Deer. She gives birth in the forest to their son, Oisín ('Fawn' or 'Little Deer').

For Celtic peoples, as for many of their Indo-European cousins, the Horse bore great significance and was at some point associated, through ritual and mythic symbolism, with the Sovereignty Goddess of the Land. As long as the people, via sacral kingship and the wisdom of the sacerdotal class, remained in harmony and right relationship with that divine feminine power, the Land and the people would flourish. As Macha's tale makes clear, however, to sin against that divine power, to attempt to exploit her, disdain her generosity, or take her for granted, means to inevitably decline in an accursed state of being.

This tale of Macha, and all stories containing the archaic motif of the goddess or animal spirit woman marrying into human life and society, recall to us the intimate proximity of the spirit world, now largely forgotten to us. In early societies, this intimate proximity was acutely felt, and, particularly as witnessed and expressed through the concept of animal spirits, was known as something truly critical in the daily life of the people. In hunter-gatherer societies, intimate and visionary knowledge of the outward movements as well as the deeper, unseen spiritual currents of animal life on the Earth is quite literally a matter of life and death. But the stories that recall these archaic truths to us persist even into the modern era, and are preserved wherever human beings are living in close proximity to wild land-scape (whether ocean, forest, plain, or mountain).

Reciprocity is also a key lesson or insight to be garnered from the narra-tives that share in this motif, as is the inherent spiritual relationship (whether properly seen and respected by the protagonist or not) between human beings and animals, human beings and the Otherworld. There is always an element of these stories that calls forth the innate need humans have for such relationship. That relationship is explored in terms of its implications for health and well-being in human life and affairs—again, whether this falls within the human protagonist's conscious field of perception or not. Often this is expressed by the grief and ill state of affairs that follow when the human individual or community somehow breaks trust, disrespects the sacred dynamic, and the relationship is severed.

It's interesting to note that in what seem to be more recent renditions of the motif (e.g., in the Gaelic 'Woman of the Sea' tales), the ultimate cause of the animal spirit's departure from the human community is her longing to return to her own people, rather than an offense or breach of relational har-mony on the part of the human spouse. Though in these particular expres-sions of the motif, a common element is that the woman has been somehow tricked into staying with the man and marrying him—for example, by his theft and hiding of her Seal skin. This is quite different than what seem to be the more archaic versions of the narrative, in which the animal spirit woman appears of her own accord, and tells the man quite bluntly that she has cho-sen him; in other words, the feminine theophany of Otherworldly origin initiates the relationship and seems initially to have control over its terms. This latter element changes when the spirit woman makes herself genuinely vulnerable to the risks of the relationship, and in some sense places her own well-being in the hands of the human spouse. This scenario, of course, yields much in the way of metaphor.

The 'softening' of the motif to free the human protagonist from respon-sibility for the spirit woman's departure might be a development that arose as these tales passed into times and cultural contexts in which direct, inti-mate relationship with the natural world, the animal world in particular, and the animal spirit world most precisely, was no longer seen as critical for human survival. The shamanic functionary was no longer needed, then, to forge and maintain those Otherworldly relationships for the health, wholeness, and survival of the people. The divine feminine spirit of the Land receded gradually from human view and experience. The Well Maidens were raped and left for dead, their sacred springs sapped to desert dryness, and the living Earth began her cataclysmic transition into wasteland (or 'Waste Land', as it's often rendered in the old Arthurian tales), by agency of the imbalanced, masculine human ego and its dominator agendas.

With a supermarket on nearly every corner, collectively offering any kind of food one might desire in sterile, tidy packaging—indeed, with a total disconnection of consumers from their food sources, and from the Earth herself—what role has the one who communicates with and honors the animal spirits, who can tell the movement of herds? What role has his or her stories, brought back from Otherworld voyage, given (at least in part) to convey the profound needfulness of reciprocity and harmony with the animate world of Nature? Agriculture, complex machinery, and eventually industrialism and mass production can certainly be seen as likely causes of such mythopoetic erosion, of the breakdown of the human community's once ubiquitously shared perception of interbeing, and of the proper ways to navigate our critical relationships with all other creatures on the Earth.

Once you have self-sufficient 'man' in isolation as a socio-cultural (and mythic) model, propped up by the religious imagery and hubris of 'heavenly ascent', the archaic motifs begin to slip into obscurity of meaning—they lose their edge of imminence and are adapted or altogether replaced. Then you're well on your way toward a Waste Land reality.

Now more than ever we stand in need of atonement, of restitution to the untamed divine, the feminine divine, and the spirits of the sacred Land; of restoration to the archaic values and the mythopoetic truths contained in these ancient tales of human souls and communities in intimate relationship with wild and Otherworldly forces; of the timeless insights and invitations of our ancient Ancestors.

We have, in a sense, come full circle. Though in a slightly different manner, under different ecological pressures and concerns, and with a vastly more complex set of inward and outward challenges, once again we find ourselves in a position in which our very survival will depend on whether or not we understand deeply the souls of the animals, of the plants, and of the sacred, living Earth. Our survival and our flourishing will depend on whether or not we can bring back our shamanic sacral functionaries, to serve our communities as true spiritual guides, to lead our children through the holy process of initiation, to make whole what has long been sundered. Our responsibility now is to create the soil-bed, the necessary conditions, to bring about that return, and to turn our focus to the needful project of deep, authentic ancestral reclamation.

One of the chief ills in contemporary Western cultures is that most of us who inhabit those cultures have set ourselves at odds with the wild, feminine mysteries of the Earth, with the sacred dreaming of the Land. We've set ourselves at an obfuscated, antagonistic angle in relation to the light of Nature: a position both tragic and self-perpetuated.

In native Celtic traditions, the wild, feminine mysteries are expressed and accessed in a wondrous array of forms—all elegant, all complex, all carrying great wisdom. One of those expressions, as we have seen, is the pan-Celtic Horse goddess—in Ireland, Macha; in Wales, Rhiannon; on the Continent, Epona.

Rhiannon birthed a son to Pwyll, but the child was stolen in the night while she slept. The three nursemaids whom Rhiannon had entrusted to watch over the child were negligent in their duties and gave way to slumber. When they awoke, they discovered that the child was gone. Rather than accept the consequences of their negligence, they instead concocted a scheme to frame Rhiannon for the murder of her own child, spreading Pig's blood around the lodge and on her mouth, and, feigning horror, publicly accusing her of cannibalistic infanticide.

What the nursemaids failed to consider in their evil scheme is this: when Rhiannon suffers, when Macha suffers, when Epona suffers, all humanity suffers with her. Earth herself suffers. All the plants and animals suffer, for the sacred bond of reciprocity and mutual care has been broken: the values of Nature have been cast out in favor of the values of ego, human exceptionalism and self-obsession. Sovereignty is put in chains, and so the human community wanes into stagnation, disconnection, isolation, ignominy, and suffering.

Like the guilty, anxious nursemaids who framed Rhiannon to protect themselves from blame, we've thoughtlessly condemned the wild mystery, both within and all around us, resigning her—and ourselves—to a humiliating and ridiculous sentence of demeaning punishment. From the Mabinogion:

'And the penance that was imposed upon her was, that she should remain in that place of Narbeth until the end of seven years, and that she should sit every day near unto a horseblock that was without the gate. And that she should relate [her] story to all who should come there, whom she might suppose not to know it already; and that she should offer the guests and strangers, if they would permit her, to carry them upon her back into the palace. But it rarely happened that any would permit.'[16]

Along with the foolish nursemaids, we, too, have fallen asleep on the job of tending to the health and flourishing of Creation—which includes tending to our own place in the vast knotwork tapestry of interbeing, of loving and honoring the wildness of the Land and of our own deep humanness. One could make a symbolic connection here with the Gospel image of the bridesmaids who slumber when they should be watchful, letting the oil in their lamps run out.

We've exiled the wild Horse goddess, who embodies our connection to the sacred Land. As a result, we are plagued by increasingly alarming data about the current and forthcoming effects of human-aided and human-en-

---

[16] Lady Charlotte Guest, trans., *The Mabinogion: From the Welsh of the Llyfr Coch O Hergest* (London: Wyman & Sons, Ltd., 1877), 354.

gendered climate change. Our relationship to the feminine divine within the landscape is now, and always has been, of critical importance. Whether that relationship is one characterized by neglect, avoidance, irresponsibility and abuse, or by good sense, affection, and unity will determine the fate of humanity and many other species on this planet.

❦

Beneath the puritanical and scientistic chastity-belt Western peoples have forced over our own marginalized native origins lies the quiet, pulsing revelation and the deep-soil memory of the Sovereignty of the sacred Land. In that wild territory, ownership is a self-evident absurdity, commodification and materialism the most foolhardy offenses—repression, institutionalized rigidity, and immutability the antitheses of all that is truly sacred.

Imperialistic Western societies have long raped and pillaged, plundered and boasted of stolen material privilege—and now we are paying the price: an environment that daily becomes more uninhabitable; a corrosive and terminal lifestyle that many have yet to realize or accept is unsustainable; a deep sickness of body, spirit, and mind; pervasive addiction; isolation; loss of soul. The dominant, overarching culture of materialism that now constitutes Western societies—and especially American society—is not only trivial and destructive, but also childish and unconscionable: a deadly combination of elements.

Now we come to an ever-shortening list of productive options. It seems to me that the last truly meaningful option we have is, as it were, the first: to in some sense go back to the beginning, to reflect on our present socio-cultural (and existential) situation in light of our own rejected indigenous traditions, whatever those happen to be. If we do so, we are certain to encounter in ourselves the reality of a self-imposed alienation. And until we directly face that alienation, there is no possibility of healing for us or for the planet, no possibility of experiencing—or understanding in any capacity—what it means to live holistically, to embody what Christian tradition has termed the 'ministry of reconciliation'.[17]

In practice, our systemic and individual alienation appear as arrogance: thinking we can go it alone, assuming that, because of our scientific and technological acumen, we know something about Reality, something more about life than our ancient Ancestors did, or than other cultures still operating under different paradigms do; assuming our material prosperity and technological development give us superior knowledge about how to tend to the affairs of life on this planet.

The truth, however strange it might now seem, is that the ancient myths and folktales of our archaic Ancestors—which we have generally resigned to the nursery—can tell us far more about Reality and about how to live on this Earth than anything produced by the mechanistic rationalism of the present dominant culture. As John Moriarty once observed, we desperately need a *principia mythica*, a worldview-framing structure rooted in the living Earth and in the animistic awareness of our ancient Ancestors; we need recourse now to such a guiding framework far more than we need recourse to a *principia mathematica*, for the latter (and all that follows from it), however useful it may be in a utilitarian sense, can never restore us to a state of harmony and right living, or ultimately teach us anything about the actual depth, mystery, and nuance of Life.

The self-imposed exile from the rest of Nature that has accompanied our reductionistic, dominator cultural style—the style that has ruled Western life now for centuries—means a near-total divorce from our true and actual support structure, which is Nature herself.

A radical change of mind, of perception—a total *metanoia*—is necessary for us to correct these tragic missteps and restore ourselves to authentic community, to the partnership community of Nature. To move quickly and intelligently toward the landscape of indigenous, animistic, mythically saturated, folklorically constituted consciousness, which lies beyond the veil of our ordinary perception, is, culturally speaking, the only meaningful option

---

[17] 2 Cor. 5:18 (NRSV).

41

now left to us. Moriarty called this *commonage consciousness*. Nothing else can facilitate the kind of collectivity and the mythic 'rewiring' we need now to make any sustainable changes at all to our way of life and to our destructive impact on the Earth.

Commonage: community land; commonality; the stewardship of something, especially a pasture or other landscape, in common with others; the right of pasturing animals on common land; the state of being held in common. One might also say: interbeing, interdependence, *communitas* in the interlaced and ever becoming whole of Nature.

Wilhelm Grimm, that devoted and idealistic folklorist, reminds us that the commonage consciousness of the archaic wisdom-light which burns undying in the realm of every myth and every ancient folktale 'resembles a well whose depth one does not know, yet from which everyone draws water in accordance with his need.'[18]

A deep well, indeed, are we obliged to draw from now: nothing less than the primordial Well of Wisdom—: the Well of Segais, Nectan's Well, Connla's Well, which is also the Cauldron of Transformation, the holy Chalice, buried and forgotten in the depths of the Grail Castle, in the midst of the vast, toxic Waste Land of contemporary Western cultures. The Waste Land is deconsecrated and desacralized territory. The great Well—now nearly dry—is the womb of initiation, the container *sine qua non* for all of the deepest cultural inheritance of Europe. Its inextricable associations with the feminine divine and the depths of the Earth are of course no accident. Its marginalization and its hiddenness from our perception has left a massive, well-shaped void—a mythic, communal, and poetic void—right in the center of our being.

What to be done? 'Tomorrow I have only a small task for you. In the forest behind my house there is a well, now mostly dry, into which my light

---

[18] Wilhelm Grimm, 'Introduction', in *Kinder- und Hausmärchen* (Berlin: Reimer, 1822).

has fallen. It burns blue and never goes out. I want you to go down into the well and fetch it for me.'[19]

That well is the passage opening up before us, the hand beckoning inward and the whispered instruction. 'To know, and to continue to know, that any well we dip our buckets into is Nectan's Well is why we are a people.'[20]

We'll have to be spoken into, shatteringly. The voice of the ancient Earth, the voice in the blood, the voice of the Hag in the darkened wood: that is the wild, swimming voice we must catch and put our parched, hungry lips to.

⛤

The Pilgrim sets out, east of the Sun and west of the Moon. The incarnation, the ensoulment to a world ensouled, passage along the pale-root pathway, a breaking into twilight, unfolding into flower. The newly born seer is cast out to sea in a Deer-skin satchel; a boy born to the mistress of a mighty king thrown into a rushing river, impossibly alive with frenetic promises in a fresh spring snowmelt.

His salvation, his sovereignty will be found in the old witch he meets at the Well. Lost in the mapless forest, his teacher must be the Hag, the Grandmother who dwells in an ancient Oak—the Lady of Mists, Badb, An Cailleach, Cerridwen, the Old Woman in the Land.

The Gwrach y Rhibyn, Hag of the Mists, is the Welsh Midwife of Death: a figure we have come to fear, to demonize, paganize, and exile like an untouchable—forgetting the truths we once knew about Death, the ways of authentic transformation, the soul's profound need of initiation.

In the indigenous European mind—in *any* mythically and folklorically attuned mind—even the contrived medieval Christian image of 'the Devil'

---

[19]   Jacob and Wilhelm Grimm, 'Das Blaue Licht', in *Kinder- und Hausmärchen, 7th Ed.* (Berlin: Reimer, 1857), no. 116. This translation is from D. L. Ashliman, and is available on the University of Pittsburgh website: https://www.pitt.edu/~dash/grimmtales.html (accessed June 10, 2019).

[20]   John Moriarty, *Dreamtime* (Dublin: The Lilliput Press, 1994), 18.

must be subject to the greater (if unseen) authority of the Old Grandmother. This motif is explored in tales like *The Devil and His Grandmother* and *The Devil with the Three Golden Hairs*. There are certain intuitive and collectively affirmed cultural knowings that cannot be eradicated—they will always reemerge in other forms. The Cartesian rationalists, the Christian fundamentalists, and the dominator politicians will inevitably play their game of whack-a-mole, as they've done for centuries, but deep cultural memories never really die. Even if consciously forgotten, they are passed on to us epigenetically, and through the deep-dream archetypes of our unconscious. And they are with the Earth, held safely in the heart of our ancestral Lands. They can and do resurface, when we come to desperately need them again (whether we consciously realize our need or not).

There was once a widow who had two daughters, one of whom was beautiful and industrious, the other ugly and lazy. She showed more love, however, to the ugly one, because she was her own daughter; but she made the other do all the hard work, and live like a kitchen maid. The poor maiden was forced out daily on the high road, and had to sit by a well and spin so much that the blood ran from her fingers. Once it happened that her spindle became quite covered with blood, so, kneeling down by the well, she tried to wash it off, but, unhappily, it fell out of her hands into the water. She ran crying to her step-mother, and told her misfortune; but her step-mother only scolded her terribly, and treated her very cruelly. At last she said, 'Since you have let your spindle fall in, you must go and fetch it out yourself.'

Then the maiden went back to the well, not knowing what to do, and, in her distress of mind, she jumped into the well to fetch the spindle out. Presently she lost all consciousness, and when she came to herself again she found herself in a beautiful meadow, where the sun was shining, with many thousands of flowers blooming around her.

She got up and walked along till she came to a baker's house, where the oven was full of bread. And the bread cried out, 'Draw me, draw me, or I shall be burnt. I have been baked long enough.' So she went up, and, taking the bread peel, drew out one loaf after the other. Then she walked on further, and came to an Apple tree, whose fruit hung very thick, and which exclaimed, 'Shake us, shake us; we apples are all ripe!' So she shook the tree till the apples fell down like rain, and when none were left on a branch, she gathered them all together, and then went further onward.

At last she came to a cottage, out of which an old woman was peeping, who had such large teeth that the maiden was frightened and ran away. The old woman, however, called her back, saying, 'What are you afraid of, my child? Stop with me. If you will put all things in order in my house, then shall all go well with you; only you must take care that you make my bed well, and shake it tremendously, so that the feathers fly, for then it snows on the Earth. I am Old Mother Frost.' As the old woman spoke so kindly, the maiden took courage and consented to engage in her service. Now, everything made her very contented, and she always shook the bed so industriously that the feathers blew down like flakes of snow, and therefore her life was a happy one, and there were no evil words; and she had roast and baked meat every day.

For some time she remained with the old woman, but all at once she became very sad, and did not herself know what was the matter. At last she found she was homesick, and although she fared a thousand times better when she was at home, still she longed to go. So she told her mistress, 'I wish to go home—even if it does not go so well with me above as it has here below, still I long to return and be among my own people.'

The mistress replied, 'It appeared to me that you wished to go home, and, since you have served me so truly, I will fetch you up again myself.' So saying, the old woman took her by the hand and led her before a great door, which she undid; and when the maiden was just beneath it, a great shower of gold fell, and a great deal stuck to her, so that she was covered over and over with gold. 'That you must have for your industry', said the old woman, giving her the spindle which had fallen into the well.

Thereupon the door was closed, and the maiden found herself upon the Earth, not far from her mother's house; and, as she came into the court, the cock sat upon the house and called, 'Cock-a-doodle-doo! Our golden maid's come home again!'

Then she went in to her mother, and, because she was so covered with gold, she was well received. The maiden related all that had happened; and, when the mother heard how she had come by these great riches, she wished her ugly, lazy daughter to try her luck. So she was forced to sit down by the well and spin; and, in order that her spindle might become bloody, she pricked her finger by running a thorn into it; and then throwing the spindle into the well, she jumped in after it. Then, like the other, she came upon the beautiful meadow, and traveled on the same path. When she arrived at the baker's the bread called out, 'Draw me out, draw me out, or I shall be burnt. I have been baked long enough.' But she answered, 'I have no wish to make myself dirty with you', and so went on. Soon she came to the Apple tree, which called out, 'Shake me, shake me; my apples are all quite ripe.' But she answered, 'You do well to come to me; perhaps one will fall on my head', and went on further.

When she came to Old Mother Frost's house she was not afraid of the teeth, for she had been warned; and so she engaged herself to her. The first day she set to work in earnest, and was very industrious, and obeyed her mistress in all she said to her, for she thought about the gold which she would present to her. On the second day, however, she began to be idle; on the third, still more so; and then she would not get up of a morning. She did not make the beds as she ought, and the feathers did not fly. So the old woman grew tired of it, and dismissed her from her service, which pleased the lazy one very well. But the shiftless girl thought, 'Now the gold shower will come.' Her mistress led her to the door, but, when she was beneath it, instead of gold, a tubful of pitch was poured down upon her. 'That is the reward for your service', said Old Mother Frost, and shut the door.

Then came lazybones home, but she was quite covered with pitch; and the cock upon the house, when he saw her, cried, 'Cock-a-doodle-doo! Our dirty maid's come home again!'

But the pitch stuck to her, and, as long as she lived, would never come off again.[21]

❦

Old hag   old mother
old woman in the land
grand mother of ash
bone widow   veiled
cave and burial
of the vast   loam
that bore us up
like cherished seed
discarded comfort earned
at hearth   and then
forgotten   bent
digger   of roots
crooked old waterer
nourishing dark   churning
spiral sea   a moot
of strained shadows wed
the folded gray   death-
like knee   we are melting
snow to your ages
we are   the long
usury
            breath rescinds.

❦

In making an immersive study of myth and folktale, one inevitably begins to see disparately occurring images as interrelated. Truth begins to separate

---

[21]   Jacob and Wilhelm Grimm, 'Frau Holle', in *Kinder- und Hausmärchen, 7th Ed.* (Berlin: Reimer, 1857), no. 24. Translated and adapted by the author.

from fact—two things inextricably wedded only in our strange and aberrant house of Cartesian assumptions. It is certainly possible—and crucial, in my view—to hold the two in productive tension: the reasoned pursuit of evidentiary, factual knowledge sought for the greater health and wisdom of the whole, and the visionary pursuit of rationally immeasurable truths, sought for the same ends—accepting that, in the realm of direct experience of the numinous, some truths have little concern for the modern conventions of factuality. And we should be mindful that as a culture we are withering from factuality, parched near to death in the desert of reductionism, in the desert of false dogmatic certainty, of mechanistic materialism.

In one valence, the Old Woman in the Land, who is also Sovereignty in her form as Hag-Initiatrix, reveals the sacred as immanent within the whole of Creation, and more specifically in the Earth beneath our feet: the foundation and sustenance of our physical life. But such potent mythic images can never be adopted as fixed or somehow objectively verifiable. Our binary, either/or thinking will have to go if we wish to grasp the mythic wisdoms of our ancient Ancestors. We'll have to learn to think and feel and perceive again in manifold pluralities: in symbolic trinary instead of reductionistic binary.

The characteristically Indo-European experience of divine triplicity has given us the knowledge that binaries, though easy to fall into, are in fact false constructs; they are instances of incomplete and inadequate perception. Throughout the whole of Nature, diversity—of expression, of experience, of emanation—prevails. And whenever two are seen, a third hidden thing is present somewhere out of sight. It is usually that third hidden thing which resolves the tension of the illusory dichotomy, which has power to dissolve the convenient but false assumptions of duality most of us are so deeply conditioned to see, and convey an experience of wholeness.[22]

---

[22] This is a thread of natural speculation that seems to have been particularly key to Celtic thought. Similar threads were later picked up by Renaissance alchemist, Robert Fludd, and more recently by German philosopher, G. W. F. Hegel.

When we bear witness to Sovereignty—whether as Hag-Initiatrix, Bride of the King (and sole source of his authority), Earth Mother, bestower of the sustaining gifts of the Land, soul of the Land itself, shaper of cliffs and mountains, or guardian along the pathways of death—we are witnessing a particular face of divine Mystery, as light refracted through a prism.

Old Mother Frost—as Berchta, as the Witch in the wood, as Hölda, as the Wise Crone at the crossroads, as Cailleach the shaper of landscapes or bringer of the winter snows, as Cerridwen the witch-goddess, as Badb the Hag of Sovereignty—beckons us toward the Well, the Cauldron, the Chalice of initiatory trial. The archetypal choice—to assent to her call and embrace the needful trials of transformation, or continue in the fruitless patterns of imprisonment and self-alienation—is ours to make.

Today in the West, our fear of death, our neurotic aversion to aging, our immoral rejection of the elder members of our societies, our grotesque, dis-associated, materialistic ideologies—: all these indicate, among other things, a suicidal marginalization of the sanctified, archaic image of the Sovereignty of the Earth, the Hag Mother, Old Woman in the Land. As revealed in the ancient folktale of Old Mother Frost, only when we tend with great care to her house—only when we skillfully and lovingly co-manage her affairs (which are also our affairs), when we cease from condemning and imprison-ing her at the horseblock, when we give her the honor and reciprocity she is owed, when we shake well her bedding so the feathers fly freely like snow—: only then can we be in true balance and harmony with the Land and with the whole of Creation. Only then can we live in the true wealth of reflective interbeing, of holistic *communitas*; only then can we at last experience the true atonement of our homecoming, of our prodigal return.

Samhain comes, and the veil between worlds is thinning. Old Mother Winter quickly approaches, sending forth, like ghostly emissaries, white flurries of howling wind and snow. Gather in the final fruits of your harvest. It will soon be time for the singing of threshold songs.

Songs of Birth and Vision

Everything is inward / This is the distinction /
The poet thus conceals.

—Friedrich Hölderlin

[We] do justice only where we praise.

—Rainer Maria Rilke

Incarnate soul, fully born: Where are the Lion Stars? The *Logos* rains like summer storm through golden hills and grasslands of our sleeping.

Lonesome priest of burdened heart: The road you walk is Logres Road—it is Chalice Road, Grail Road: a processional pathway from the Well of Song.

Incarnate soul: You've come this far on the starry path, along the wayside, to give your blossoming gifts of Beauty, to share an ancient story, of which the Earth is source and settlement.

O priest of worlds: Let your priesthood be a sacred song—: Fox-woman-priesting, Deer-trail-priesting, Oak-bough-priesting, five-ancient-paths-priesting, twelve-ancient-winds-priesting.

O poet-seer of roots and flowing springs: You walk the Royal Road, coming out from the Mound of Hostages, coming out from the Land of Women, Land of Apples, Land of Summer Stars. In the Flower World of your dreaming are vast, unspoiled forests; on the limbs of its eldest trees are tied the prayers of your people. There dwells the Well of Darkened Speech, Well of the White Cow Mother, Well of the Long-Hidden Sacrament.

Through the unitive you will have to pass, returning at last to the bright-feathered chorus: an endless diversity of spirit, the Mag Mell Flower World of luminous forms: our shamans' radiant Valley of Truth, the world of vast Nature ensouled.

Spirit walker, let the deep voice sing in you once more the songs of all wayfaring souls, the songs of star-filled mountains now embracing you. Learn again to sing the songs of your breath, your Flower World heart, your land of mirrored pools and veils; fill your blood with the strange, pulsing rhythm.

Song in you, like speech, is gift. Song in you is cure.

❧

This tower, the fort from which we'll finally achieve it—: a grounding and remaking of perception; a transcendence of things akin to subject-object opposition. Along the skirting pathway, around its stone-stacked borders: last threaded blooms of Pulsatilla; blinked eyelight tired from rebirthing; sentences vague, one-fourth recalled from precognitive dream; a meditation on the archetype 'Magician', which you dutifully renamed. Fragmentary image— Who passed along that narrow Deer-trail? Christ who was that distant soul who crafted this model for speech, for self-reflection? The alleys of connection fraying true, you disappear and reappear—again appear, and, following the patterns of the body's reeling, step into a new cognition.

This is the space of forgetting, which is all true recollection. The fountain path to worlds' unsure departures. Yellow Finch; wind-twisted Juniper; your writing of the inward choreography. Each word-form invokes without will the strange impression of a larger landscape—a plan once mapped, perhaps, through channel of some other *nous*, now completely irretrievable. (When we arrive here finally, what becomes of us?)

And upstream, sailing—leaving all our terrible inventions. Re-invoking the White Thorn, re-invoking the spiral thread, re-invoking the gods of Sea and Sky—saying, 'Something we needed, something we needed, now betraying us,' like a mantra now betraying us. These notions may arise from print. Refraction. Toward self-reflection. Toward our collective *aisling*. To ward against the horseblock prison, and open a path of re-collection.

☙

And I beheld:

Utterance from the Well of Wisdom, weaving the floral tapestry. Raincloud. Hazelwood. Seabreak. Hummingbird. Monsoon Chaparral. Oak leaf. Coralroot and Violet. Sight in word—all felt and re-collected dream—all utterance, known as luminescent sound.

Lines like code of scattered song as symbol, reshaping in us our long lost myths, our gods, our barren vision; reshaping in us the dreaming hearts of our people; reshaping in us the taproots, the deep-soil threads connecting souls to ancient Source—a guiding voice—reshaping in us our history, our dire and heedless wandering.

Our Lost Indigenous Soul

This is what is the matter with us. We are bleeding at the roots, because we are cut off from the earth and sun and stars, and love is a grinning mockery, because, poor blossom, we plucked it from its stem on the tree of Life, and expected it to keep on blooming in our civilized vase on the table.

—D. H. Lawrence

My teacher always said that if there is to be any hope whatsoever of living well on this Earth, we have to take the ancient root and put new sap in it. That doesn't mean we need to do something new, but to do something old in a new way, which takes great courage… The answer must be found in your own backyard, where you live. The only reason to explore another culture is to be able to smell the poverty in your own. Even if you go to another culture and are accepted in some way, you still have an obligation not to abandon your own culture, but to return to your homeland and try to coax its alienated indigenous traditions back into everyday life and away from tribalism, fundamentalism, and corporatized, nihilistic greed.

—Martín Prechtel

In pre-Europa's Europe the consciousness of Altamira and Lascaux was commonage consciousness. And it seems to me that it is only in commonage consciousness that the Earth can be saved...It is time now, in Western [societies], to reinstitute commonage consciousness. We have to reinstitute it in the way you would institute a new Sacrament.

—John Moriarty

There is a language older by far and deeper than words. It is the language of bodies, of body on body, wind on snow, rain on trees, wave on stone. It is the language of dream, gesture, symbol, memory. We have forgotten this language. We do not even remember that it exists.

—Derrick Jensen

C ollectively, we've lost our grip on the magic of life: the Beauty, Mystery, hidden depth, innate sacrality and existential interconnectedness of our humanness and our part in the greater cosmic journey. Life in the Western world has for centuries now been reduced to a materialistic affair, and our way of being as embodied souls on the Earth has been twisted around in the most bizarre and grotesque manner. We're so thoroughly sick to the soul, in fact, that we have no concept of the real severity of the illness, no clue how to heal it, no idea what to replace our inherited spiritual, cultural, and ecological trauma with.

The United States, so-called leader of the free world and chief purveyor of the socio-cultural and economic norms now dominant throughout much of the Western world, bears a lion's share of the dis-ease. Any culture that can produce common idioms like 'time is money' is a sick culture indeed.

Western peoples—and particularly those of European origin—are so far severed from our own indigenous roots that we're unable to contrast any longer the profound dysfunctions of the current mode of life we assume to be normative with human life authentically lived—that is, life lived in deep, conscious interconnection with all of Nature, in meaningful community, and in fully integrated spiritual awareness. We can hardly even catch the scent of those lifeways any longer. We long for the life giving waters of the ancient Well of Wisdom, but we don't know where or how to access them.

Long ago, in a somewhat nebulous, shadowy time and place now hard to define (and through a long cascade of actions, ideas, and conditionings), we made the Faustian deal with Christian-born human exceptionalism, with fear of Nature and fear of the wildness in ourselves, with a Gnostic view of both Creation and humanity, and finally with materialism, and thus effectively rendered ourselves a cancer on the Earth. This toxic approach to human life and human relationship with the Earth found its culmination in the Protestant reformations and the puritanical ideologies they birthed, which still provide the basic foundation for Western thought and life, even if hidden now from the conscious perception of most secular Westerners.

The documents of the reformations show the appalling ideational and spiritual depravity which both marks an advanced stage of, and has subsequently facilitated, our collective descent into perilous disconnection from Beauty and from the rest of Creation. We might, for example, reflect on Ulrich Zwingli's statement in 1523 that 'everything which makes itself out to be splendid before men is a great hypocrisy and infamy.'[23] At the surface level, Zwingli refers in this statement to the use of ornamentation and creative expression in the clothing and appearance of clergy, but the statement obviously reveals a deeper assumption of the Reformers: that the human person, along with the whole of Nature, is fundamentally flawed, even wicked, and thus anything that seems beautiful to the human eye is a lie—: everything of the Earth, no matter how splendid or enchanting or spiritually alive, is in essence a sham, to be rejected in favor of a paradisal afterlife reserved for those who have followed in strict, literal, and joyless fashion the

---

[23] Ulrich Zwingli, 'The Sixty-Seven Articles' in *Confessions and Catechisms of the Reformation*, Ed. Mark A. Noll (Vancouver: Regent College Publishing, 1991), 42.

dogmatic rules set down in a series of texts imagined to be divinely originated, infallible, and themselves solely qualified as the measuring rod of truth. The Earth, then—the natural Creation—is not simply made incidental, but is made an outright enemy of human endeavor, the core of which is to escape the 'prison' of natural reality. And the body of texts in question is an idol, which circularly feeds and is interpreted by a Gnostic demonization and hatred of Nature.

Otto Rank once observed that 'when [Western] religion lost the cosmos, society became neurotic and had to invent psychology to deal with the neurosis.'[24] Of course, psychology in itself is not enough to heal the deep-rooted neurosis; it can help to remediate some of the symptoms, and to bring us each a bit closer to the core issues, but it cannot in itself unravel and resolve those foundational dysfunctions. It is certainly true, however, that when our religious institutions rejected the prominence, flow, and values of Nature within us and in the world around us, we became decisively neurotic, both as a society and as individuals.

The stark distance between what we once collectively knew and held to be both sacred and self-evident about Creation, and the hideously disconnected island on which we presently reside, is a cavernous abyss: the abyss of our Fall and the potential seal of our demise. Centuries of neurotic disconnection from our true identity and lifeblood mean that our souls are parched, nearly to death: parched from a lack of connection to the source of real Beauty and depth in human experience.

In contrast to our present state of being stands the perennial, archaic set of values and worldview components we might call 'indigenous thought', or an indigenous way of being in the world. This way of seeing and being in the world has several key components that distinguish it from modern, materialistic worldviews. The international advocacy group, *First Peoples Worldwide*, explains those qualities well:

---

[24] As quoted in: Matthew Fox, *Original Blessing* (New York: Jeremy P. Tarcher/ Putnam, 1983), 75.

'In indigenous [thought], we are all related as individuals, as part of a kinship-based community and as part of Nature, in balance with the whole. In most Western thought, society is seen as an aggregate of self-interested individuals, connected by competition with each other over limited resources, creating fear, insecurity, hopelessness, a scarcity of spirit. Indigenous societies see prosperity in Nature: resources are abundant, shared; collaboration fosters environmental stewardship and balance with Nature. In the [contemporary] Western worldview, Nature is feared, its value based on hierarchy: everything on Earth [is] ranked…with humans at the top, dominating everything below. In the indigenous worldview, humans are an equal part of a vibrant, interconnected whole.'[25]

A disturbing sign of the depth of our collective cultural illness is the degree to which our youth are damaged by the inhumane pressures, expectations, ideological and social toxicities, violence, disconnection, neuroses, and general lifelessness of the world we've created and brought them into. As Derrick Jensen summarizes, a comprehensive national study published in the late 1990s estimated that, in the year 1993 alone, 'approximately 614,000 American children were physically abused, 300,000 were sexually abused, 532,000 were emotionally abused, 507,000 were physically neglected, and 585,000 were emotionally neglected. 565,000 of these children were killed or seriously injured.'[26] These numbers, we can logically assume, have continued to rise over the last twenty years or so, as the population increases and our collective crisis grows ever more lethal and entrenched. We cannot possibly imagine it to be coincidental that teen suicide in the United States is rising at an alarming rate. Such signs of destruction, social decline, and the devaluation of Life itself should act as a barometer that shows us how sick

---

[25] 'The Indigenous Worldview', at *First Peoples Worldwide*, www.firstpeoples.org/video-media.htm (accessed May 30, 2018).

[26] Derrick Jensen, *A Language Older Than Words* (White River Junction, VT: Chelsea Green Publishing Company, 2000), 39.

our pattern of living has become—but of course they don't. Instead, denial, avoidance, and immoral habits of justification—rooted in the equally sick religious and cultural ideologies that have birthed this violence—continue to prevail. We continue to look the other direction, to refuse to cast off the lens of our delusional cultural conditioning which tells us that all this is 'normal', just the way it is in the world, the product of our irrevocable sin or 'fallenness' as human persons, and that our actions are justified, or, at very least, morally irrelevant as we await the 'second coming' of some illusory salvific figure popularly described beneath a thin veneer of historicity. (We speak here, of course, of the largely unknowable life of a first century Galilean mystic and social radical.)

Jensen rightly asks, 'What is the relationship between [this violence] and our culturally induced isolation from the natural world and each other, from the social embeddedness in which we evolved?'[27] The answer is that the relationship is directly and totally causal: the endemic patterns of cultural and ideological illness that have birthed, constituted, and perpetuated Western civilization (so-called) and its dominator agendas *are* in essence patterns of unprecedented disconnection from, and toxic abuse of, the natural world. These patterns are inseparable from the destruction of the lives and potential futures of ourselves, our children, and scores of innocent creatures who populate the vast web of interbeing on this planet—the web we have delusionally told ourselves again and again we are not actually part of, is insignificant, illusory, or even outright evil.

Addiction to pharmaceutical drugs and the chronic use of antidepressants are likewise indicative of a culture in a state of sharp decline. As I write this, synthetic opioid addiction and overdose are beyond epidemic. Journalist Andrew Sullivan summarizes some of what has led to these crises in American society: 'Take away the stimulus of community and all the oxytocin it naturally generates, and an artificial variety of the substance becomes much more compelling.' In other words, we have lost the experience of real

---

[27]   ibid.

community, which we naturally crave—not just with fellow human beings, but with animals, plants, and the whole of Nature.

Sullivan references a study in which laboratory rats were offered morphine in water bottles in two different environments—some in cages and some in pleasant, wide-open recreational landscapes. The study showed that rats isolated in cages drank many times more morphine than rats in the 'parks' and died rapidly from the substance. These rats were self-medicating in response to the horrendous pain, anxiety, and despair that invariably come with disconnection and isolation. As Sullivan observes:

'One way of thinking of postindustrial America is to imagine it as a former rat park, slowly converting into a rat cage....Ever-more-powerful market forces actually undermine the foundations of social stability, wreaking havoc on tradition, religion, and robust civil associations, [ironically] destroying what conservatives value the most. They create a less human world. They make us less happy. They generate pain....What has happened in the past few decades is an accelerated waning of all [the] traditional American supports for a meaningful, collective life, and their replacement with various forms of cheap distraction. Addiction—to work, to food, to phones, to TV, to video games, to porn, to news, and to drugs—is all around us. The core habit of bourgeois life—deferred gratification—has lost its grip on the American soul. We seek the instant, easy highs, and it's hard not to see this as the broader context for the opioid wave.'[28]

The mass pharmaceutical opioid crisis presently plaguing American society is a sign, a symptom of the foundational sickness we collectively carry. Think of it as one microcosmic indication of the vast macrocosmic crisis we have unthinkingly created: one showing among an ever-increasing plethora of symptoms. What American culture—and dominant Western culture more broadly—has helped invent and propagate the world over is a cut-throat socio-economic style rooted in philosophical and consumeristic materialism, ideologically (and especially religiously) justified genocide, violence, and domination, rejection of Nature, and an individualistic

---

[28] Andrew Sullivan, 'The Poison We Pick', in *New York Magazine*, February 19, 2018.

denial of the importance of community—a way of life that leaves its people starved on every level of being: spiritual, social, psychological, and physical. Pharmaceutical drug abuse (tied inextricably to the greed of the aforementioned political-economic systems) can be understood as part of a matrix of symptomatic manifestations, which also includes the systematized degradation and abuse of women (and the feminine more broadly), the horrors of cultural genocide inflicted by Western dominator culture on indigenous populations that still maintain at least a semblance of connection to the realities of Nature, the thoughtless destruction of entire species of non-human animals, the raping of natural resources—: all signs of the cancer we've become.

It's as if we as a culture unconsciously (some of us perhaps consciously) wish to destroy everything that is life giving and natural, everything which gives testament to the values of Nature, of the native wisdom of our Ancestors we have violently and foolishly rejected. Destroy all the evidence that we are insane, psychopathic, self-toxic, and perhaps we can collectively get away with continuing to pretend we aren't. If we continue to put our fingers in our ears and obnoxiously intone, like toddlers, then perhaps the crushing reality of our own catastrophic failure, our own treachery, our own imminent demise, will simply disappear. We all know the popular definition of insanity, though perhaps we no longer even expect different results with each repetitious moral breach, with each violence. Perhaps we're completely apathetic and resigned to our own corrosive way of being in the world. As Jensen again summarizes: 'Another way to say this is that within any culture that destroys the salmon, that commits genocide, that demands wage slavery, most of the individuals...are probably to a greater or lesser degree insane.'[29] And I can't imagine at this stage any argument justifying a psycho-social description of dominant Western culture that does not include, front and center, the descriptor 'insane'.

---

[29]   Derrick Jensen, *A Language Older Than Words* (White River Junction, VT: Chelsea Green Publishing Company, 2000), 61.

The foundation of our collective cultural crisis is essentially spiritual. 'Spiritual' in this context indicates that the illness lies at the deepest level of our being. In other words, it is existential. Therefore, it cannot be resolved by dealing with external, political factors alone. The infection is too deep and too pervasive, and those factors alone cannot penetrate deeply enough to effect a change at the root, where the illness dwells. There has to be a radical and total rejection of the entire cultural construct—basically the whole way of life now taken for granted as normative in Western societies will have to be cast off, both inwardly and outwardly, and a viable alternative created, adopted, and sustained in its place. An alternative that draws heavily from the native, Land-based wisdom of the Ancestors.

It is far past time we instigated such radical change in our culture, in our religion, in the way we live day to day. The refusal to do so becomes, effectively, a willful act of damnation: a damnation of ourselves, our children, and the planet to an ever worsening and grotesque existence, stripped of real health and dignity. Ideational and worldview changes are just as needful as outward solutions to create sustainable remedies to the cataclysmic problems that presently face us, but the ideological and assumptive—which is to say, that which operates at the level of worldview—is really the decisive factor: it is at this level that our cultural models and lifeways must first be revolutionized. Otherwise, the same destructive patterns will simply repeat unabated.

To really move forward, we will have to make the unpopular statement that apathetic inaction and denial are not merely unacceptable, but are clear and profound evils—perhaps the greatest evils of our time. They are also the most prevalent evils now displayed on the stage of Western idiocy. Some of us are awake to the toxicity we've collectively created—and probably most of us sense it (unconsciously) in our hearts—but instead of us each saying, 'I will not rest until this is totally changed and I've helped to create, in partnership with others, a meaningful and more humane alternative in my own local context,' we generally just shrug our shoulders, say nothing can be done, and carry on with business as usual, at best merely Band-Aiding the wounds where we can. This, of course, is an utterly insufficient approach to the problems that plague us. It seems, moreover, an alarming approach to life itself, a barbaric way of being in the world. I recall here Terence McKenna's statement that in the Western world of the twentieth century we invented a new sin: the sin of robbing our own children of a future worth living in.

As things become increasingly cataclysmic in the world around us, gradually a few individuals—reflective people who are concerned with Beauty, dignity, and the preservation of life—are beginning to realize that the values and behaviors long advocated for and enforced by economically and militarily dominant Western societies are both deeply unwise and patently unsustainable. But, simultaneously, social ills seem to rise more and more to the surface in reaction to what many perceive as a threatening dissolution of enshrined socio-cultural boundaries. Voices from benighted corners of the social fabric, like those of racism and sexism, or those speaking from profound spiritual illness like the crypto-Gnostic Evangelical fundamentalism which longs for a literal 'second coming' and condemns the Earth and its resources to death and destruction while looking toward a fantastical scenario of 'rapture'. Such ideas seem to increasingly dominate or otherwise subvert our public discourse, in both subtle and overt ways. In an absurd and dangerous cultural feedback loop, consumeristic media sustains itself largely by highlighting and giving platform to these toxic voices, by breeding controversial argumentation and exaggerated polarization, preying on the lowest common denominator of the caged and endemically conditioned masses.

Meanwhile, anxiety, depression, isolationism, addiction, and psycho-spiritual dis-ease of every kind constitute a widespread socio-cultural epidemic the likes of which the Earth has never seen. We are collectively and individually sick with Western civilization, afflicted now perhaps beyond repair with the consequences of the idiocies of scientistic reductionism, consumeristic materialism, Protestant literalism, repression, rejection of the living Earth and Her natural, theophanically revealed values, Abrahamic fundamentalism of every variety, human exceptionalism, cultural self-negation, and the corruption of myth and symbol to serve the male dominator program of control.

None of these phenomena are isolated from one another, though it's common for us to discuss them in isolation. In my perception, each of these limiting cultural factors is connected to all the others, collectively comprising one grand, intractable crisis. The central issue might be described, *en précis,* in the following terms: By way of its devotion to materialism in every form, its total disconnection from the natural world, its adoption of destructive mythologies and worldview assumptions, the Western socio-cultural milieu has become decisively corrosive to itself and to the planet. Thomas Merton astutely observed that 'the reason for the inner confusion of Western [humanity] is that our technological society has no longer any place in it for wisdom that seeks truth for its own sake, that seeks the fullness of being, that seeks to rest in an intuition of the very ground of being.'[30] Wisdom and truth, I would add, imply a conscious, felt awareness and direct experience of the interconnectedness of all things, an intuitive attunement to the vast spiritual ecology of Nature. They imply, above all, an experience of *communitas,* a relationship to the indelible isness of the Great Mother, the World Soul, and to the myriad of souls present around us in nonhuman form, both this-worldly and Otherworldly.

I contend that the central catalyst for the long formation of this cancerous quality of Western societies is that they have, each and all, abandoned their own indigenous roots. This means that Westerners have abandoned all those things that would naturally convey to them the authentic, deep-rooted wisdom regarding how to live well on the Earth. These indigenous roots forsaken by Western peoples contain the very lifeblood of perennial, collective human wisdom which knows how to live in harmony with the Land, and with all of Creation. In other words, they contain the skills, knowledge, and worldview elements we now most desperately need—the only ones that could truly save us at this late hour.

---

[30]   Thomas Merton, *Faith and Violence* (Notre Dame, IN: University of Notre Dame Press, 1968), 217.

Intelligent, introspective, and well-intentioned people in modern Western societies have very few meaningful alternatives to the living nightmare in which they find themselves embedded, except perhaps to flee from it in one form or another. Of course, fleeing is becoming less and less viable as the whole world is consumed by postindustrial Western commerce and ideology—and, at any rate, to flee means necessarily to abandon the sinking ship and leave its crew members to a dire fate: it ignores, in several significant ways, the core human mandates of collectivity and mutual creative transformation. It cannot be realistically disputed that all people in this cultural milieu are desperately starved of real nourishment—spiritually, emotionally, intellectually, and on some level even physically.

In looking toward the possibility of the reclamation of our own native wisdoms, it must be acknowledged that Western societies have passed so far beyond a humane, natural way of life that most of us are incapable of consciously recalling the fact that such a way of life ever really existed. Still, unconsciously and epigenetically, at the deepest levels of our being, we know it to be true—and so we suffer, many of us, in a kind of unconscious 'nostalgia for Paradise', having no accessible recourse to a tangible alternative, no measurable ability to restore or recreate a life of real substance, interconnectivity, health, and meaning. This is hard for people to admit, and hard for some to even perceive, but it's becoming more and more self-evident—and it's crucial that we begin to include this layer of depth in our collective conversation about the state of things.

The aforementioned cultural factors all reflect a loss of our 'indigenous soul' as Western peoples—a soul-loss both individual and collective. The indigenous soul is, most fundamentally, a way of seeing. It is a thing we each still possess at the deepest level of being, though it must be actively pursued, recovered, restored, and nurtured. That process begins with no longer allowing ourselves to be lulled into the collective delusion that has long since severed us from our deepest roots and kept us bound, controlled, brainwashed, trivialized, and powerless. We must cease from continually trading our authentic personhood, our ancestral wisdoms, our rightful human inheritance for the trivial and misguided concerns that generally dictate our daily thoughts and activities: materialism, consumerism, wealth, power, convenience, control, addiction to vapid and distracting pastimes.

There is a deep, soul-level pain in the fact that these things dominate our reality—a pain from which a great deal of trauma, anger, violence, unprocessed grief, angst, and fear will continue to arise until we face these dimensions of our own tragic history and our own present circumstances head-on. Our unprecedented disconnection from our deepest selves, from our own true origins, from Nature, from the authentically sacred, has produced a living nightmare that each of us are forced, to one degree or another, to inhabit. We are right to call this benighted state of being 'hell'.

In the deepest and most relevant layers of Christian metaphysics, hell is not a place we go after death, but rather a state of being created here and now by our own thoughts and actions. This of course means that heaven is likewise a state of being we are invited to co-create and enter into here and now: the 'Kingdom of Heaven', the Mag Mell Flower World of Beauty and Otherworldly vision. At the chthonic level of meaning, the notion of hellish or heavenly states has nothing to do with speculation regarding an afterlife. We each stand perpetually at a crossroads in which we are invited to choose between two basic pathways: business as usual—a road paved with materialistic anti-values, addiction to convenience and false modes of security—or a redemptive path of true atonement. Sadly, the dominant choice made in our cultural milieu has long been the former.

It is crucial that we adequately and intelligently name the rather desperate condition in which we now find ourselves as a culture—not that we might despair about it, or address it from a place of emotional reactivity, but rather that we might take a truthful and realistic account of the situation, of the deep structures of sin we've woven ourselves into, and thus create real opportunities for correcting the course.

The medicine we need will be found not in the false promise of a technologically perfected future, but rather in the deepest threads of our past;

not in the contrived, mechanistic endeavors of this world, but in the leaves of an Otherworld Tree, the Tree of Life. We should guard against the temptation toward anachronism, and instead keep our focus on an authentic reclamation of the deepest wisdoms of our Ancestors, which, being sensibly and realistically integrated with the realities of our current contexts, can restore us again to deep connection, health, and a more meaningful, sustainable way of life.

If one queries the average Westerner today regarding whether or not they have (or ever had) an indigenous culture, almost invariably the reply is in the negative—or otherwise they glaze over in bafflement at the question. Say the word 'indigenous' to contemporary Westerners and typically what comes to their minds are peoples of North or South American nations, African tribal cultures, or Australian Aboriginal peoples. In other words, most people afflicted with the dis-ease that is Western dominator culture do not even realize any longer that they have, or ever had, their own indigenous history and traditions. This is a testament to how long and how thoroughly we in the West, regardless of our ethnic origins, have been divorced from our own cultural roots. This divorce is particularly tragic because it means the loss of precisely the knowledge and wisdom we most need now as a human race—the knowledge and wisdom that can save the human endeavor and protect the vital health of the planet.

The task at hand, then, is a genuine restitution of these indigenous wisdoms, and, resultantly, a reclaiming of the true wonder and beauty of life on this sacred Earth. We should each look to the restoration of our own native traditions, whatever those happen to be, to accomplish this aim: to attain once more to a lived state of feeling, being, and perception rooted in the animistic worldview that forms the basis of all ancient indigenous cultures, and its attendant experience of reciprocal, interdependent relationality with the whole of Life. We've had far too much of the crypto-colonialist appropriation and resultant cultural erosion of the indigenous traditions of others. The pattern of cultural appropriation as inflicted by the dominator culture of the West is damaging to both afflicter and afflicted. Moreover, our own indigenous ways hold special value for us precisely because the unique wisdoms of our Ancestors—their particular stories, images, archetypes, and spiritual gifts—are especially suited to our psyches, our personal challenges. They hold deep, epigenetic memories of the human struggles, victories, and insights particular to the peoples from whom we descend.

The answer to the question of how to authentically accomplish such a reclamation of indigenous traditions for the transformation of both individual and society lies in the territory of direct, personal, and culturally integrated experience. An efficacious approach to this task must be one which equips and supports individuals in the broader culture with tools and opportunities to personally experience an indigenous alternative to the dominator model. This implies a conceptual and practical tapestry of delicately interwoven threads—a body of efficacious initiatory lore and technique, creatively and sustainably integrated into our daily lives and worldviews.

In ancient European cultures, as in all native cultural traditions, people officially became recognized as adults in their societies through undergoing the process of a radical, life-altering initiatory experience, or 'rite of passage', wherein they were set apart temporarily from the social structure and guided by sacral technicians into a state of initiatory crisis—often to the very threshold of death—before being 'reborn' and subsequently reincorporated into the community as fully matured human persons. A folkloric memory of such initiations can be discerned in the motifs of many European folktales. Most often these experiences probably happened once in a person's life, during adolescence (as is common in most tribal cultures), though if a person's particular vocation dictated it—for example, if one were called to a life of sacerdotal service as a priest, shaman, poet, or healer—then a number of such initiations throughout one's lifetime might be requisite, each experience drawing the individual deeper into his or her authentic personhood, into the truth of his or her vocation, into deeper connection with spiritual allies.

These deep and life-altering initiations were from the earliest times overseen by shamanic figures with expert knowledge of entheogenic plants. Such plants were in nearly all cases a primary tool for effecting the necessary transformative experiences of initiates. Without this kind of initiatory experience, people remain spiritual children. So a society—and a religious system, of whatever variety—that has lost the spiritual technology for efficaciously facilitating these necessary trials of legitimate initiatory rebirth is effectively a culture constituted and overseen by infants, and a religion that has lost hold of its true purpose, which is to be a facilitative and supportive structure for radical personal and communal transformation.

As Terence McKenna notes, in all archaic cultures 'the onset of puberty was the signal to the social mechanisms of the people to begin the administration of psychedelic plants—: to carry people into adulthood, to carry them into a feeling-toned relationship with the mythological material that they had learned as children, but that they now would be expected to exemplify as realized adults within [their cultures]. We, in our anxiety...have interfered with this, and we have [resultantly] enforced upon ourselves a kind of infantilism. We have become more and more soft, more and more infantile, and the final phase of this was the decision that we never needed to grow up at all, we never needed to find out about the nature of our relationship to Being, and so the psychedelics were suppressed. What you have in the pre-adolescent child is an extreme expression of ego...and in a sense we got hung up at that place, or we "fell" into it.'[31]

Aldous Huxley once humorously (and rightly) observed that the loss or denial of this spiritual technology within the Christian tradition 'does no harm to the distillers [i.e., of alcohol, to which people turn instead as a coping mechanism], but is very bad for Christianity. Countless persons desire self-transcendence and would be glad to find it in church. But, alas, "the hungry sheep look up and are not fed". They take part in the rites, they listen to sermons, they repeat prayers; but their thirst remains unas-

---

[31] From a talk given at *The Esalen Institute*, Big Sur, California (date unknown).

suaged.'[32] In contemporary religion people find no deep and meaningful alternative, in other words, to the expedient and addictive medications of consumerism, alcohol and drug abuse, distorted and compulsive sexuality, and all the rest. These they abuse in a desperate, unconscious attempt to fill the existential void that haunts them—and of course these desperate efforts yield only more misery, since nothing can satiate the soul but authentic, ego-reducing transformation in immersive *communitas* (in both the human and nonhuman communities in the greater web of Nature), along with a real discovery and actualization of one's deepest vocation, the gifts one has to offer to the Great Community, the vast ecology of souls. These are precisely the things that materialistic Western cultures and religions are utterly unable to provide support in, which is an appalling tragedy since these are the only things that could ever scratch the existential itch which naturally arises from the circumstances of being human. Thus, we go on and on with our psycho-spiritual complexes, our trivial and destructive behaviors, our existential thirst forever unassuaged.

Just as when no discernment has been done regarding a person's true vocation and they fall unthinkingly into patterned expectations and dominant social norms, then inevitably wind up miserable, so it is that when no deep, authentic spiritual initiation is experienced by individuals in a given society those individuals remain effectively lost: clueless about their deepest identity, their proper role in the culture, and their own nature as human beings on the Earth. In the contemporary West, this foundational disconnection from authentic selfhood and vocation—combined with our general isolationism, our severance from real relationship with the Land, and from the indigenous wisdom of our Ancestors—has shown itself to be unequivocally lethal. It is a pervasive infantilization that has thoroughly infected all dimensions of contemporary Western societies, and, increasingly, non-Western societies afflicted with our materialistic agenda.

---

[32]   Aldous Huxley, *The Doors of Perception and Heaven and Hell* (New York: Harper & Row, 1954), 69.

Resultantly, we find ourselves in a social world created, governed, and populated by directionless, uninitiated children, who have never glimpsed the spiritual depths of Nature, never discovered the deepest truths about themselves, and are therefore severely deficient in the realm of authentic human values. Such people are largely incapable of understanding themselves, of grasping what it really means to be human, of discerning and fulfilling their proper relationship and responsibility to the human communities in which they dwell or to the rest of Nature outside the human community. A sense of where they come from, where they belong, and where they are going, both culturally and metaphysically, is effectively absent, and thus their unconscious minds are wracked with anxiety. Foundational anxiety of this depth must eventually spill over into conscious, waking life, and into the biological life of the organism, effectuating pathologies of every kind. Often folks proceed through the whole of their lives in this juvenile, dis-eased, self-centered manner, pursuing ultimately inconsequential or destructive aims at the expense of other beings, abandoning familial and communal responsibilities (if they ever learned them in the first place), their lives shaped by a narcissistic obsession with their own egoic impulses, which are continually fed by the dominant, ego-driven culture.

The consequences of living in such a world are apparent for all to see: this mode of being is driving us rapidly off the proverbial cliff. It is imperative now that we quickly reverse the course, and do so in a way that is not reactionary or impulsive but stable, gradual, deep, and sustainable. Only such a path can redeem the human endeavor.

In normative Western religion there has long persisted a tragic and pervasive mistake: the mistake of assuming that religiosity means 'belief'—and usually belief in some sort of materialistically conceived mythos (e.g., a literal, historical reading of Jesus and the Gospel texts). In other words, religion is assumed to be about having the right ideas. In the Christianized West, religious systems have long been subject to the twin evils of the neurotically anthropocentric dimensions of the Judaeo-Christian mythos, and the resultant and yet more neurotically anthropocentric paradigm of materialistic rationalism. This has yielded a truly disastrous vision of the human person, and a disastrous way of being in the world.

The loss of indigenous wisdom, folk tradition, and proper initiatory technologies, along with the cultural apparatuses that support them, has sadly yielded for most religious participants a surface-oriented experience consisting largely of facades, stand-ins, emotional onanism, and ineffectual placebos. It has produced a conglomeration of signs with no signified substance, symbols stripped of their original meaning, which have therefore become hollow objects around which are built an infantilizing culture of non-participatory, empty, and/or routine ritual actions performed for their own sake, or for the attainment of a low-grade, fleeting emotional easement.

Conspicuously absent from all modern, establishment religion is the capacity for actual personal transformation; and long removed are the perceptible fruits of any such transformation, relegated to a distant, fantastical realm or imaginal historic era (e.g., the time of the saints, the time when God still actually worked tangibly in the world to transform it, still cared to sanctify prophets and seers). It presumably goes without saying at this juncture that such an imaginal situation is not only delusional but appallingly fallow and resigned, utterly lacking in the necessary courage and energy to reclaim something of real substance for the human experiment.

While there are many causal factors related to this degradation of culture and religion, one possible factor that has not yet been examined seriously enough is what Terence McKenna referred to as the 'gradual profanation of…psychoactive plant sacrament[s].'[33] I take this to mean not only the plant Sacraments themselves within a given cultural context, but also the ritual, mythic, and ethical context that natively frames the transformative, visionary experiences afforded by such efficacious Sacraments. The long process of the degradation of these things in a culture, McKenna explains,

---

[33]   Terence McKenna, *Food of the Gods: The Search for the Original Tree of Knowledge* (Bantam Books: New York, 1992), 122.

yields an 'abandonment of the original psychosymbiotic mystery', resulting in 'the substitution of completely inactive materials for active ones.' I interpret 'active' and 'inactive' here in both a literal and figurative capacity. Finally, in the most advanced stage of this amnesiatic process, 'symbols are all that is left. Not only are psychoactive plants out of the picture, but plants of any sort have disappeared, and in their place are esoteric teachings and dogma, rituals, stress on lineages, gestures, and cosmogonic diagrams. Today's major world religions are typical of this stage.'[34] Apart from the use of entheogenic plant Sacraments in specific, the key issue described by McKenna is, it seems to me, the erosion of efficaciousness in Sacrament and ritual more generally: the erosion of original intent, function, and meaning of the ritual and communal iterations we now find in Western religion to be almost completely hollow, trivialized and stripped of their transformative edge, their capacity to facilitate radical change in persons or in larger socio-cultural environments.

I personally have found no more compelling theory for the origin of human consciousness as we know it, or for the associated advent of language, culture, and religious experience than the archaic discovery of entheogenic plants. But whether or not we take McKenna's description to be indicative in a total way of the process of degradation that has long plagued Christianity and all normative modes of religiosity in the Western world, or take it merely as one possible (and perhaps abstruse) angle on the situation, the basic process he describes is, I think, self-evidently true, and can be easily witnessed directly by anyone who clearly examines the present realities of mainstream religiosity. Again, the most central point is not the exact, original nature or identity of an efficacious, plant-based sacramentality, but rather the more foundational and more troubling fact that religion has lost the only valid purpose it ever served to begin with, having lost the knowledge, wisdom, and practical tools necessary to uphold and carry out that purpose.

---

[34]   ibid.

It is certainly possible to reclaim those original aims and methodologies, but it will require a totalizing kind of reform. In the final estimation, the deepest dimensions and meanings of faith are only to be found in the humble surrender of our return to Nature: our return to the bosom of the Mother. An authentic religiosity for our time will only be uncovered through such a metaphysical and existential homecoming. The prospect of meaningfully and completely engaging such a process is, to say the least, a decisive challenge for most people in postindustrial Western cultures, owing to the radical extent of our prodigal errancy, our disconnection from the foundational realities of Nature. Nonetheless, a restitution of this kind—a reentry into balanced, reciprocal, and sacral relationship with the whole of Creation—is the only real path to atonement.

Our most pressing need is to learn to trust and be nourished at every level of being by the supernal gifts and values of Nature. Religion, if it wishes to become relevant and effective once more, must become totally permeable to that need, to the processes that will facilitate its fulfillment, and to Nature herself. It will have to actively and seriously engage the work of authentically reclaiming the indigenous wisdoms that grant, illumine, and support the necessary unfolding of such an atoning reclamation.

In a way of being that is truly oriented toward authentic atonement, we align ourselves with the redemptive *telos* of Nature and the Gaian intent—that 'tender and terrible energy that is, for those with eyes to see it, love'[35]—and find, in the experience of surrendered, rooted faith (not 'belief') in such dynamic flow, that real transformation, real illumination, real redemption is actually possible. This is a critical intuitive experience, a gift of the indigenous worldview, of the animistic way of seeing, needful of recovery not just by religious systems but by all people in the world.

---

[35] Christian Wiman, *My Bright Abyss: Meditation of a Modern Believer* (New York: Farrar, Straus, and Giroux, 2013), 36.

We are each called to become educated about and to actively resist the socio-cultural and ecological evils we encounter in this thoroughly toxic and dysfunctional dominator culture. We must simultaneously hold in our minds, however, the reality that putting out localized fires, while crucial, will never quench the source of the blaze. We will have to peer through to the obscured foundation of the outward atrocities of the culture, to the underlying myths and ideologies, and seek first and foremost to transform things at that foundational level.

One thing is certain: the transformation we need must be total, and begin within each individual. It will never come from a political movement or a new ideology. It will only come when we're restored to deep connection with the soul of the Earth, to right relationship with all that is sacred in us and in the whole of Creation. Toward this end, a few structural premises may be worth establishing. There are four basic components I propose as remedies to our present crisis—building blocks for establishing a restored future in Western cultural environments.

The first foundational principle is a return to deep, integrative, and harmonious reconnection with the natural world and all its creatures. This implies the metaphysical position of animism. The second principle is a reclamation of indigenous ancestral folkways and wisdoms. This is the kind of cultural framework that can properly restore and support in Western consciousness the aforementioned animistic worldview, and reimpart crucial values—namely, the values of Nature—necessary to redeem Western societies. The third is a return to a localized, tribally inspired, interdependent and sustainable way of life and mode of community. The fourth principle is an authentic reclamation of the feminine divine (in whatever cultural framework), and a simultaneous sloughing off of male dominator modes of language, authority, value assumptions, and social organization.

The doorway to actualizing each of these principles is opened only by admitting—not just in word, but deeply—the profound dysfunction of the dominant culture that houses us and constitutes much of our life and perception. As the old therapeutic axiom reminds us, one cannot begin to heal until one admits one has a problem. The dangerous illusion that all is well must be shattered. We will have to be willing and able to step completely outside the normative ways of thinking, seeing, and being in the world that we've been so thoroughly conditioned with. The cultural assumptions and rhetoric we're continually fed—through media, through the voice of those subject to and embedded in the dominator system—must be roundly rejected.

The term 'resist' has recently become a buzz word in contemporary American politics, typically used by individuals who find the current course of American society to be unacceptable. I think the word is well chosen, because resistance is indeed necessary, not just in North America, but everywhere: resistance to the corrosive worldview assumptions, socio-political and economic systems now long inherent to the Western cultural milieu. (In some sense, the present normative culture of the United States is like an icon of the dominant Western ethos at large: the most grotesque and virulent expression of the deep-seated illness which has plagued the whole of Western consciousness and society for many generations.)

In my assessment, the need to resist is much broader and much deeper than most people who use the term in the aforementioned context are aware, because the requirements for redeeming the human endeavor, and preserving the optimal health of the Earth on which it has thus far played out, point to a resistance not of one isolated political trend or another, but of the entire dominant worldview, the dominant approach to social organization, religion, spirituality, economy, and culture, which underlie every normative social structure.

A succinct statement or 'manifesto' of the modes of resistance which I think are now most needful might look something like the following:

By reclaiming your own indigenous, animistic roots, folkways, and wisdoms, resist. By reuniting with the spiritual dimensions of Nature, resist. By rejecting the materialistic, male dominator ideologies of the present culture, resist. By seeking truth and spiritual depth instead of banality, resist. By throwing away your television (or its current equivalent), resist. By rediscovering the true magic in your life and in the whole of Nature, resist. By reclaiming the feminine divine, resist. By establishing localized communities of genuine interdependence, resist. By banishing fear, resist. By putting yourself on the line and seeking radically transformative initiatory experiences, resist. By rejecting the ideology of convenience, and all that promises meaning or fulfillment but demands no measurable change in you, resist. By living a life of introspection and contemplation, resist. By condemning the Protestant work ethic and its sickening, dysfunctional relationship to time, resist. By learning traditional arts and life skills, resist. By rejecting the false promise of happiness through consumerism and acquisition, resist. By rejecting the foundational assumptions of capitalism and trading them for natural human values, resist. By embracing the fact that ultimately the only valid measure of what is real and true will be your own direct experience, resist. By refusing to accept the endemic dis-ease and inhumane pressures of the present socio-cultural and economic systems, resist. By fervently dismissing all forms of fundamentalism, reductionism, materialism, and literalism, resist. By reclaiming the poetic and the great virtue of Beauty, resist. By boldly dissolving all unhelpful cultural boundaries, resist. By casting off all unfounded optimism and denial of the true horror of the situation in which we now collectively find ourselves, resist. By locating and embodying true hope, resist. By discovering who you truly are, where you come from, and what you came here to do, resist.

Let us leave the mythic land of gross excess, of disconnection from Nature, of violence and artificiality. Let us leave in search of a better country, in search of a deep, ancestral home, a landscape of spirit. Let us leave in search of truth.

And whoever so journeys—as Fintan or Bran or St. Brendan once journeyed on the vast, surging seas—may they be blessed to find the transformative light they seek—: the light of *metanoia*, which breaks over a deep, interior horizon, and reveals the dawn of true atonement.

For the great efforts we each must make in the years and generations to come, in order to redeem the project of human life on this planet, to reclaim the lost threads of Western indigenous traditions, and for the necessary wisdom, will, and grace to accomplish these most needful tasks, I offer the following prayer.[36]

Mother, it is time: Loose from the mountain peaks the wild, electric currents. From the deep-rooted groves of Aspen, shake out the fire of liminality. Consume us with unforgiving Beauty. The dry, brittle gold of the not-yet-fulfilled awaits our slow becoming. Let us sing Your songs of untranslatable grieving; landscapes never seen. Let us cast the dry leaves of former years to the holy flame of sacrifice, and ready our feeble hearts for rebirth. Let the charge of your sweet death come, not with the fragrance we wished or imagined, but another sort of wind, cool and dry and colored with deeper notes. Bring us Your hidden light from the Land; show us the bright decay; teach us the hymn of leaf and loam. Let it be to our foolish minds a mystery beyond all measure. Bring us at last to that vision which disturbs us, unravels us—and, being shattered, connect us once more to the secret Life of Your Being, that we may know in full the luminous strains of those songs our Ancestors, radiant in some vast and sacred distance, still long to sing.

---

[36] The phrasing in the first lines of this poem is inspired by Rainer Maria Rilke's *Herbsttag.*

An Axis Altar on the
Bay of Dolphins: New and
Ancient Gospel from Beyond
Europa's Distant Shore

O n Inis Mór, the pilgrimage group I'd been guiding through the
holy wilds of Fódla ambled round the narrow roads, skirting the
perimeter of the limestone-covered island, past Cows and Goats
being brought down for summer grazing in the lower pastures, past little
family Potato crops where seeds had not long before been sown.

As is often the case in sacred pilgrimage, the most shining gifts of that
day's journey came billowing out of the unexpected—which is why true
openness of heart, stillness of mind, and depth of listening are the three
most foundational prerequisites for making true pilgrimage.

Thus it happened that we stumbled unexpectedly into an ancient holy
site not included in our itinerary. I had, in fact, never before set foot inside
its small, sacred walls. It was the deceptively diminutive, devastating majesty
of Teaghlach Einne—'Enda's Household' or 'Enda's Hearth': originally a
monastic hermitage established in the late fifth century by St. Enda of Aran,
now marked by the ruins of an early eighth-century church—that awaited
our unsuspecting hearts.

Walking down into that elegantly ruined little church, hidden beneath the protection of grassy bluffs, there was hardly space in me for breath, no space at all for language. I was overwhelmed by a palpable sense of profound hospitality, by the feeling of untouched spiritual wildness—: a gentle wildness, buttressed by centuries of prayer and devotion not disconnected from the felt presence of Nature. It was a hospitality not always found in ancient monastic sites: one that graciously welcomed every part of me, and every part of my ancestral inheritance. Not only welcomed it, but lovingly affirmed it. It was a place that seemed to knowingly hold with tender care the indigenous, pre-Christian wisdom of the Land alongside the later Christian tradition. It was a place of reconciliation, of communion in the broadest sense, of real prayer in its deepest dimensions.

As I reverently stepped through the tiny archway of the entrance, which faced out toward the Sea, moving slowly and with wonder past ancient carvings of knotwork, of horse and rider (Macha, the Horse goddess, image of Sovereignty? Likely not, in historical terms—but mythopoetically, imagistically…), I was overcome with affection, with an Otherworldly stillness. I knelt down at the old stone altar, somehow pristinely preserved through the centuries. Someone had placed little offerings there: small stones, candles, a few dried flowers. Carved on the altar's face, side by side, were Neolithic-style spirals and crosses, as if in this place there had never been a suspicion of incompatibility between the variant worldviews and spiritual expressions these respective symbols signified.

Placing my forehead on the surface of the holy table, I was instantly transported to a deeper plane of Presence, as if ushered into a hidden, Otherworld parallel of the same physical and temporal frontier. (I think now of the medieval Irish accounts of people seen sailing in boats through the Sky not far above, while those in the boats perceived they were sailing on the Sea.) The sensation that rushed over me then I can only describe as a totalizing embrace. Suddenly I felt clearly in my heart that *this* was the only place in which my Catholic Christian priesthood any longer made sense— the only place it was ever intended to make sense. To be sure, it no longer made sense in the stale walls of failing modern institutions, filled more with excessive privilege and fear and absurd attachments than with prayer and sincere pursuit of transformation. It made no sense in structures designed to shut out the natural world; it made no sense in any context where apathy and confusion, concern for monetary security, for institutional survival (to what end?) occupied more space than anything resembling authentic spirituality, let alone the ancient Mysteries of prayer and of Sacrament.

But *this* place on the wild and pristine extremity of Inis Mór: this was a true shelter—: a 'serious house on serious earth', to reference Philip Larkin: a house in which I could authentically and without regret, without any feeling of misplacement, continue to live out the sacramental vocation of my life as a Catholic Christian priest who has also been called to the ancestral office of *fili*, or, 'poet-seer'. There, in that still, remote chapel, my priesthood made sense again. After the ravages attendant to my earnest attempts at inhabiting a space in which I could never really fit, trying to challenge and transform from the inside a religious institution self-condemned to spiritual unfruitfulness, triviality, and dissolution, I finally breathed once more the fresh air of hopeful clarity, of the peace that can only come from knowing one's proper place in things—even if it also implies the hard work of shedding safeties and supports we've come to depend on.

The sheer luminosity of a place so long devoted to the earnest pursuit of wisdom, of natural sanctity and transformation, of the truth of interbeing, somehow redeemed the priestly aspect of my vocation; it redeemed the pain of my involvement with a questionable and ultimately ineffectual institutional edifice; it invoked in me the purity and simplicity of my original call to Christian life, and to sacerdotal life in that context. It embraced me as a child is welcomed home.

The thing is, it was a homecoming that also shattered once for all,—like the final blow to a cracked clay vessel—my confidence in, and interior commitment to, the professional and communal structure to which I'd at least provisionally entrusted my heart, my time, and my livelihood. It somehow dealt a deathblow to whatever affection I retained for the broken institution that half-heartedly lifted me up and then set me adrift; the institution which showed no desire to house me, which could no longer shelter my soul or receive the words it longed to offer. It seemed to mark a heavy but graceful ending of my years-long experiment of infiltrating, prophetically and trans-formationally undermining the assumptions of a cultural-religious structure long bereft of real life and spiritual potency.

Though cautioned and tempered by at least a semblance of humility, I have nonetheless found myself thinking frequently of late on Jesus' thir-ty-eighth saying in the Gospel of Thomas: 'You have often longed to hear the words that I am speaking to you. You have no one else from whom you can hear them. But the days will come when you will seek me and you will not be able to find me.' I have seen these words in my mind's eye written on the last crumbling walls of Western Christianity.

D. H. Lawrence wrote in 1924, 'the adventure has gone out of Christianity,' and I think he was right. We stand now in the final hours—perhaps the final moments—of its twilight, and, the adventure having long since passed out of it, there seems to be very little left worth preserving. Certainly the ancient mysticism, the liturgy, the sacramentality, but only in their most archaic and now distant iterations, icons of a time before the apathy and torpidity of established Western Christendom set in to erode their deepest meaning and purpose from the consciousness of the institution itself, and nearly all its members, save a few errant mystics here and there throughout the centuries. 'We must start on a new venture towards God,' Lawrence said.

As the curtain unequivocally falls on institutional Christianity in the Western world, the question beginning to speak itself is: What will be our 'new (ad)venture towards God'? Wisdom, it seems to me, negates the pos-sibility of any time at all wasted in grieving the loss of something that's become but a pale, dim shadow of itself. Why, after all, lament the fall of a house that in the end held so little depth, that could only offer a foun-dational, exponential misperception and avoidance of the real purpose and potential of religion?

No, our new adventure lies ahead. That much seems abundantly clear. And so in lieu of bold critique or lamentation, today I bring good news: I bring the gospel of a small, persistent light at the furthest end of the known European world—an obscured but potent flame alive and well on the periphery of this cultural and religious darkness that surrounds and all too frequently constitutes us—a light standing poised to seed that darkness with the necessary elements for an upending and alchemical transmutation, which could set a new holy quest in motion.

I bring news that in a ruined little monastery established in the late fifth century on the uttermost margins of Western Europe, remembrance of the true and perennial quest, the natural and indigenous quest, the chthonically rooted quest, lives on, if only in pregnant potential. It is not the meandering and misguided quest of Western Christianity as we've known it these many centuries, sullied by dominator agendas, but the quest embodied in the grand, dreamlike experiment of early Irish Christian syncretism: an entirely different animal, whose gifts and invitations would make the psycho-spiritually constipated, dogmatic, crypto-colonialist ideologies of even the most progressive mainline Christian recoil in terror. Neither is this particular adventure of which I speak the same lost adventure Lawrence referred to when he wrote of early medieval monasticism saving Western cultures from the ravages of the Dark Ages (though certainly Irish monasticism played a leading role in that effort, as did St. Enda himself)—: that adventure, as Lawrence affirmed, is long over. New horizons must now be sung. Sung like a seer sings in the spirits.

Truth to tell, friends: salvation always and inevitably arises from the margins, from the outlandish periphery, from beyond the pale of established cultural mechanisms. Such was the case with those early Christian monastic adventurers, those stout-hearted pilgrims who took the last remaining treasures of a cultural milieu in its death throes and sheltered them, fermented them, ruminated on them deeply and breathed them into new flowering, somewhere hidden quietly from view—somewhere in the proverbial forest, in the desert, in the wilds: out far beyond the bounds where the gaze of the expected fell. Out in the Atlantic ocean, for example, at the edge of Inis Mór.

The hope and spiritual enfoldment I experienced in that blessedly naked, roofless little sanctuary at the blue-green edge of the world was the gift of a more archaic and more liminal reality: a soul-level reality, an Otherworld reality, a deep-Earth reality which holds court equally for the ancient gods of Land, Sky, and Sea, and the new gods that came from the East—so long as the latter have paid proper dues, shown rightful honor and respect, earned their keep. It receives *first* the untamable wildness of Macha, and the radical, sacrificial love of the Earth Mother, of the reciprocity She rightly asks of us—and then, only when those fundamentals have been set in order, does it move toward reflection on the sacrificial love of Christ. First holy Brigid and the undying flame of ancestral wisdom; then Christ the dying and resurrecting god, the shamanically soterical god who was sacrificed on the Tree of Worlds.

This deep-Earth reality, this blessed air of the axis altar, by its very nature rejects all forms of the diminution of native ancestral streams, all forms of colonialism and oppression. Equally, it rejects all dogmatism, all repression of authentically expressed human soul, human dream, human life. It makes little space indeed for Patrick and his imperialistic agenda, or for any of the conformist Roman toxicity that followed closely on his heels.

In this archaic sanctuary there is, I am happy to report, no room for the lukewarm, the half-baked, the fundamentalist, or the manipulative; there is no room for whitewashing, sanitizing, or subjugating. Here in this humble place beyond the boundaries, the sacramental dream of 'Church' is restored to an initiatory body, a sacral space of true natural Mystery: nothing more and nothing less. It is restored to a body that can actually perform the real, deep functions of religion in its most authentic and most needful manifestations.

In this holy space, Anu, Macha, and Badb receive the first portion of every sacrifice. The first drink of the Chalice is offered to the Spirit of the Land, the life giving Mother, from whose compassionate and endless generosity its metals—and the holy drink it holds—were born. On the altar of this sanctuary rest natural icons of the three holy realms of Earth, Sky, and Sea (it is, after all, into this wholly good, ensouled reality of Nature that the Wisdom of God became incarnate). On its surface the three Worlds converge in intimate nearness, and the hand and sight of Manannán's abundant oceanic plain—the plain of endless flowers, an ordinarily unseen but always already present heaven, like the Flower World of the Ancestral Puebloans—draws wondrously close, to offer vision and to bless.

This altar is not only an altar of Christ-Sophia, the Holy Wisdom of God, but a druidic altar, an ancestral altar, a shamanic altar at which the ones who walk between worlds and speak the sacred, poetic Word of Otherworld wisdom must preside. An altar at which those first sacred functionaries, returned to us again to perform the holy, atoning work of re-humation, like long-forgotten spirits suddenly resurrected from the forests of our ancient folktales, must attend and give voice to the deepest longings and the deepest griefs of our people. Indeed, it is such priests—and *only* such priests—that we now need desperately restored to our midst, that we should now make room for round the hearth-fires of our collective dreaming.

'But the learned say that whenever a wondrous apparition was revealed to royal princes in olden times—as when the phantom spoke to Conn, and the Land of Promise appeared to Cormac—that it was a divine visitation which came in that semblance, and not a devilish visitation. It was an angel which used to come to their assistance, for they were faithful to the truth of Nature; for the precept of the Law was served by them.'[37]

Without question we are beset now collectively by a desperate hunger of the soul. And a spirit-starved world is a world that needs to be blessed by the breath of real, rooted seership—: seership with roots as deep as the Tree of Worlds. By all that's sacred, we need now more than ever our native shaman-ists, our spirit-walkers, our shapeshifters, our poet-seers, our myth-tellers, our wisdom keepers—who, if they are to be priests, must first be seers. And we need the kinds of cultural-religious frameworks that can adequately shel-ter and support them, and facilitate the authentically redemptive work they are meant to perform, which is the salvific work of restoration to wholeness,

---

[37] From *Scél na Fír Flatha* ('The Tale of the Pledges of Sovereignty'), an early medieval Irish text found in both the Book of Ballymote and the Yellow Book of Lecan. This translation from Whitley Stokes and John Carey. cf. Carey's excellent work, *A Single Ray of the Sun: Religious Speculation in Early Ireland* (Aberystwyth: Celtic Studies Publications, 2011), 37-38.

the 'ministry of reconciliation' to our own deepest roots, to our souls, and to all of Creation—I dare say, the true work of Holy Wisdom, of Christ, which the Church as we now know it could never begin to grasp, let alone accomplish.

As Charlotte Du Cann wisely observes, 'The spirit needs the archaic things, the earthly things, the encounter with the nonhuman, with the ancestors…otherwise we remain only half a person, unrealized, like stunted trees.' A fruitful paradox: wisdom is in the soil; wisdom is an Otherworldly affair. At some primordial moment it erupted into this sensorily perceptible realm of incarnate human experience and birthed all mythopoesy, birthed the shamanic vocation, birthed the sacred speech of poetry and ritual, opened the door between worlds, shaped the druidic vision and its grasp of the journey of souls—by way of our 'ancient Grandmother, who first ate the Apples.'

My intuitive feeling, crystalized at Teaghlach Einne, is that early Irish Christianity, in its still druidically co-constituted form—as well, perhaps, as the earliest expressions of Christianity in the other Celtic nations—not only retained these archaic truths, but understood them as perennial and indispensable. The stubborn, world-shattering light of those truths, like Brigid's flame, housed in some long-invisible shrine, still waits to illumine the way for our next holy pilgrimage, whenever the ancestral councils deem it ripe for unfurling.

If we are to embark on a new adventure toward wisdom, toward real communion with the holy, then I wager we could do no better than to start at the mythic source, than to trace back the life giving spring of Beauty, with her white-robed sisters of sensory perception, flowing from the primal Well of Wisdom into this manifest world, set loose by the untamed, anti-authoritarian hand of the White Cow goddess.

It is, you see, and always has been about Beauty. About re-membrance—: restoration of the body, in every valence. Restoration to the wholeness of conscious interbeing, 'the truth of Nature'; to the known, immediate experience of the soul's eternal sojourn. A return to the primal Word of Wisdom, the poetic and translinguistic Word, which is heard, felt, beheld through the rupture of the mundane plane of experience, through the rending of veils and the bridging of worlds. And here we stand in stark need of the return of our shamanic figures, of the true priestly function, the deepest work of the altar, which dwells at the axis: the reconciliation of worlds, the way-crossing, the tending of the threshold. Singing into this world the Wisdom-Word of the Other. Work fit for a druid, for a seer. Work fit, too, for a dying and resurrecting god, a god of three worlds, a shamanic god who brings from the unseen realms salvific knowledge of the soul's eternal nature. 'Christ is my Druid', St. Columba proudly sings.

Perhaps, if we're fortunate, the Mother of fire and holy well, of the shamanic arts of smithing, medicine, and poetry, of the birthing and protection of the lambs, will graciously preside over the *leitourgia* of our re-membrance. What other gods, what spirits, what holy ancestors might wish to preside, I wonder, over such majestic work, over the birthing of that new and ancient venture, that primal and endogenous *mysterium*?

On our return to the mainland from Inis Mór, passing through Doolin Bay, a school of Dolphins surrounded our boat, playfully guiding us back to shore. Their gracefulness, their natural joy, their precision and attentiveness shone forth with such astounding soul. I recalled John Moriarty once saying, 'The Dolphins are coming up into Doolin Bay, and they're trying to tell us something.' Evolutionarily speaking, human beings went the way of attempting to shape the Earth to suit us, he said; Dolphins, by contrast, went the way of harmony with Nature, of saying to the Earth: 'You shape us to suit you'.

I don't claim to know what, but I'm confident that the Dolphins, could they speak our form of language, would say sooth, with many wise words to impart. I can only imagine that chief among those words would be that it's long past time we remembered how to be in reciprocal relationship with the Earth—long past time we remembered how to listen. It's long past time we remembered, like our distant forebears, how to be 'faithful to the truth of Nature', for that, indeed, is the only Law that was ever worth keeping: a Law not birthed by political agendas, not writ by human hands.

At St. Enda's hermitage, as in the hushed Hazel forests and limestone caves of the Burren, or on the windswept shores of Achill, or in the silent cairns of Loughcrew, the only sensible thing to do is listen and listen deeply. Whatever brings us to that stillness, that pregnant receptivity, that irreducible awe in the face of an obviously ineffable Mystery, it is *that* we're most in need of. For only in the oratory of such profound silence might we hear the counsel of the Old Ones, whispering to us the needful shape of our next individual and collective sojourn.

The adventure of Christianity having long ago passed out of this world, we are beckoned now to a new kind of pilgrimage—though it is equally an ancient sort, perhaps the quintessential or archetypal pilgrimage. Whatever the nuance of its shape, may it blossom as a quest for the Grail, in only its wildest, most sensual and poetic iterations. May it unfurl as a quest for true wholeness, for restoration to natural unity, to a clear, animistic awareness, to deep ancestral wisdoms, to a conscious state of reciprocity and interbeing with the mysterious, sacramental, and living worlds of Nature.

In that quest we will certainly face the fierce squalls and billows of the wide, surging ocean. The waters of Wisdom make no definite promise. Bóann is robbed of an eye and two limbs. As with the venture of incarnate life adopted in this Middle World, we know only that the journey will be challenging, unpredictable, and will not leave us unscathed. The same risk applies to the spiritual quest: the courage to make real sacrifice, to meet danger and death, to step into the wild unknown, is requisite for transformation. Though we're not given to know where those blessedly untamed currents will guide us, I say—I sing—that we must soon embark, for the hour now enveloping our wayward endeavors of culture and religion has grown tremendously late. May we set out with hearts attuned for seeing in the unseen ocean valleys—set out in Earth-born coracles, formed of the stories of our ancient Ancestors, over the broad, timeless seas of dreaming, of reclamation, of sacred adventure.

Roots of the Wild Wood

The Holy is too great and too terrible, when encountered directly, for [people] of normal sanity to be able to contemplate it comfortably. Only those who cannot care for the consequences run the risk of the direct confrontation of the Holy.

—Jaroslav Pelikan

Where the glacier meets the sky, / the land ceases to be earthly, / and the earth becomes one with / the heavens; no sorrows live / there anymore, and therefore / joy is not necessary; / beauty alone reigns there, / beyond all demands.

—Halldór Laxness

L iminality does not conceal truth, but reveals it.

The nature of divinity, as revealed in our manifest world of embodied, sensory experience, necessarily appears as paradox. The paradoxical, the 'both/and/neither' is the doorway to Mystery, and when it breaks into our linear world, it opens with profound invitation. We can then be fairly certain we're coming up against something substantive, something with real truth-value, something sacred.

Closure is therefore the enemy of the true, the unhappy offspring of existential insecurity and philosophical materialism. The enemy of the true is the friend of the merely factual.

The supreme liminality is the transition to and from embodied existence. This is where any authentic religion must direct and lead. It is the soil-bed of true initiation. Any form of religious practice that does not lead to a direct encounter with this veil is ultimately ineffectual, an aborted endeavor which has lost the memory of its original purpose, and the memory of what it means to be human.

The *fili*, the poet-seer, gazes in two directions simultaneously: at the revelations of this world, and the revelations of the Other. It is also true to say that the *fili* gazes in three directions simultaneously, for he or she possesses the ability to see in all three worlds, and to bring back visionary experience, word, and wisdom from those worlds in order to help maintain the health and wholeness of the people.

Dusk reveals the not-yet-night, the no-longer-day. This is the threshold and the gateway of wisdom.

A number of twin- and triple-faced stone figures are found in the Celtic archaeological record, among them the stone figure on Boa Island in County Fir Manach, Ireland, still in place today where it's stood for more than two thousand years. The druidic gods and holy Ancestors are those who see in such a way: simultaneously in the depth of this world and of the Otherworld. They can help us to intentionally and productively cross over the various thresholds we encounter on this pilgrim journey. They can help us to navigate the seas of liminality, where they mysteriously dwell and are perennially emergent.

The beginning of authentic spiritual formation is attunement to the Other, to the unseen. The unseen is not only the unmanifest, but also 'What no eye has seen, nor ear heard, nor the human heart conceived.'[38]

The *fili* is the primal source of language, the proto-magician, the shamanic explorer who steals the seed and fire of linguistic art and manifests

---

[38] 1 Cor 2:9 (NRSV).

them here in this sensory world. The origins of language and the origins of magic are one and the same. They emerge from the ecstatic crisis of the same initiatory moment.

The *fili* is an explorer of Otherworld landscapes, a hollow bone for ancestral and divine remembrances, for the utterances of the unseen.

The journey toward wisdom, toward illumination, is a journey of eternal unfoldment—like the pilgrimage of the soul, it is a road without discernible advent or end.

Amergin, the great poet-seer of the Milesians, setting foot for the first time on the sacred Land of Éire, declared: 'I am a wind on the sea, I am a swelling wave, I am a voice of the ocean, I am a stag of seven clashes, I am a hawk on the cliff, I am a dewdrop in sunlight, I am the rarest of herbs, I am a boar of great battle, I am a salmon in a pool'.

The Welsh poet-seer, Taliesin, declared in the opening of his visionary poem, *The Battle of Trees*: 'I have been in a multitude of shapes, before assuming a consistent form. I have been a sword, narrow and variegated. I will believe when it is apparent. I have been a tear in the air. I have been the faintest of stars. I have been a word among letters. I have been a book in the origin. I have been the light of lanterns...I have been an eagle, I have been a coracle on the seas...I have been a raindrop in a shower'.

The Mazatec shaman, Román Estrada, entering the ecstatic state of the mushroom Sacrament, declared: 'I am the big lightning, says. I am the lightning of rocky places, says. I am the light of the dawn, the light of day, says.'[39]

María Sabina, the great Mazatec *curandera*, from the depths of her mushroom *velada*, declared: 'I am a Cross Star woman....I am a woman who flies. I am the sacred eagle woman, says. I am the Lord eagle woman, says. I am the lady who swims, says. Because I can swim in the immensity. Because I can swim in all forms....Because I am the sacred opossum....I am

---

[39]   Henry Munn, 'The Mushrooms of Language' in *Hallucinogens and Shamanism*, ed. Michael Harner (London: Oxford University Press, 1973), 111.

the woman book who is beneath the water, says…I am the shepherdess who is beneath the water, says. I am the woman who shepherds the immense, says….I come, going from place to place, from the origin.'

When Gordon Wasson met Doña María Sabina in the Oaxacan mountains in 1955 and was introduced to the archaic shamanistic traditions she maintained under tutelage of the divine mushroom Sacrament, *teonanácatl* ('flesh of the gods'), he reflected broadly—and rightly—on the implications of such a profound hidden treasure of religious experience:

'We had attended a shamanistic rite with singing and dancing among our Mixeteco friends which no anthropologist has ever before described in the New World, a performance with striking parallels in the shamanistic practices of some of the archaic Palaeo-Siberian peoples. But may not the meaning of what we had witnessed go beyond this? The hallucinogenic mushrooms are a natural product presumably accessible to men in many parts of the world, including Europe and Asia. In man's evolutionary past, as he groped his way out from his lowly past, there must have come a moment in time when he discovered the secret of the hallucinatory mushrooms. Their effect on him, as I see it, could only have been profound, a detonator to new ideas. For the mushrooms revealed to him worlds beyond the horizons known to him, in space and time, even worlds on a different plane of being, a heaven and perhaps a hell. For the credulous primitive mind, the mushrooms must have reinforced mightily the idea of the miraculous. Many emotions are shared by men with the animal kingdom, but awe and reverence and the fear of God are peculiar to men. When we bear in mind the beatific sense of awe and ecstasy and *caritas* engendered by the divine mushrooms, one is emboldened to the point of asking whether they may not have planted in primitive man the very idea of god.'[40]

One thing that Wasson—who was not a trained folklorist and who lacked familiarity with archaic European traditions, particularly Celtic traditions—failed to imagine was the possibility that the lost Sacrament of

---

[40] R. Gordon Wasson, 'Seeking the Magic Mushroom', in *LIFE Magazine* (June 10, 1957).

the Celtic poet-seers and their attendant visionary rituals might have a profoundly intimate relationship—in terms of form, substance, and mythopoesis—with the Sacrament and ritual of María Sabina.

Notwithstanding, an Otherworld gate was opened up before Wasson and his companions there in the Oaxacan village of *Huautla de Jiménez*, and, by extension, that gate was also opened up, at least *in potentia*, to the rest of the world. Sadly, the publication of Wasson's monumental discovery ushered in a tidal wave of American colonialist destruction and shameless cultural appropriation in Oaxaca—hardly different at all, in fact, from what's happening now in South America with the present Ayahuasca craze.

But for all its subsequent tragedy, Wasson's quest did open up profound and revelatory modes of experience—ecstatic, visionary experience. And it reintroduced to a spirit-starved world the holy Sacrament that had from earliest times facilitated such experiences, long lost to Western consciousness but an archaic friend of European peoples. And that, of course, is a profound gift. I suspect it was also a divine grace, a gratuitous gift of Spirit, of Nature herself, handed back to us at the crossroads—: a potentially soterical gift of the gods. To be sure, Spirit can and will find a way to work through anything. But the work of salvation is always participatory. As the clichéd colloquialism would have it: it takes two to tango.

In the Celtic world, the gods have certainly continued to weave their way into the fabric of society, by all manner of luminous and creative expressions—even in the midst of unfriendly socio-cultural territory, of colonialist iterations, self-hatred, unprocessed grief, and all the rest. Perhaps as the holy ancestral councils see fit, and the souls of their kin are reborn into this world now poised at a decisive crossroads of planetary fate, the archaic threads of wisdom are being resurfaced and set to the loom, brought once more into the light of day, where they await our wise and careful reclamation.

Naomh Brìghde ('Holy Brigid' or 'Saint Brigid') is an elegant icon of the relatively seamless maintenance of pre-Christian, indigenous Celtic traditions in the Christianized Celtic nations. As a goddess and divine ancestress—

patron of poet-seers, smiths, and healers—Brìghde seems to have been incarnate on this Earth, in one form or another, during archaic times, the time of the Tuatha Dé Danann. But she was later born again on the Earth as Brigid the Abbess of Kildare—fittingly, the daughter (or in some stories, niece) of a renown druid teacher, and guardian of a sacred landscape at Kildare where once was maintained a druidic Grove of holy Oaks (*Kildare* means literally, 'Church of the Oak'), a fire sanctuary that from the earliest of Celtic times housed an 'eternal flame', as well as a college or 'Mystery School' of druidic training. She was also said to have been present with Mary in the manger at the birth of Christ: Mary's midwife (fitting for a holy patroness of healers) and Christ's wet nurse. Thus, she is called in Ireland and Scotland a 'second Mary' or 'Mary of the Gael'.

How might it be that the same divine soul could have existed in all these forms over vast spans of time? In spite of how it may appear at first glance, the aforegiven explication of the three lives of Holy Brigid is not merely a contrived attempt at loosely Christianizing a pre-Christian deity (though that, of course, is one dimension of the matter). As a metaphysical proposition, taken on its own terms, such a notion only makes sense where an indigenous Celtic or druidic worldview has persisted, because within such a worldview, the soul persists forever on an eternal pilgrim journey, and can be born or incarnated in any number of worlds—or eras of this world—throughout the whole of time. This applies to all souls that ever were. Certainly this includes first and foremost the gods and holy Ancestors, the 'first ones' of the arts of wisdom, the Shining Ones, the radiant ones of unsurpassed illumination. Brìghde, I would assert, is one such soul.

On the holy Feast of Imbolc, Naomh Brìghde is thought to return in spirit from the Otherworld to visit the homes of those who show her devotion. Many customs survive even to the present day of preparing a place in the home for Brigid's return, of making and laying out special ritual objects for her to bless upon her return (e.g., the *Brat Bhrìghde*, a piece of cloth representing Brigid's protective mantel, or the emblematic 'Brigid's Cross', woven from wild rushes). In some parts of Ireland and Scotland, a bed was made in the house for Brigid on the Eve of the Feast of Imbolc, also known as *Lá Fhéile Bhríghde*. Often in each home a dinner table was set for her before a freshly swept hearth (a number of the traditional prayers to Brigid are related to kindling or smooring the hearth fire, and Brigid has always been in some way associated with fire as a sacral, life giving, transformative, and sacrificial medium). A small effigy, known as a *Brídeóg*, was also made and carried in procession through the villages on Imbolc Eve, to signify Brigid's return and her presence among the people on that night.

The assumption that Brigid can and does return in spiritual form on this holy night each year—just as all the Ancestors (and other spirits who may populate the Otherworld) are able to pass through the veil and return to this manifest world on the holy night of Samhain—implies a free and lively movement of eternal souls. Indeed, in native Gaelic understanding (and probably throughout the vast world of ancient Celtic cultures), the gods—including those gods who can be accurately described as the souls of large-scale natural phenomena—are seen as Ancestors—sometimes, though not always, Ancestors in the flesh, but always Ancestors in spirit, kindred along the great starry road of eternal pilgrimage.

The 'pan-Celtic' worldview, to the extent that such a thing existed and can be realistically recreated, seems to have given a place of centrality and great honor to the Ancestors and the ancestral, as did the Neolithic cultures that preceded the Celts in their Westernmost homelands. These cultural groups inhabiting the Isles have always held a deep respect for the power and influence of the Ancestors (or the Saints, in more contemporary parlance): for their wisdom, their power to create desired change in the lives of their living or presently incarnate descendants, but also for their potential to cause mischief, and even to bring us prematurely through the veil of death.

In an animistic worldview such as that embodied and expressed in ancient Celtic cultures, ancestral souls understood to be divine may be—or may once have been—spirits of natural phenomena; they may also be heroic figures of battle and/or of wisdom, great poet-seers, druids, and sages who once inhabited human form. There are also stories from both Gaelic and Brythonic traditions of what might technically be called 'totem animals' (long-lived animal spirits who act as guardians, icons, and points of connection for their particular species, and who are often considered patron protectors and helpers of individual souls and tribal communities) being described as 'Ancestors', and there are likewise many tales of souls inhabiting animal forms before returning to human or divine form, in a process of *metempsychosis* or 'transmigration of souls'. In a worldview in which all things are known to be ensouled, the lines that ordinarily frame our conventional and culturally constituted categories like god or goddess, Ancestor, totem, nature spirit, etc., are often blurred or completely absent. This may frustrate modern minds not reared in animistic cultural environments, but the reality is that for those of us who frequent Otherworldly domains, one thing becomes inevitably clear: the cosmos is far more complex, far wilder, and far stranger than our comfortable, expedient clinical categories could ever truly express. This is the witness of all shamanic pilgrims, of visionaries and poet-seers.

We might speculate that ancestral souls who are overtly divinized, presumed to be especially holy or illumined, possess a greater power and agency with which to navigate the worlds. Perhaps for those souls, rebirth in fleshly form at some point comes to a close. We do have attestations in Irish tradition that there was, at least in the early Christian centuries, a precedent for the idea that gods 'die' and pass out of this world. This does not mean their souls cease to exist, but rather that they, like us, can die to certain forms they've long inhabited, and take on other forms in the great river of cosmic becoming. Some of our holy Ancestors, and perhaps our gods, may now dwell indefinitely, then, in an Otherworldly state—or an inter-dimensional layering of states—vulnerable to our prayers and petitions, and able, through the power of their wisdom and magic, to respond as they see fit, though they are no longer seen among us in this Middle World as they once were. Celtic thought asserts, too, that the veil between worlds may always be crossed in both directions, and so divine and ancestral souls dwelling now in the Otherworld are able to revisit this earthly realm in both corporeal and non-corporeal forms, particularly when the wheel of seasons turns to a place of pronounced liminality and the veil becomes especially thin.

☙

If, as we see in the tales of Fintan Mac Bóchra and others, the soul can enter into the forms of animals such as Salmon, Hawk, or Stag, then could the soul not also enter into Grove, Spring, Stream, or Ocean? If the Arthurian tale of the nine maidens of the sacred Wells contains some authentic survival of animistic belief, then we might deduce that the spirits of natural phenomena can indeed die, pass out of the world and on to some other form and place, just as human souls do. An understanding of the spirits of natural phenomena as ancestral divine figures has precedent in many indigenous cultural contexts. It is certainly possible that deities like An Daghda or Manannán Mac Lir (gods associated with Storm and Sea, respectively) were mythically understood as ancestral figures in ancient Gaelic cosmology.

Regardless, what is clearly implied by any worldview built on the foundation of a vast and interwoven ecology of spirit, such as the pan-Celtic worldview heretofore discussed, is the shared experience of being situated in an eternal and all-pervasive community of souls. In this worldview there are not 'human souls' and 'other souls' (as distinct from human souls), but there are simply souls, which can inhabit any number of forms—or a potentially infinite number of forms—throughout the course of endless ages.

Perhaps the best (and most concise) definition of animism is therefore: 'Nature ensouled'.

The traditions surrounding Naomh Brìghde, along with traditions related to many other divine and/or ancestral figures, such as Fintan Mac Bóchra or Finn Mac Cumhaill, constitute an organic mythic flowering of a worldview which assumes the doctrine of *metempsychosis*—the transmigration of souls—as a foundational fact of being.

☙

In native Celtic traditions, the gods are often given three names or titles—three being the holiest of numbers, and a signifier of sacrality.

The Daghda, though he has many other monikers, bears three primary names: An Daghda ('The Good God' or 'The Fire God'), Eochaid Ollathair ('Horseman All-Father'), and Ruadh Rofhessa ('Red One of Great Knowledge' or 'Red One of Great Science').

He is also called Athgen mBethai, 'Regeneration of the World', and is associated in the insular texts with *druidecht* (i.e., druidic magical arts), as a bearer of great spiritual might and potency. He is Daghda nDuir, strong or mighty as the Oak, bearer of all-powerful knowledge. He is also Cerrce and Fer Benn (perhaps 'Striker' and 'White-Peaked or Pointed Man', respectively),[41] names that some have suggested could link him to the 'Horned One' or 'Antlered One'—Cernunnos in Gaulish tradition, and perhaps Conall Cernach in later Irish sources—but could just as easily confirm his origin in the tradition of an archaic Indo-European 'Sky-Father' and storm god associated with lightning and the Oak, wildfire (and therefore fire more generally, as something descended from the heavens), rainfall, and regeneration of the Land.[42]

A majority of the epithets and symbols of the Daghda seem to link him with lightning strike, thunder, storm, and, by extension, sacred fire, fertility, renewal of crops and of the sacred Land. Scott Martin notes that the unusual Irish description of the Daghda's club as a 'wheeled fork' (*gabol gicca rothach*) may well confirm these attributions, with the 'fork' representing the forked appearance of lightning, and the 'wheel' the sound of thunder (presumably by connection to the sound of chariot wheels).[43] In the Irish text, *Tochmarc Étaíne* ('The Wooing of Étaíne'), we read: 'There was a famous king of Ireland from the race of the the god-peoples, named Eochaid Great-Father.

[41] cf. Scott A. Martin, *The Names of the Dagda* (2008), at http://www-personal.umich.edu/~samarti/dagda.pdf (accessed April 15, 2018).

[42] cf. William Sayers, 'Cerrce, an Archaic Epithet of the Dagda, Cernunnos, and Conall Cernach' in *Journal of Indo-European Studies* 16, 1988, 341-364.

[43] Scott A. Martin, *The Names of the Dagda* (2008), at http://www-personal.umich.edu/~samarti/dagda.pdf (accessed April 15, 2018).

He was also called the Dagda [the 'Good God'], for it was he who used to work wonders for them and control the weather and the crops. As a result of which men said he was called the Dagda.'[44]

The 'Good God' is the one who assures the abundant gifts of the heavens, in union with the abundant gifts of the Land (whom he is said to mate with each Samhain), to sustain the collective life and health of the people. It is therefore intuitive to link the Daghda with the Roman Jupiter, the Greek Zeus, and the Norse Thor, each as unique cultural expressions of a more ancient, common Indo-European deity often described as a 'Sky-Father', associated with rainfall, lightning and thunder, with the Oak tree, fertility, and fatherhood (in a variety of capacities). Mark Williams also points out a possible connection with the Norse Odin, by way of the epithet 'All-Father' applied to both Odin and the Daghda.[45]

Apart from all this there are a formidable number of additional references to the Daghda and his characteristics throughout the insular Irish texts, sometimes contradictory to one another. This dizzying array of references, possible literary and mythic valences is characteristic of the Celtic mythic inheritance. Scholars have long lamented the cognitive dissonance created in attempting to reconcile the Celtic gods in their appearances as divine or semi-divine Ancestors with the gods as spirits of Nature or as deities in a more Classical sense. No doubt part of the reason for this dissonance is that the ancient Celts neither naturally possessed nor valued these particular intellective structures, which to them would have seemed foreign. They apparently did not feel the need for such linear categorization of the sacred.

That being said, it is nonetheless possible to find some clarity regarding the infinitely faceted sacred in these cultural streams. On occasion, the principle of Ockham's Razor may be useful in sifting through the inherited content.

---

[44] Mark Williams, *Ireland's Immortals: A History of the Gods of Irish Myth* (Princeton: Princeton University Press, 2016), 87. cf. also O. Bergin and R. I. Best, *Ériu* 12 (1938), 137-196.

[45] ibid.

With regard to the Daghda, it seems most sensible to conclude that he was originally a divinity associated with rain, thunder, and lightning, of the basic Indo-European type described above—an archetype which evolved in a variety of ways within various European cultures over time. He would then be cognate with the Gaulish Taranis ('The Thunderer'), and distinct from the Gallic Cernunnos, who holds a different set of symbolic attributes.

The Daghda, we can imagine, might naturally take on a druidic patronage and association with druidic arts and powers by his association with lightning—a seemingly magical natural phenomenon giving rise to fire, which is in turn not only sacramental in druidic ritual but also a supernal symbol of wisdom and illumination (á la the 'fire in the head'), the chief aim and virtue of archaic Celtic religion—as well as by his association with the Oak, which was the great sacred tree of the druids, icon of the cosmic World Tree, and etymologically related to the term *druid* itself (meaning, in essence, 'Oak Wisdom' or 'Wise One of the Oak'—that is, one who possesses the sacred wisdom of the Oak). It is also interesting to note, in view of the Daghda's close association with druidic arts, that lightning has been connected in other Indo-European traditions with the seemingly miraculous appearance of entheogenic fungi.

Like other Indo-European storm gods, the Daghda possesses a club which 'strikes' like lightning, and can either kill or give life, just as storms can either destroy (e.g., by lightning strike and resultant wildfire) or rejuvenate the Land (e.g., by rainfall, and the resultant nourishing of plants and animals). The epithet 'Horsemaster' could also be a metaphoric reference to thunder, with the rumbling of horse hooves on the Earth being audially akin to the sound of thunder. He may also be represented in the 'god of the wheel' depicted in various forms of pan-Celtic art, e.g., on the Gundestrup Cauldron, perhaps similarly associated with thunder by the sound of chariot wheels, and with the heavens by a symbolic resonance with the cyclical nature of the turning seasons and celestial bodies.

Jean Markale suggests that An Daghda's sacred objects—magical harp, club, and cauldron of abundance—make him All-Father of the three social classes of Celtic societies: the sacerdotal class, the warrior-artisan class, and the producer or laborer class, respectively.[46] This is a compelling possibility.

I would assert, however, that this does not make An Daghda equivalent to Caesar's 'Celtic Dis Pater', described in his *Commentarii de Bello Gallico* as supreme Ancestor to all the Gallic tribes. All Celtic divinities can be made, in one way or another, to fit symbolically in one or more of the traditional social classes. If all the ancestral deities in Celtic cultures are connected in some way with one or more of the three primary social classes, and if the druids are the most important figures in the entire social structure, held up as sacrosanct, as the very mediators between Otherworld, gods, Ancestors, and humanity, then more naturally the druids' chief patron, their great vocational Ancestor, their 'first one', would be counted as progenitor of the people—at least as imagined and taught by the druids themselves. This 'first one' seems most convincingly to be Cernunnos (and his equivalents in the various Celtic cultures).

It is compelling to consider that the Daghda incorporates into his repertoire of magical symbols and divine attributes elements normally associated with the feminine (particularly the Cauldron of abundance and regeneration, and his intimate connection with the fertility of the Land). The Daghda in this sense can provide a rather beautiful model for harmonizing masculine and feminine elements in the human psycho-spiritual journey. As Peter O'Connor points out, 'He would appear to be an advance on the singularly masculine gods of the ancient Greeks, which have played such a powerful role in shaping the psyche of Western man.'[47]

This model presented by the divine figure of the Daghda offers a vision of life and spirituality in which the feminine and masculine dimensions are balanced, and the rational, more egoic impulses of the masculine are properly harmonized and integrated in a worldview in which the source and

---

[46] Jean Markale, *The Druids: Celtic Priests of Nature* (Rochester, VT: Inner Traditions, 1999), 92.

[47] Peter O'Connor, *Beyond the Mist: What Irish Mythology Can Teach Us about Ourselves* (London: Orion Books, 2000), 31.

impetus of Life is ultimately feminine. (Anu, the Earth Mother, is, let us recall, 'Mother of the Irish Gods'.)

We might do well to reflect on the differences in worldview (and therefore world) produced by such an integrated model of divinity, versus an unbalanced, male dominator model, as has been normative for most of Western history. In this latter category we would have to place everything in Western religious and cultural endeavor that has been born of Roman, Hellenistic, Judaeo-Christian, and other Near-Eastern and Mediterranean assumptions about divinity, as epitomized in male dominator figures like Yahweh and Zeus.

One other possible reference to the archaic figure of An Daghda in Irish insular tradition—and an instance of text which bears a great deal of symbolic significance beyond the discussion of his nature and identity—is to be found in the tale of *Finn and the Man in the Tree*, preserved in an eighth-century manuscript. In this evocative and undoubtedly very ancient narrative scenario, Finn encounters a mysterious, disguised figure seated in a great tree (mythopoetically, we can easily imagine it to be an Oak tree, though the text does not specify). The Otherworldly encounter is recorded as follows:

'One day as Finn was in the wood...he saw a man in the top of a tree, a blackbird on his right shoulder and in his left hand a white vessel of bronze, filled with water in which was a skittish trout, and a stag at the foot of the tree. And this was the practice of the man, cracking nuts; and he would give half the kernel of a nut to the blackbird that was on his right shoulder while he would himself eat the other half; and he would take an apple out of the bronze vessel that was in his left hand, divide it in two, throw one half to the stag that was at the foot of the tree and then eat the other half himself. And on it [on the stag? on the tree?] he would drink a sip of the bronze vessel that was in his hand so that he and the trout and the stag and the blackbird drank together. And then his followers asked Finn who he in the tree was, for they did not recognize him on account of the hood of disguise which he wore.'[48]

Finn, having himself received the initiation of a poet-seer and consumed the Salmon of Wisdom, and who is thus able to glimpse the truth of all things in vision by placing into his mouth the 'thumb of seership', answers and reveals the identity of the mysterious Otherworld figure. He is, Finn says, *Dercc Corra Mac hUí Daighre* (or, *Dearg Corra Mac hUí Daighre*): 'The Peaked Red One, Son of the Flashing One'.

As Anne Ross notes, 'The above anecdote seems to stem more convincingly from original cult legends than almost any other in the vernacular tradition.'[49] There are many layers of esoteric symbology in this image of *Dercc Corra*, and we will explore here but a few.

The 'trout' in the chalice seems likely to be cognate with the Salmon of Wisdom, and the nuts the man is cracking and sharing with the Blackbird seem likely a reference to the Hazelnuts which are said to fall from the nine Hazel trees surrounding the Otherworld Well of Wisdom, which the Salmon eats, thus coming to embody all knowledge and Otherworldly vision. The Blackbird is also an ancient Celtic symbol of Otherworld contact and communication, much represented in folklore and mythology, and bearing in its Gaelic name, *Druid-dhubh*, a seeming connection to druidic knowledge. Apples are of course a quintessential symbol not only of the Otherworld in general, and of certain landscapes visited by mythic travelers in Otherworld realities (e.g., Bran Mac Febal), but more specifically of Otherworld food— the sacramental food which gives one access to the Otherworld in felt, immediate experience. The Hazelnuts, the Salmon, and the Apple are all, in fact, likely symbolic representations of the lost entheogenic Sacrament of the poet-seers.[50] The Stag is, in Celtic traditions both insular and continental, a frequently recurring symbol of sacred wilderness, and, as Ross notes,

---

[48] Kuno Meyer, trans. 'Finn and the Man in the Tree', in *Revue Celtique*, XXV (1904), 344-349.
[49] Anne Ross, *Pagan Celtic Britain* (Chicago: Academy Chicago Publishers, 1996), 421.
[50] I explore this theme in depth in a forthcoming work.

'an otherworld animal, luring the living into the realms of the gods.'[51] The Stag is also closely associated in continental Celtic iconography with the antlered deity, Cernunnos, who seems to be Caesar's 'Celtic Dis Pater', a guardian of Otherworld roads (i.e., of the pathways between this world and the Otherworld), a deeply archaic ancestral figure, perhaps seen as 'first one' among the Celtic tribes (and/or among the proto-druidic sacral class), and therefore also a psychopompic and prototypically shamanic figure. Indeed, the name of Dercc Corra, 'Peaked Red One', is tempting to connect with the 'peaked' image of antlers, and therefore with Cernunnos or the antlered god more broadly. However, I strongly suspect a different—or at least an additional—association embedded in the name (though this does not necessarily rule out the possibility of Dercc Corra as a figure in some way analogous to Cernunnos).

In Irish sacral and mythic terminology, the color red seems ubiquitously associated with wisdom and illumination, as well as with Otherworld landscapes (e.g., in the description of Otherworldly foods, such as 'raw flesh' or the red of Apples, or in the characteristically red ears frequently attributed to Otherworld animals). We've already seen this Otherworldly red associated with the Daghda in his epithet, *Ruadh Rofhessa*, 'Red One of Great Knowledge'. Red is also naturally associated with fire, which, as we've also noted, is in turn associated with knowledge and wisdom, particularly with the illumination or 'fire in the head' of the poet-seers, like Finn.

In a more universal scope, terms like 'red', 'peaked', and 'knowledge' (particularly in the sense given here in Irish tradition, as wisdom and seership related to normally unseen truths and realities) can all be intuitively and materially linked with traditional descriptions of shamanic ecstasy— and especially shamanic ecstasy induced by entheogenic plant or mushroom Sacraments. The images of Otherworldly foods contained in the scene of 'The Man in the Tree' likewise point to this archaic set of ritual techniques.

How might all this relate to the figure of An Daghda? I think it relates to him principally in Dercc Corra's surname, Son of the Flashing One. As we

---

[51]   Anne Ross, *Pagan Celtic Britain* (Chicago: Academy Chicago Publishers, 1996), 423.

have seen, the Daghda is continually associated through his various epithets with phenomena related to lightning, thunder, and storm, placing him, in my view, firmly in the divine category of the Indo-European storm god or 'Sky-Father'—'for it was he who used to work wonders for them and control the weather and the crops.'[52] Ross likewise makes this connection, seeing 'the tribe of the flashing one' as related to 'Leucetius, "Lightning"...Taranis, "Thunderer" and others descriptive of aerial phenomena.'[53]

The 'hood of disguise' described as an attribute of Dercc Corra in his appearance to Finn and his followers is possibly, but not necessarily, a negation of the idea that Dercc Corra could be an insular Irish expression of the Cernunnos deity type. One fundamental deciding factor would be whether 'hood of disguise' is meant literally or in a purely figurative sense. For if we are to imagine the figure of Dercc Corra as an antlered divinity, we can scarcely imagine him as simultaneously wearing a hood, which would seem an awkward accoutrement indeed for one with Stag's antlers protruding from the top of his head. However, if the attribution of the hood is given figuratively, or simply to indicate that the figure of Dercc Corra was symbolically 'cloaked' or 'veiled' in some unspecified fashion and therefore unrecognizable to Finn's followers, or, more interestingly, that he wore something akin to the fringed masks of Eurasian shamans, found in European shamanic burials as early as 9,000 years ago (e.g., the 'shaman of Bad Dürrenburg'), then the identification with Cernunnos could stand. Ross seems to want to make the connection between the two figures, but is also hesitant: 'It would be unrealistic to suggest that the Irish "Peaked Red One" is identifiable... with Cernunnos in his role as nurturer of animals, but nevertheless, it can hardly be held that the cult legends which gave rise to symbolism of these monuments can have differed greatly from those in which this extraordinary

---

[52] Mark Williams, *Ireland's Immortals: A History of the Gods of Irish Myth* (Princeton: Princeton University Press, 2016), 87. cf. also O. Bergin and R. I. Best, *Ériu* 12 (1938), 137-196.

[53] ibid., 422.

scene, described in a later Christian milieu, but in which the pagan details would seem to have been so faithfully preserved, originated.'[54]

Perhaps the Irish figure of Dercc Corra is indeed connected to the continental figure of Cernunnos, as the 'Celtic Dis-Pater', so-called, guardian and wayshower of Otherworld roads, seated in the Tree of Worlds, itself the axis or way between this Middle World, the Upper World, and Lower World, and thus patron of the archaic technologies that facilitate Otherworld travel—that is, the arcane and holy Sacraments and their associated ritual uses. And perhaps An Daghda, along with his continental equivalent, is father to Dercc Corra, making the latter, 'Son of the Flashing One'. These possible connections must, of course, remain provisional and exploratory, but they are certainly compelling in their implications—and there is, within a mythic narrative as rich as *Finn and the Man in the Tree*, much we *can* know and rediscover, and much that can lead us, at least in potential, back toward the Otherworld Well.

While there is no way to convincingly determine, in intellective or rational terms, what the intent of a medieval author of an eighth-century tale was regarding a single phrase (in this case, 'hood of disguise'), and while the real nature and identity of a figure like Dercc Corra may, at least in the surface layers of human mentation, never be known, I would argue that instances like these (of which there are many) should not discourage us in the project of indigenous reclamation. For, like most things connected to the realms of the Otherworldly, deep-rooted in native traditions, such sacred knowledge must ultimately be attained through visionary experience, through direct reconnection with the ancestral, and with the Otherworldly sources of wisdom. Scholarship, while crucial in its own ways, can never lead us to the Well of Wisdom. A tale like that of *Finn and the Man in the Tree*, if nothing else, reminds us of the tools that can indeed take us back to that wellspring of ancestral knowledge and spiritual nourishment: they are tools of the visionary, of the 'archaic techniques of ecstasy', of the multivalently symbolic, the mythic, the sacral and the poetic.

---

[54]   ibid.

Vision, Orality, and Mythic Reform

For I did not imagine that things out of books would help me as much as the utterances of a living and abiding voice.

—Eusebius

When a tradition loses its living practitioners, it doesn't mean that the tradition is lost; like water, it goes underground, and it finds another place to come up.

—Caitlín Matthews

The path of the old spells is languishing in the west without refuge. // Rich the body of the mountains with remembrance of days gone by / Blessed the face of the ocean with the dream of a time that has passed / Shining is each season with the spirit of a wind of tranquility / O, days of esteem, your nobleness, your affection! // O radiant days of love, with your bright, virtuous customs / O times of joy, with your laughter, cheer and music / O generation of divine fortune, of beams of knowledge and discernment, / Why have you gone and left no noble light to reflect your honor?

—Donald Sinclair

Storytelling reveals meaning without committing the error of defining it.

—*Hannah Arendt*

As the folktale sees I see. / As the folktale lives I live. / And the path to my door, that too is a folktale. / Coming here, you either undergo what people undergo in a folktale or you'll never lift my latch. // Little wonder I so rarely hear my latch being lifted.

—*John Moriarty*

The song I hold may appear in this world as imperative—a kind of manifesto or offering of instruction. This is the effect of a momentary glamor, a strange and passing refraction, a necessary play of light. The song that breathes in me is Connla's, it is Fintan's, the silver sound of white blossom bells. My song finds its home in the wild, mythic field, in the Hazel wood, in the cool, gentle waters that flow forth from the sacred spring in Coill Bhoireann, where one may be pleased to wander eternal, as over the ocean plains of the West, across Mag Mon, over the honeyed streams, in the valley of endless flowers. 'My song is love unknown'—: the breaking-in, the wild return to myth, the language of the sacred Earth.

To decolonize the soul, to exhume the transformative capacity of our most deep-rooted mythic memory, to restore, re-enliven, and unapologetically reclaim the ancestral inheritance that was long kept hidden from us, buried beneath an amnesia-producing battlefield of ego-toxicity and mechanistic materialism: this now must be our labor, our watchword, our central guiding aim.

The doorway of and to the mythic, the archaic, the indigenous, is our portal of atonement-*in-potentia*, a faint hope of salvation from the dew-covered night of our strange and alienating exile from the Real, our misguided sojourn into the corrosive theater of techno-patriarchal rationalism and the delusion of endless material progress.

Presently the voice of the author is expected to avoid a posture of certainty; perhaps to unfold the subjective experience with a kind of *emotive* certainty, but at all costs to abnegate the surety of large-scale claims about reality, to avoid the imperative modality altogether, and to cease from imbuing even the consciously subjective, the 'I', with any real degree of power and potency.

These things may be part and parcel of postmodern convention, but they have no part in the way of the *fili*, and would seem to most indigenous worldviews a bizarre and probably neurotic aberration. So long as the dynamic spirit of inquiry, of searching is maintained and the demons of dogmatism are kept at bay, the sure prophetic voice should sing once more. The visionary ecstasis of the poet-seer, the shamanic explorer, the mystic affirms and draws its resultant power from the truth-value of the felt presence of subjective experience. Language that emerges, then, from that state is by nature prophetic, divinatory, curative, and magical. It contains the mark of Otherworldly power, and therefore has transformative capacity: capacity to cause real change in the manifest world.

Our socio-cultural and ecologic hour here in the contemporary Western world is growing late, and the strange, overly self-conscious dance of postmodernity may be ill-fitted for the needful tasks of revisioning and restoration to wholeness. It's quite possible that the deafened ears of most cannot at any rate hear the subtleties implied in that continuously reflexive approach; it's possible we can no longer afford to play with such delicate maneuvering.

Golden herb of twilight. Sacred Well of many names. Poetic ecstasy of seers—the only ones who can realistically declare, with resonant veracity: 'I am a god who kindles fire in the head'. To these it seems we must now return.

'Our species thinks in metaphors and learns through stories', Mary Catherine Bateson observed.[55] Many of the foundational stories we've adopted and perpetuated throughout the last two thousand years of Western history have been profoundly destructive, alienating not only to the human soul (and the whole human person), but also to Creation, to Nature and all Her nonhuman children. I think this is clear enough to see for anyone who examines the matter with even a modest degree of focus.

The mythic narratives that underlie our conscious reality determine the course of our lives, both collectively and individually. Often they are simply the 'water we swim in', and go largely unexamined. Thus, a process of excavation is needed—an exhumation of our current mythic assumptions, as well as the buried, forgotten, or rejected archaic worldviews of our distant Ancestors, which we would do well to re-encounter and intelligently reclaim.

Jung once said of his sojourn into myth and symbol: 'I had to know what unconscious or preconscious myth was forming me, from what rhizome I sprang.'[56] That is the sort of excavation we in the Western world are desperately overdue for; but our process of transformation cannot stop there—it must unfold into an active mythopoetic revolution, in which the corrosive myths or mythic components we've inherited are cut out, and the atoning myths of our deep ancestral inheritance are reclaimed and properly tended in their stead.

One element that all the corrosive mythic threads of Western cultures seem to have in common—whether they be products of Cartesian-Newtonian rationalism, or of Judaeo-Christian religious speculation—is that they are decisively reductionistic. Oddly, these two worldviews have been co-creative of one another throughout much of the last four hundred years of Western history. The linguistic-ideational memes and myths created by this strange pair of unlikely bedfellows have become cancerous to

---

[55] Mary Catherine Bateson, *Peripheral Visions: Learning Along the Way* (New York: HarperCollins e-books, 2008).

[56] Carl G. Jung, *Symbols of Transformation* (London: Routledge & Kegan Paul, 1956), xxv.

us insofar as they have birthed and perpetuated a closed, unnatural, repressive, world-denying, and institutionally sanctioned set of assumptions that have fueled the destructive practices of dominator power structures. Such power structures have in turn facilitated the cultural and ecological disintegration we are now witnessing on a planetary scale. The memes and myths that undergird them must therefore be rejected. It is our duty, in fact, to refuse to carry these destructive ideologies any further in the course of human endeavor.

The problem is that such ideologies, supported by deeply engrained mythic assumptions and institutionalized hierarchies, tend to be inherently resistant to critical self-examination. Occasionally the alarm is raised, but the force of its sound tends to die off rather quickly as existential placeholders and/or careers are threatened. Too often the needful fervor is short-lived, if it's ever fully actualized at all.

As an example, theologian Matthew Fox, in his book *Original Blessing*, looking at the destructiveness of the doctrine of original sin—an entrenched and twisted Augustinian reading of the Creation narrative(s) of Genesis—can rhetorically ask, 'How much pain and how much sin have come about because of an exaggerated emphasis on the doctrine of original sin?' and at the same time suggest that the doctrine needs merely to 'find its proper and very minor role in theology.'[57] This could certainly qualify for one of the great understatements of the last century. Weak statements like this, along with the attitude and approach they reflect—which on some level placate and perpetuate defective institutional power structures—plainly lack the force of will needed to bring about any real transformation in religion and culture. My intention is not to demean Fox or his work (I think the aforementioned book has notable value, particularly given the time of its publication), but rather to highlight this very problematic phenomenon of unwitting self-sabotage by placation, subtle or overt, of the institutional structures that support us and seem to give us security—and, by extension, the large

---

[57]   Matthew Fox, *Original Blessing* (New York: Jeremy P. Tarcher/Putnam, 1983), 50.

scale socio-cultural sabotage that goes on continually in the popularly sanctioned contexts that are most in need of restructuring and reformation.

Might we not say instead that there is absolutely *no* acceptable place any longer for the kind of destructive, world-denying doctrines Fox discusses in his book? Might we not say without hesitation that such nonsensical and harmful concepts are anathema, being antithetical to the values of Life, to its flourishing and preservation? Can we afford to be worried at this stage about offending the neighbors, the mayor, the Church authorities, or anyone else? Is it not incumbent upon us now, seeing the severity of the consequences of allowing their perpetuation, to decisively banish such dogmas from the realm of theology altogether (and from the realms of religion and public discourse more broadly)?

And yet the 'progressive' theologians carry on—apparently unaware of the latent contradiction—operating within the very linguistic and ideational framework that has perpetuated the doctrines they often half-heartedly decry, with a few fresh translations of Greek or Hebrew terms thrown in here and there to unwittingly legitimize that same oppressive framework. They remain bound to a conditioned obsession with text and textuality, which keeps their ankles shackled to the rock of absurdity and corrosion.

This is a truly caustic phenomenon, because these systemic ideational structures, along with the texts that support and perpetuate them, nurture the very myths which have long eroded Western cultures. Typically, academic theologians omit from their work all meaningful examination of myth, even ignoring in many cases the metaphoric dimensions of their own mythic tradition (i.e., the Christian tradition): the very things the stagnant institutions they inhabit are most in need of encountering. Instead of tending to this work, however, what seems normative now is repetitiously flogging the proverbial horse of postmodern critical theory.

It may well be that, at this historical moment, the jig is finally drawing to a close. No longer can we (nor *should* we) tolerate the kinds of institutionalized foolishness—theologies of original sin, Biblical literalism, Puritanism, human exceptionalism, 'cultural evolutionism', and patriarchal dominance, for example—that have so long been upheld as authoritative and normative in the West, without proper critique. Their immunity to proper questioning is rapidly falling away—and not a moment too soon.

It is plain to see the disastrous kind of world those ideational cancers have helped to birth and perpetuate, and it's long past time now that we were educated and empowered to reject them, forcefully if needed. *All* such ideologies should be boldly and unapologetically cast off. But rejecting them in itself isn't enough. In fact, it's merely the first step. The ultimate task is to replace these things with modes of thought, community, metaphysical speculation and sacred cultural practice that are actually life giving.

There is no compelling reason to engage in this kind of difficult work apart from love: love for Creation, for the Ancestors, for that which is good and beautiful, for that which is truly sacred. We are collectively in desperate need now of people who are willing to step out and compassionately but decisively say 'no' to these deep-seated, corrosive ideological constructs, to articulate to the world how and why they are toxic, and, most importantly, to present in their place some truly viable options for a better way of living on the Earth. None of us can afford to sit idly by any longer. Like cancerous cells, the ideologies that have landed us up in this horrendous state of affairs must be exposed for what they really are: false, inhumane, and destructive to all life on this planet.

Where Christianity in particular has gotten into the most trouble is where it has done violence to the mystery of its own inheritance by trying to conform it to a literal, historical, and rational framework. This is, without exception, a terrible intellectual move, and it often conceals—or at least conveniently bolsters—a dominator agenda. The central textual object—in this case, Judaeo-Christian Scripture—having been fashioned into the idol of all idols, conveniently supports this move, and keeps the mind bound to its contrived significance like a mule tied to a post. And one is bound to wander in endless, myopic circles, being tied to such a narrow, absolutist ideology—being tied to such a deceptive material object. Such entrapment,

I would submit, cannot produce—and, in fact, can only disallow the production of—healthy, whole, and life giving ways of being in the world.

The idolizing of text, rational interpretation, ideation, belief, and a fixed, literal-historical vision of religious truth is the deathly aberration of Western religiosity, and of Judaeo-Christian or Abrahamic religious systems in general. The direct, personal experience of the numinous—and the related pursuit of real, soul-level transformation in the individual (and, by extension, in the human community)—which is the only true purpose of religion itself, has been effectively cast out of these systems in favor of those cancerous notions aforementioned. In such a thought- and text-obsessed model of religion, salvation means simply 'having the right idea': a cheap, trivial approach to the endeavor of human development, a corrosive factor to the human soul, and, by extension, to the Earth. Thomas Merton articulates this dichotomy well in his comparison of Christianity with Buddhism. He observes that the heart of Buddhism is direct, personal experience, whereas:

'This is in a sense the exact opposite of the situation in Christianity. For Christianity begins with revelation...communicated to us in words, in statements, and everything depends on the believer's accepting the truth of these statements. Therefore Christianity has always been profoundly concerned with these statements: with the accuracy of their transmission from the original sources, with the precise understanding of their exact meaning, with the elimination and indeed the condemnation of false interpretations. At times this concern has been exaggerated almost to the point of an obsession, accompanied by arbitrary and fanatical insistence on hairsplitting distinctions and the purest niceties of theological detail.'[58]

As Merton also points out, however, the absence of an experiential and transformative focus in Christian practice and tradition is neither inevitable nor irreversible. The same could be said for Christianity's incessant and corrosive obsession with textuality: with dogmas, beliefs, credal statements, and ideation, all of which have replaced a true and proper focus on direct

---

[58]   Thomas Merton, *Zen and the Birds of Appetite* (New York: New Directions, 1968), 39.

experience, on the real, existential transformation of the human person. 'This obsession with doctrinal formulas, juridical order and ritual exactitude has often made people forget that the heart of Catholicism, too, is a *living experience* of unity in Christ which far transcends all conceptual formulations.'[59] That is to say, at the heart of Catholic Christianity in its deepest and most authentic expression, which is as a Mystery Cult, is an elegant system of initiatory and ascetical transformation aimed at realization of one's own immortality, mystical communion with Creation and Creator.

One wonders how different the face of Christianity might be today if its practitioners lived the deepest insights, symbols, and pursuits of their own misunderstood and misappropriated religious system; if they were, like Jesus, grounded in orality rather than obsessive textuality; if they applied themselves sincerely to a practical path of spiritual transformation within their own set of religious tools, their own mythic and imagistic framework; if they continually asked themselves the question: 'How might each of the religious words and concepts I hear, recite, pray, and reflect on point toward a dimension of needful spiritual change in *me?*' As John the Evangelist lamented, if only people would continually seek the 'life and spirit' of the tradition, its profound mythopoetic depth, rather than chasing a misguided, literal, and materialist shadow: a mere shell of the once mythically potent Christian Mystery Tradition.

What the vast majority of Christians don't realize, because they have not been formed in a legitimate system of religious transformation, is that any authentic encounter with spiritual depth naturally gives rise to the openness of heart and mind that allow for a living, organic revision of assumptions— *all* assumptions—: individual, collective, and institutional. And the revisitation of mythic threads or underlying narratives in light of what might be optimally life giving for the whole is simply an obvious result of that fresh openness. It is only the ossified, rigid institution or institutionally minded person that can resist the free-flowing and dynamic waters of Spirit, which are the Waters of Life: what the Chinese call *Tao,* or the Way of Nature.

---

[59]   ibid.

Only the most spiritually insensitive and dull-witted can fail to see that anything which goes rigid to and resists the dynamic flow of Nature is destined for miserable failure, and cannot possibly be in alignment with the verity of cosmic or divine will, whatever that may be.

Resultantly, the basic and intuitive notion that key religious texts (or portions of texts), along with their mythic transmissions and the interpretive accretions they've accumulated, may need to be intentionally transformed or otherwise rejected altogether appears to be off the table for all institutionally sanctioned Christian thinkers, regardless of how 'progressive' they may consider themselves to be. In other words, Biblical texts and the mythic images they concretize have straightforwardly been made into idols—a reality which should, at very least, draw our reflection to the dangers of an overemphasis on textuality and a loss of the gifts of oral tradition.

We see in these pseudo-religious games long played by dominator institutions the 'sacred cow' phenomenon writ large, wherein texts—as fixed, linguistically constituted objects—are superstitiously assumed to hold an innate, immutable power. We also see the age old political power grab, wherein certain sacred texts—or carefully selected portions of texts, interpreted according to the political ambitions of those in positions of power—are wielded like weapons by dominator groups who wish to control the rest of the population. The kind of mental and spiritual enslavement produced by these idiotic cultural-religious dynamics, whether willful or otherwise, is in itself inherently antithetical to the values of Nature, and thus to the values of indigenous philosophies and lifeways.

This anti-Nature, anti-freedom, anti-Spirit, anti-Beauty oriented idolization and political manipulation of text is a phenomenon both inconceivable and blasphemous to the indigenous Celtic heart and mind. In light of the long, systemic abuses enshrined in and facilitated by Abrahamic religious texts and their various institutional manipulations, one need reflect only for a moment on the ancient druidic insistence on an exclusively oral maintenance of sacral tradition to imagine what strongly recommends the ancient Celtic approach. The notion of all-authoritative, inerrant, and immovable dogma ossified in textual objects would no doubt inspire disgust in the context of any ancient oral tradition. But the institutional inertia of contemporary, dominant culture and religion keeps us bound to these unhealthful and death-dealing practices, separated from those things that legitimately give rise to and perpetuate holistic values or the ways of Life— again, what Taoists, and probably all animistic traditions, would consider to be the 'Way of Nature'. We therefore assume these unhealthful approaches to be normative, while in reality they are, in the larger scheme of religious endeavor, completely aberrant.

৺

Terence McKenna once defined evil as 'anything that trivializes a mystery'.[60] This strikes me as a very apt definition, which highlights the central problem of Western societies and cultures. The dominant, overarching culture of consumeristic materialism by its very nature trivializes anything that rises above the surface of collective (and even individual) experience, commodifying it, marketing it, whoring it out as the next fast-food answer to all our problems, that it may further line the pockets of the economically and politically powerful—whatever the moral, psychic, physical, or spiritual cost might be to the foolish and victimized consumer masses or to the planet. The promise implicit in this pattern, which Western dominator culture cannot even begin to deliver on, is the filling of the existential void that persists in the center of each member of the society, controllers and cogs alike. That hole in each person's soul is so vast and imponderable that most can't approach it consciously, let alone understand its origins or the medicines that might begin to heal it. It's the great dis-ease in us that's veiled from our perception but to which all the slags of opportunistic materialism are continually marketing.

The worldview assumptions that have caused and perpetuated the opening of that existential chasm in us—plunging us into the hell of isolation, of total divorce from an authentic and holistic relationship with the rest of

---

[60] From the interview, *Psilocybin and the Sands of Time*, recorded at Esalen Institute in Big Sur, California, 1982.

Nature—are direct results of the Cartesian-Newtonian and Judaeo-Christian brands of crypto-Gnostic, world-denying, reductionistic materialism, which have long infected Western cultures. Not only the outward but also the metaphysical implications of these worldviews are far-ranging and severe.

The dominator agendas that have been built and sustained on these wrong-headed foundational assumptions eschew and subvert the authentic values of Nature, of Life, which, *en précis*, might be defined as follows: conscious relationality and interbeing; psychological, physical, and spiritual freedom; ecologically minded, reciprocal, and cooperative community (inclusive of the non-human); respect for and preservation of all manifestations of life on the living Earth; Beauty as supreme cosmic value and *telos*; celebration of novelty and diversity; the pursuit of wisdom and direct, experiential knowledge of the sacred as the highest aims of culture and human endeavor; the mythic, poetic, and metaphoric as truest signs of the presence of the holy.

What is imminently needful, then, is to move from the false religion of self-imposed exile to an authentic religion of return, atonement, transformation, reciprocity, and unity with the whole of Nature, seen and unseen. The values of Nature are our true birthright. We might consider them, in mythically redeemed terms, as constituting the holistic, unifying consciousness of Eden, of the dawn-time. We might also call this atoned state of being the Holy Grail, for 'the Grail [means] being in perfect accord with the abundance of nature, the highest spiritual realization, the inexhaustible vessel.'[61]

❧

The only sensible and integrous thing a culture in our present state of calamity—or, indeed, an individual situated within such a culture—can do is aim to correct the course, quickly and at all costs. To quote from Mario Savio's famous speech at Berkeley in 1964: 'There is a time when the operation of the machine becomes so odious, makes you so sick at heart, that you can't

---

[61] Joseph Campbell, *Reflections on the Art of Living: A Joseph Campbell Companion* (New York: HarperPerennial, 1991), 161.

take part—you can't even passively take part—and you've got to put your bodies upon the gears and upon the wheels, upon the levers, upon all the apparatus, and you've got to make it stop.'

That means, firstly, to either radically reshape or discard outright the corrosive, world-denying narratives that have too long forged our individual and collective destinies, and to replace them with something that is life giving, generative, re-humanizing, and salvific for the whole of Creation—: to replace them with something that, for starters, rejects absolutely the false and grotesque notion that the human person somehow stands apart from the rest of Nature, that the Earth and all her nonhuman creatures are dispensable chattel, material resources to be stripped, extracted, commodified, bought and sold at will for the egotistical purposes of human groups and individuals. The same principle, of course, applies equally to the treatment and view of any disenfranchised group of human persons. And it applies to the interior disenfranchisement of the spirit, of the body and embodied experience, to mystical pursuit, the 'Great Work', and to the archaic, shamanic quest for direct, personal experience of the sacred, toward the blessing and wholeness of all beings.

Within the boundaries of Christian religion, resistance to the project of mythic reformation is endemic. There is, as previously discussed, a deep-seated fear of such reshaping based in part on the notion that Scripture is God-breathed and therefore out of bounds for any serious revisitation or revision. It is a strange fate, indeed, to be beholden to a mythic system that idolizes a singular, culturally constituted construct—in this case a collection of texts, translated and redacted a thousand times over—to the point that the text itself is elevated to godhood (that is the only metaphysical category that can reasonably be given to something that is conceived of as inerrant, divinely constituted, and immune from intelligent and spiritually sound alteration). This is a rather bizarre aberration in the vast field of human cultural and religious history. Combining this idolizing of text with the literalist hermeneutical style that arose largely from materialistic rationalism has yielded a truly abhorrent and neurotic set of reflexive ideologies.

The notion of God-breathed text, somehow passed down uncorrupted by human hands, is totally lacking in rational veracity, and in any defensible philosophical basis. It is a false construct functioning all too easily as a strong arm of dominator culture and its institutions—but it is also an arbitrary and self-imposed barrier to some of the most needed transformations in our world. It further happens to run counter to the inherited wisdom of most (if not all) ancient indigenous cultures, which for countless generations thrived culturally and spiritually on the primacy of oral tradition. To be sure, that archaic and perennial approach to sacred teaching and folklore in which orality is the supernal vehicle of transmission is 'in marked contrast to modern times, when oral tradition is deemed untrustworthy and must be confirmed by written documents ("Get it in writing").'[62] The modern approach is merely a product of changing historical circumstances and the biases they have produced in the Western world.

My assertion is that any textually obsessed mode of religion—which means a culturally ossified one—is contrary to the pursuit of real, expansive human transformation, being out of step with authentically transformative spiritual experience and with the natural development of human cultures. Such religious modes are actively destructive, and self-evidently so. They are therefore too dangerous to be maintained. As John Moriarty once observed, 'All our statements, all our creeds, all our cosmologies, all our cosmogonies, all our sacred texts [must] be vulnerable to further experience.'[63]

The transition from oral to print-based culture gave rise in Western societies to a host of new cultural and religious pitfalls. A text- or print-based culture, as history now informs us, all too easily sets its feet on the slippery slope toward becoming a culture that idolizes textual objects, that imagines textual objects to hold some kind of inherent, indissoluble author-

---

[62] Alan Dundes, *Holy Writ as Oral Lit: The Bible as Folklore* (Oxford: Rowman & Littlefield, 1999), 17.

[63] From the audio recording, 'Six Stories', *An Evening in Eden* (Dublin: Slí Na Fírinne Publishing/The Lilliput Press, 2007).

ity: a culture which is tumbling almost inevitably toward fundamentalism, set to begin the employment of thusly enshrined textual objects as tools for the abuse of power. If a society, a religion, or a subcultural community is inhibited from natural growth because it is unable to move beyond or intelligently and realistically revise a guiding document, then it has made itself invulnerable to further experience, and is thus radically diminished in its ability to meet the unique challenges of the age.

Systems of writing—and particularly the preservation of 'sacred' teachings in textual form—have of course given much to the world of human endeavor; but they have also become weaponized in a variety of ways, and have wreaked a great deal of havoc in Western societies, particularly in bringing about forms of religious and political fundamentalism, in which the mythopoetic, the Natural, and the numinous are all but totally exiled. As Huxley once cautioned, 'we can easily become the victims as well as the beneficiaries of these systems.'[64]

Often a literalist or fundamentalist hermeneutic is tied up with fear of change, and with an unexamined psycho-social pathology, namely, a pervasive inability to live in what Keats called a state of 'negative capability': the ability to hold two seemingly opposing things together in tension without an irritable grasping at reason. In other words, fundamentalism often arises from and perpetuates an egoic fear related to loss of rational control, or an unconsciously perceived inability to rationally quantify and strictly organize reality.

Personalities and cultural groups unable to understand and accept paradox, individuals and societies disconnected from the manifest truths of Nature, who labor under the tragic delusion that control is both possible and desirable, are generally the ones who throw in with literalism. This phenomenon is in essence the product of uninitiated cultures and individuals who have not excavated the depths of their own existential fears and impulses, and therefore have not yet begun to work those things out in the clear light

---

[64] Aldous Huxley, *The Doors of Perception and Heaven and Hell* (New York: Harper & Row, 1954), 74.

of silent awareness. The clear heart and mind, by contrast, perceive that the very notion of quantifying, codifying, and controlling the lived experience of being in rational terms is both absurd and impossible.

Calling into question the assumption of textual authority and the presumed ability to rationally quantify the cosmos should not, however, imply a descent into total relativism. This is particularly important to mention in the present discussion because the sustainable mythic reformation and renewal we now desperately need cannot be based merely on the whims of the moment; nor can it be based solely on the ideation of present-day subcultural movements. Instead it must be deeply rooted: in the deep soil of the Earth, and in the deep history of human experience. Rather than being based on an imagined and arbitrary inerrancy or supremacy of certain textual objects, it must find its ground in a healthy and appropriately critical veneration of ancestral wisdom, arising out of ancient oral tradition.

Oral tradition is, in indigenous worldviews, at once both authoritative and *open*, rather than authoritative and *closed*, as in print-based traditions. What do we mean by 'open'? 'Open' in this context indicates that a narrative or poetic creation is never imagined to be finalized or closed down, impervious to alteration; rather, it is considered to be *living*. If it is in a textual form, then it is a kind of materialized extension of oral tradition, rather than a source of inerrant, unquestioned, or 'pure' authorial intent. It is always therefore permeable to the realtime, real-life experiences of those who read and interpret it, always open to addition and amendment. But this does not mean that amendment and addition are done in a haphazard manner. There must be a supportive structure of meaningful discourse, a legitimate wisdom tradition, and a system of artistry and aesthetics (in the broadest sense) to safeguard the process.

In an oral tradition, this process is endemic to the fabric of the culture itself, and is often a formal part of the formation and vocation of the sacral class, which possesses its own norms and practices for the living, dynamic, and faithful preservation of narrative, song, poetic law, prayers, etc. The consciousness of orality, which we might also call the folkloric consciousness, is radically different than the consciousness presently dominant throughout

Western societies. The latter is largely the product of a long-standing and aberrant obsession with textuality, and particularly with sacred documents. This textual consciousness affects nearly everything we think and assume about culture, about human experience, about reality itself, whether or not we're consciously aware of that fact. An oral consciousness—and, by extension, an oral culture—is simply not equipped for producing the kinds of repressive fundamentalist thinking that have destroyed Western cultures and are now threatening to destroy the planet. This fundamental difference is a matter of life-or-death importance.

What sort of world would we now have had Christianity come down to us as a living, oral tradition focused on the transformative mystical capacity of its *mythos*, and on the beautiful and dynamic narratives it preserves, rather than an ossified, world-denying, legalistic, text-based tradition focused on control and moralistic injunctions for 'right living'?

Within contemporary domains of progressive Abrahamic theology, perhaps predominantly in Christian contexts, there has been great—and, in some cases, noble—effort to transform these inherited mythic-religious frameworks into sets of spiritual tools and ideas that can actually address contemporary global crises. The chief example of this, to my mind, is effort made on the part of some Christian thinkers to put focus on certain elements of Christian text, mythos, and traditional praxis which might be harnessed toward the causes of ecological justice, i.e., to attempt to remediate, through localized action and political advocacy, the critical factors in climate change and in human destruction of natural environments and resources. The central idea here, in principle a sound one, is to reference the inherited textual object in a way that serves the needs of the present time and culture.

It is only natural that leaders and functionaries within such an institutionalized religious framework, who genuinely care about the cause at hand but feel unable to draw from resources outside the set of expected and internally enforced norms, would desperately fish for any possible scrap of supportive imagery or language that might support their rightful aim.

The problem, however, is that the Judaeo-Christian mythic-religious milieu is simply too impoverished of the values of Nature, of natural imagery, of Life-honoring mythic threads, to be useful in this regard. In fact, it is precisely this cultural-religious aberration, this strange and devastating impoverishment, which has led to the problems that now plague and threaten human cultures and the living Earth. Ultimately, a text can scarcely be made to yield something it simply never contained to begin with.

Just as thought cannot be used to end thought, hatred used to end hatred, or the tools of a dominator culture used to dismantle that same culture, so the Judaeo-Christian mythos and religious ideologies cannot be utilized to transform the ecological or other injustices which they themselves have unwittingly facilitated. We have seen borne out over many centuries the inevitable results of their myths and ideologies, and those results are simply unacceptable, being oppositional to the very values of Life, and therefore to the creative forces of Nature. The world they have helped to build is, as it were, a kind of hell.

The 'Good News', however, is that we still have access to deeper ancestral threads, to ways of Life, Beauty, and harmony, and to the eternal heart of Nature herself; we have access to those ultimate and needful resources, if we would but choose to avail ourselves of them. This will require a serious mythic reformation, a redirection of values and ideological commitments, and a radical openness to the possibility that our collectively accepted cultural-religious structures, historically taken for granted by most as sacred and effective, may have in fact been rotten and non-efficacious from the beginning. We may, in fact, have been duped by a cascading series of dominator agendas, each building on the previous structure, each leaning on a corrosive and commonly held set of foundational ideologies that have from their inception promulgated a negation of Nature and the living Earth, domination of others, repression of natural humanness, vilification of the Other and of indigenous worldviews.

True liberation, in our current context, can only come from the margins, from what has been rejected, excised, silenced: it can only come from the indigenous soul. In potential, that voice is within us all. It lives in our genetic and epigenetic memory. It is from *this* deep inheritance that we must draw again if we wish to save the sinking ship of Western cultures, of human planetary presence, and of the life and well-being of the living Earth and all her children. It is, by contrast, foolish to continue grasping for spiritual resources in a mythic and ideological desert, where precious few such resources have ever existed. Rather, it is incumbent upon us all to look for those Life-preserving and critical resources in the place where they have always been waiting, and still can be found: in the Well of Wisdom, in the Mag Mell Flower World of Otherworld vision, of deep ancestral wisdom—: that font of Beauty which seeks to uplift, to magnify, and to perpetuate the endless diversity of Creation; which seeks to protect and further the natural, universal values of Life, of the truth of interbeing.

Some version of the Judaeo-Christian mythos might be preserved, but only if we're willing to radically alter it, and to give up the dead-end task of sifting through scraps for images, stories, and language that will support legitimately sacred values in harmony with the whole of Nature, in places where such values are simply not to be found.

The horrendous ideological aberrations that have brought Western cultures to the present state of crisis need not be a perpetual prison, for the option of atonement, of true salvation, still lies before us: the option to make right the wrongs that have catalyzed our collective undoing. Through transforming or replacing those foundational elements of the cultural-religious inheritance that has landed us up in this proverbial Desert of Zin, and reclaiming the native values and wisdoms of our own pre-Christian Ancestors, a new cultural pattern can begin to be laid in the Western world, which can inspire, support, and facilitate the concrete outward steps that must be taken toward total alteration of lifestyle, commitment, and behavior—not only at an individual level, but, by extension, at a collective level as well.

The answers we seek lie not in *Paradisum* or in some externalized 'second coming', nor are they to be found in substitutionary atonements, fanciful eschatologies, culturally bound and corrosive Biblical moralities, or theories of original sin; rather, they will be found in Mag Mell, in a Flower World Kingdom co-actualized here in our midst, on and with the body of the sacred Earth: an Eden reclaimed, with its Tree of Life, its Tree of

Knowledge, its hidden sacraments, forbidden by dominator patriarchs, and its Well of Segais, from which flows the River of the Waters of Life. Such an atoned state of being, alive in Beauty and in the truth of interbeing, continuously oriented toward, and constituted by, sacramental, incarnational consciousness—Earth Mother, White Cow Mother, Sacred Well Mother consciousness—by the poetic, the mythic, and the folkloric—is not likely to wander down avenues of literalism, fundamentalism, or world-denying ideation, and thus it is protected from the possibility of becoming something which instigates the kind of fall into corrosive worldview patterns and social practices that has constituted Christianized Western history. In fact, it is only the radically salvific water from that Otherworld Well that can redeem our collective human experiment.

❦

It's true that the genie of print-based culture cannot be put back in the bottle. And the information landscape morphs ever more rapidly, as digital technologies alter drastically the way we receive and conceptualize text, or any other form of data. The complexities and potential gifts brought to bear on our circumstances by the rise of commonly accessible and widely distributed digital media in audio and video forms is a fascinating additional dimension to explore, though it is one which lies outside the boundaries of the present work. For our current purposes, we should simply note that the principal invitation, in looking toward an authentic reclamation of indigenous wisdom in the midst of our now irrevocably text-based (and *digital* text-based) cultural milieu, is to re-emphasize orality as a foundational religious style and orientation, along with its attendant worldview elements and practices, and to creatively discover ways of doing so inside the current social, religious, and material framework. The aforementioned non-textual digital media could prove to be potent tools for actualizing these aims.

It may come down to the planting of new memes: subversive memes of orality, scattered in the soil of the dominant culture—including its normative modes of religiosity. Germs of orality to undermine the dominator obsession with control, and to diminish the primary fuel for that fire—namely, reductionistic rationalism, mechanistic materialism, and their beloved prison, textuality. The level and kind of transformation implicated in such a cultural upending is staggering, and, so far as I can tell, would touch everything from personal and social liberation, to psychological health, to cultural justice and preservation, to ecological justice and restoration.

In other words, such an approach could actually address the core problems with Western religion and cultures hitherto discussed. These problems are now more broadly talked about in the arena of popular culture (e.g., by popular intellectual figures like Sam Harris), which is a good and necessary thing. The diseased cultural elements must be brought to light, for nothing that is not brought into the light can really be healed. But the problem I see with much of the current discourse is that it suggests nothing meaningful in place of those destructive ideologies. Or, if it does suggest an alternative, it is simply further emphasis on mechanistic materialism and the idol of scientific progress—which can only compound the deepest problems we presently suffer from, rather than heal them.

To throw out religion and spirituality altogether, or to dismiss the wisdom of ancient traditions, is certainly not the answer; rather, to facilitate the restoration of religion and spirituality to their most authentic, integrated, and life giving modalities, in the context of deeply rooted oral tradition, seems to be the best option we have. To restore religion to the only authentic purpose it ever had, which is to guide us toward real transformation. We will have to enter deeply into myth and folklore, not just academically but experientially; we will have to hear the old stories and songs again, sung round the fire, in the dark wood, on the sacred Land, and allow them to move and breathe in us, to 'rewire' our hearts, minds, and bodies to the deep mythic threads we still retain in our epigenetic memory, which cause in us an inexplicable longing—: which cry out against the horrors of our present way of being on the Earth.

We might do well to consider how radically Western religious ideology and practice would change if in our religious communities we simply shifted the focus away from textuality—and the idolization of text—back toward legitimate oral tradition. If the body of sacred stories we tell was allowed not only to expand and to re-root us to our own indigenous traditions, but also to organically evolve, as all folk traditions must, to adjust to new landscapes, to the ever expanding ethical and cultural circumstances of the actual flow of human life, then our cultural state of being would inevitably begin to shift. Certainly that process would take time, but it would at least be one concrete and practicable path toward a better world. To be unshackled from the repressive fundamentalist and rationalistic assumptions that have colored Western cultures now for hundreds of years would be a great liberatory boon.

All that would really be required to set such a restorative process in motion is for us to collectively abandon the false ideologies that keep us bound to the unhealthful, death-dealing assumptions already mentioned, and to begin to tell again the ancient stories—*our* ancient stories—in a context of reclaimed, authentic indigenous lifeways. To reclaim those lifeways may seem a daunting task, but my intuition is that to simply *begin* re-membering them is all that is needed to set the process in motion and create willingness to follow faithfully the wisdom of the Ancestors on where and how to take each subsequent step. To allow the old stories themselves to speak in and through us, to teach us, to reorient our way of being in the world.

One of the great problems of Western cultures today is the rather sudden erosion of meaningful civil discourse. It seems to me that this is, in large part, the result of a lack of attention to, training in, and inclination towards the art of true listening. Increasingly, people lack the experiential knowledge of how to actually listen, and, consequently, the will to do so. They lack sustained attention or the ability to meaningfully focus on someone or something for any extended period of time and actually grasp something of the real depth in it. This is, of course, creating a trivial and surface-oriented cultural experience, at every level of being, internally and externally, individually and collectively.

The inability to truly and deeply listen constitutes, in essence, a deficiency of presence. It is also a deficiency of feeling, which allows us to dissociate from the horrors of our actions, disabling us from truly feeling what it is we're collectively doing in eroding the health and integrity of life on this planet.

I submit that if there is anything at all still available to us that could genuinely remediate this lethal deficiency, it is the archaic lifeways of our ancient Ancestors, and the gifts of oral tradition. Reclamation of the same could be our last remaining hope for reconditioning ourselves and our societies significantly enough to turn the ship around before it sails irrevocably over the ledge.

If people were taught again to sit with one another in intimate and sacred communal space, around the firelight, to listen to the deep, rich fruits of their ancestral traditions—not to analyze them, but simply to receive them with openness of heart and with curiosity, and allow them to begin to organically penetrate their souls and speak into their lives—then perhaps the organic morality of Nature, the willingness and ability to truly listen to one another and to the Earth, to abide in true, conscious interbeing, would begin to spring up in our hearts and in our cultures once more.

Once seeded, the memes of orality, of the deep, Earth-born mythic traditions,—deeply rooted as they are in our epigenetic and cultural memory—will begin to erode the hold of dominator power structures and their propaganda. This is because the indigenous memes of oral traditions are like threads leading back to our soul-home, to the ancestral values of Nature herself. It's also because dominator cultures in our time are irreducibly built on the unexamined assumptions of textuality and textual primacy. Oral tradition can therefore act as a productively deconstructive force, and can draw us back to the only medicine that will ever truly heal the hopeless longing, existential displacement, grief and alienation we feel. This invitation is one that calls for the adoption of a sensible hermeneutic of openness, of realistic breathability, balanced by a healthy veneration and application of indigenous wisdoms.

To say it in a slightly different way: this points to a shift of perceived authority from texts to oral and folkloric dispensations of myth, wisdom, and ancestral lifeways—and to the direct revelation of shamanic-priestly figures who have been called by the Ancestors and legitimately formed by vocational mentors in service of the community. In such a world, the Ancestors hold the staff of wisdom and authority, and it is known and accepted that no textual object can ever contain or shut down that authority, because by its very nature that wisdom stream is always living and dynamic—as Nature herself is.

Our ancestral traditions must therefore once again be brought to life, and part of what's implied in a living tradition is that it's allowed to retain its organic nature as a folkloric structure that grows, evolves, and adapts according to the authentic needs—not the momentary whims—of its carriers. In a Celtic cultural context, wherein the Ancestors are held near to the heart and offered profound veneration, the ancient traditions are naturally accorded a place of prominence. But simultaneously it should be understood that tradition in a healthy and life giving form is never static, never fixed or closed down. If it becomes static, then it will shortly become rigid and die.

In an oral tradition, that risk of stagnation is inherently lesser than it is in a text-based tradition, but it is certainly not absent from the field of play. It remains always a risk, particularly in Western cultural environments since the Cartesian revolution. Given this, it seems to me that we have a responsibility to live clearly and dynamically within a liminal space that facilitates two things simultaneously: (a) the reclamation and honoring of ancestral inheritance; and (b) bringing that reclaimed inheritance to life again, which means making it viable, life giving, and permeable to ethical advancements. It means assuring that its lived expressions are speaking in some way directly to the current challenges and crises of our own time and place.

The life giving alternative to reductionistic rationalism is not irrationalism, but *transrational experience*. One significant expression of this experience in indigenous cultural environments is hearing of the divine Voice, primarily effected through the vocational works of the culture's shamanic practitioners, the *filidh* or poet-seers in Celtic tradition. Hearing of the divine Voice implies 'a modality of reason in which the logos of existence enunciates itself.'[65] In the interior sacred space, transparent to the holy, one hears, too, the wisdom-voices of the Ancestors. The ground from which such hearing unfolds is the territory of *henosis*, of vision, *ecstasis*, poetic utterance, and divine communion. This can theoretically occur within any individual, but such communications are spoken into the broader culture through the vocation of the shaman who has been called to serve that mediating function in the society. The shamanic figure is one who is innately drawn to this vocation, a quality evinced in part by his or her natural affinity to the Otherworldly, the unseen.

The moment we idolize the illusion of something fixed irrevocably in time and form, we have denied the living reality of the sacred and have lapsed into the worship of death, rather than the worship of Life. Nothing ultimately good can arise from a culture that has begun to worship what is dead—that is, what is imagined to be unendingly fixed in time and space, supposedly immutable. *Panta rhei*. All flows. That is the immutable truth of Creation and Creator(s).

Our new mythic model must be an ancient one, arising from a serious and reflective reclamation of our deepest ancestral inheritance, and returning us to the perennial wisdom of the dawn-time, the origin-point of human culture and language, the birth-moment of our conscious relationship to the sacred. This means a full embrace of the eternal flow and dynamism of Nature, what Jungian thought often refers to as the 'chaos' of the primal Source-Mother, the unbounded feminine Origin, who expresses the cosmic qualities of Creation, Sustenance, and Dissolution.[66] It must reconnect us

---

[65] Henry Munn, 'The Mushrooms of Language' in *Hallucinogens and Shamanism*, Ed. Michael Harner (London: Oxford University Press, 1973), 98.

[66] 'Chaos' is an ill-fitted descriptor, in my thinking; I suggest we would do much better to think here in terms of cosmic dynamism, unending movement, vitality, life-force, novelty, and the eternal pursuit of Beauty.

with the spiritual dispensation of that mythic dawn-time, which is the predominantly oral stream of wisdom and archaic techniques leading to experiential knowledge of the holy, the unseen, the secrets of death and rebirth, of how to live in harmonious relationship with the whole of Creation, both in its seen and unseen dimensions.

This is the hope to which we should now collectively look; it is the small but radiant seed of promise which bears the innate capacity to dismantle the apparatuses of dominator culture, of the destructive narratives we've received, accepted, and perpetuated to this point in history—and, most pressingly, to derail the runaway train of reductionistic, crypto-Gnostic rationalism, along with its demonic children, materialism and consumeristic capitalism.

❧

'Don't leave us in darkness or blind us', sings the shaman, the Mazatec mushroom medicine woman, Irene Pineda de Figueroa. 'Let us go along the good path. The path of the veins of our blood. The path of the Master of the World. Let us go in the path of happiness.'[67]

Here the 'Master of the World' is the feminine Creator, the Mother, along with Her informing Voice of Holy Wisdom, heard by the shaman in ecstasis. The 'good path', the 'path of the veins of our blood', the 'path of happiness' is the ancestral way of the dawn-time, the way of timeless indigenous wisdom, the holistic way of interbeing, the way of Nature. It is the way which continually re-members our rightful relationship to Creation and Creator(s).

Our own invocation must come to harmonize with Irene's—with the invocation of all shamanic voices from the advent of human culture onward. How we might restore our present traditions to happily accommodate once more those deep songs of our blood, bone, soil, and soul is the great task at hand. To authentically and sustainably fulfill it, we will have to rid our-

---

[67]   Henry Munn, 'The Mushrooms of Language' in *Hallucinogens and Shamanism*, Ed. Michael Harner (London: Oxford University Press, 1973), 97.

selves of any structures that limit, inhibit, or resist that needful reclamation and rebirthing. Among those traditions, the container of Christianity—still carried in one form or another by so many in the Western world—can and should be made to accommodate an indigenous approach to living, as it was made to do in the context of the adopted Christianity of my ancient Celtic Ancestors—or, indeed, among the Mazatec peoples of Oaxaca. Whatever dimensions of Christianity's current shape cannot accommodate the values and aims of Nature, and of our own indigenous wisdoms, should be finally dispensed with.

☖

Joseph Campbell summarizes the chief problem in contemporary Christian thinking with the phrase, *misunderstood mythology*. He explains that this implies a misunderstanding of Christian tradition, by Christians, 'consisting in the interpretation of mythic metaphors as references to hard fact: the Virgin Birth, for example, as a biological anomaly.'[68] Interestingly, it is only the Modern mind that assumes literal or 'hard' fact as the sole measure of truth. In the ancient European world, mythic valence and the use of metaphor in all sacred discourse was assumed and expected. It was the water our ancient Ancestors swam in. The water we presently swim in is of course radically different. It is Newton's ocean we inhabit, in which everything is measurable, quantifiable, knowable and definable to the human intellect—from which spirit and mystery are exiled.

It is worth noting that the anomalous occurrence of attempting to deliberately confuse the lines between the mythic and the literal-historical is to be found in isolation within certain schools of Christian thought as early as the fifth century. It just so happens that those specific schools won out in the contest for establishing 'orthodox' doctrine. At Ephesus in 431 CE, a literalist reading of the tradition of the Virgin Birth, among other things, was formally cemented as orthodox and anyone with a divergent reading of the

---

[68]   Joseph Campbell, *The Inner Reaches of Outer Space: Metaphor as Myth and as Religion* (Novato, CA: New World Library, 1986), 27.

tradition (particularly a metaphorical one) was declared heretical. There was probably always a sense among the proto-orthodox Christian groups that the Crucifixion and Resurrection were expressed in literal historical events, but rarely if ever were these things considered to be *reducible to* literal historical events. Campbell and others have suggested that the novel blending of metaphor and myth with the perceivable events of historical time made Christianity stand out amongst the other Mystery Cults of the early centuries of the common era, making it especially compelling as an ideational framework. This accompanied the appeal of Christianity as a radically liberative and subversive religio-cultural movement giving equal authority to the initiated regardless of their social status, and disallowing imperial military service amongst the initiated.

But a notable—and, in my view, disastrous—result of this novel combination of mythic and historical elements in developing Christian thought was that the mythic dimensions of the Christian Mysteries were slated to be marginalized, and in fact were almost totally lost over time, as the emphasis was placed more and more on a literal-historical sense of the tradition, culminating with the ascent of a post-Cartesian reductionistic rationalism, intimate in its relationship with Christian theology. Why the scale tipped in that direction can only be potentially understood in light of a very complex unfolding of socio-historical and psychological factors, a study which lies outside the scope of the present work; but it is clear on the face of it that the imbalance was, in time, devastatingly total. As Campbell notes, 'both the psychological and the metaphysical connotations of the metaphoric symbols have been all but lost in the pathos of the screen.'[69] This 'screen' of obfuscating and confused notions was combined with the fruits of scientistic rationalism to create a perfect storm of corrosive ideologies.

The cure for a foundational cultural and ideational illness such as this is not, I think, a rejection of the whole system—of Christianity, to remain with the present example. That would, in fact, amount to a rejection of 'the metaphors as lies…thus scrapping the whole [Western] dictionary of

---

[69]   ibid., 33.

the language of the soul…by which [humankind in the West] has been elevated to interests beyond procreation, economics, and "the greatest good of the greatest number".[70] In other words, if we scrap the whole system then we toss out the baby with the bathwater, losing the real depth that lies beneath the surface of the tradition—which, granted, has been thoroughly buried under many generations of stupidity and inadequate leadership, but is certainly not lost. The myths and symbols retain their innate and sacred potency, regardless of whether or not we've really tapped into them.

So the answer, again, is an authentic reclamation of the mythic, of mythic consciousness, a restoration of the proper metaphoric sense and aim of religious tradition in general, and a reclamation of our native ancestral inheritances more specifically. The potent, shaping insight we need will be found in the cultivation of an actual, revelatory hearing (or re-hearing, as the case may be) of the divine *Logos*.

The experiential pathway that can equip us to re-enter and reclaim the mythic in our time and place—and to hear again the voice of Holy Wisdom—is the pathway of our innate, intuitive, and indigenous knowing, our indigenous way of seeing the world—what Martín Prechtel has termed the *indigenous soul*. This soul still exists in all of us, spiritually and epigenetically, whether we're aware of it or not, and regardless of how deeply it's been buried beneath the mire of modern and postmodern tomfoolery.

This indigenous soul emerges now our most promising remedy, in part because it cannot conceive of—let alone immerse itself within or frame its life around—a mythos that has been confusedly and contrivedly merged with the literally factual, which separates the human being from the rest of Nature, from the Otherworldly; which isolates the human person while objectifying and abusing all non-human members of the web of being. Such a way of life and thought, which we're now profoundly immersed in, is simply inconceivable to the indigenous soul.

Restoration to the authentically indigenous and mythically sound means an emergence from the flood of half-consciousness in which we've

---

[70]   ibid., 31.

been drowning for generations, stripped of soul. It means a sacramental re-surfacing, a return to deep breath, a re-rooting in the living Earth.

❦

Mission San Miguel in Santa Fe, New Mexico, is the oldest Christian sanctuary in North America, built in 1610. It's a strange feeling to sit there in its small wooden pews, surrounded in the dark by ancient adobe bricks, by the quaint yet brutal icons and carvings brought by Spanish priests and friars; to think of how it all came to be, the hands and minds that fashioned it, the cruelty of the culture and ideology that conceived and actualized it. To think also of the thousands of Masses prayed inside those walls, the rosaries said, candles lit, petitions made.

It strikes me as a microcosm of our contemporary cultural lot—a 'weedy lot', as it were: a tangled, self-contradictory mess of egoic desires, brutality, and unfulfilled psycho-spiritual needs—: a product of the self-inflicted wounds of our cultural abnegation, our Faustian deal with materialism, and the crypto-Gnostic violence of our errant, misunderstood appropriation of a foreign (Christian) mythos.

To keep this structure standing is a perpetual labor: the external facade of the adobe structure requires re-mudding every few years, and maintenance is constant. While allowing it to fall completely to the elements, to be reclaimed by Nature, would clearly defy the sensibility of most individuals with any concern at all for the witness of history or the artistry of human ingenuity (myself included), I can't help but reflect on the fact that, at least metaphorically, that is precisely what needs to happen. This facade—and the whole tangle of destructive, dominator ideologies that underlie and are iconically represented by it—must collapse and be reclaimed by the truth and wildness of a feminine sacrality, by the truth and beauty of the Land, of the indigenous peoples whose blood was unjustly spilled on *this* Land, and whose cultures were nearly eradicated in order that this fragile structure might be erected and maintained.

In this house of mud-brick, decorated with icons of a bloodied Christ, in this house of quietude and violence, this place of thinly veiled catastrophe, I wonder if redemption is really possible for us. A flood of Christian and Modern European cultural assumptions washed over the indigenous peoples of this Land like a lethal infection. They had washed, too, over our own indigenous Europe. And what that tidal wave of cancerous ideologies produced is a ruin: a house bereft of Life and of the values of Life.

Is there a way to let Spirit and Earth, breath and ancestral wisdom, back into our decrepit house of concrete and rubble? Can we be graced once more, flesh and soul, by the embracing wind of our eternal Mother? Can we somehow be touched by and touch that power, through the walls we've so foolishly erected around our existential insecurities, our wrong assumptions about ourselves and the world in which we dwell? Can we surrender those assumptions once for all, along with the way of curses they've produced for us and for the Earth, and receive in their place a way of blessing?

Here before us stands the foundation of our bizarre, misguided endeavors, our prodigal journey through history. And here before us stands, too, all the lessons potentially learned—the error, knowledge, and confusion of historical time. What now will we do with the whole strange lot of it?

At summer's end, just before the season of Samhain, I prayerfully immerse my head three times in the River Boyne—: the great Cow Mother, granter of visions, flowing forth from the primal Well of Wisdom. I think of Moriarty baptizing himself out of Western Christianity, out of modern European culture, placing his head inside a Hare's form in the Heather, asking Nature to give him a new mind, a new story, built from scratch, starting with the building-blocks of naked sensory perception.

Is there yet something salvageable in our errant course? Is a purificatory conflagration, a new kind of Baptism,—a Baptism *out* of the content of our education and ideation—our only possible way forward to a better life? Or could it be both, a kind of *via media*?

Perhaps the *via media* of our own time, quite apart from the Reformation disputes that initially gave rise to the concept, is a middle ground between the best of Christian tradition—its mysticism, its sacramentality and liturgical integrity, its mythic symbology and archaic initiatory patterns—and the richest fruits of our pre-Christian indigenous traditions, which promise to water our parched souls, and God's parched Creation, more deeply.

The collective inheritance of the Celtic traditions invites us to seek sacrality in the radiant in-between, in the landscape of the liminal, in the dreaming, in the visionary depth of Otherworld Earth and Sky and Sea—to seek our answers in fertile ground betwixt and between the seeming binaries that continually haunt us. Can we follow that path into restorative Otherworld landscapes without denying or undercutting the radical reparation, the reclamation that must certainly unfold now within and all around us in this physically manifest world?

Little White-Thorn walks into the dewy meadow of dawn, barefoot and half-dressed, and finds there the mysterious golden herb that bestows true vision. Once she eats it, blessed by the holy Ancestors, she can understand the languages of birds. She hears truly the language of Nature, who wishes to guide her toward justice, redemption, and atonement. In following that voice, the damage wrought on her life—and the life of her mother—by powers of the dominator culture is healed. Her life and the life of the Mother are restored. White-Thorn receives the supernal gift: the gift of wisdom: of the abundance that wells forth for anyone united in love to the deep flow of the animating life-force of Anu, the Earth Mother. This is the deepest meaning of justice. To use the old bardic phrase, it is 'the truth (of Nature) against the world (of isolated and imbalanced, egoic human endeavor)'.

In the raw, naked twilight, I walk barefoot up the Hill of Tara, while Blackbirds sing of Otherworldly knowledge.

In Mission San Miguel, furnace of endings and beginnings, I light a candle, and pray that somehow, poetically, our collective way would be illumined.

Strangers to Mystic Beast and Bird: An Eco-Theological Reflection on the Feast of Rogation, and a Vision of Holistic Incarnational Atonement

There are two sentiments loose in this world, and you're not going to get through this life without taking sides: Do you believe that our destiny is in another dimension made of light on the other side of the Universe? Or do you believe that we should clean up the rain-forests and save the planet?

—*Terence McKenna*

The rising hills, the slopes, / of statistics / lie before us. / The steep climb / of everything, going up, / up, as we all / go down... / To climb these coming crests / one word to you, to / you and your children: // *stay together / learn the flowers / go light*

—*Gary Snyder*

The Christian Feast of 'Major Rogation' originated with the pre-Christian Roman observance of *Robigalia*, and was formally incorporated into Church practice around the turn of the sixth century. Robigalia was an annual occasion in the spring when a ritual procession ventured from the city into the surrounding countryside to bless the year's planting, and a sacrifice was made to ask the gods and spirits of Nature to spare the crops from blight. Similarly, in its Christian iteration, the occasion has historically been understood as a time to ask for divine protection and blessing on the year's food crops. The name 'Rogation' is derived from the Latin word, *rogare*, meaning literally, 'to ask', or, 'to petition'. As the quintessential agricultural Feast of the Church, Rogation is one expression of the pan-European practice—probably observed since the beginnings of agriculture itself—of ritually marking important times in the planting and harvesting cycle. This mode of ritual observance seems almost inevitable in a society which revolves around the movements of the Sun and other celestial bodies, in connection with the rhythms of planting and husbandry.

But what of its application in our own mechanized, postindustrial context—in an environment wherein most of us no longer know anything at all about the origins of the food we consume? In a global ecosystem brought to crisis by human agency? Outside those remaining areas where agriculture is still a dominant economic force, it seems fair to say that the more practical dimensions of Rogation no longer apply in our present cultural context. But we might do well to examine some of the metaphysical assumptions underlying this now relatively marginal Church observance, to see if those threads could yield something spiritually rich and timely for our beleaguered psyches and cultural-religious institutions—and for our suffering planet.

In pre-Christian times, a ritual observance such as Rogation would have been focused on petitioning the guardian or totem spirits of plants and animals, and the souls (i.e., gods and goddesses) who presided over the dimensions of Nature that were determinative in the success or failure of crops. The singularizing of divinity and the closing off of human consciousness from the animacy of all living things outside the domain of human experience, which came with the import of Judaeo-Christian myth and ideology into Europe, meant that when the observance was appropriated into Church practice its original sense and aim had to be shifted radically. The focus was no longer to connect directly with, to honor, petition, and bless the multitudinous spirits in Nature that the human community depended on, but rather to ask the singular God, imagined as utterly transcendent of the natural order, to look down and bless a host of inanimate plants and animals, increasingly understood as chattel and consumptive 'goods'.

This alteration of the sense and aim of the observance in question represents, in microcosm, a massive shift in perception and worldview within the European psyche—and, in my view, a rather detrimental one, not only for human beings but for the whole of life on the Earth, 'our island home'. The manner in which the human community at large, and particularly those cultural modes that can be described as dominant in our current temporal location, understand themselves in relation to the rest of Nature, in relation to the whole of non-human Creation, may ultimately decide the fate of the human species. It has already decided the fate of many non-human species who have shared the planet with us. Historian of Western ideas, Lynn White, wrote in 1967:

'Especially in its Western form, Christianity is the most anthropocentric religion the world has seen....[It] not only established a dualism of man and nature but also insisted that it is God's will that man exploit nature for his proper ends....In Antiquity every tree, every spring, every stream, every hill had its own *genius loci*, its guardian spirit....Before one cut a tree, mined a mountain, or dammed a brook, it was important to placate the spirit in charge of that particular situation, and to keep it placated. By destroying pagan animism, Christianity made it possible to exploit nature in a mood of indifference to the feelings of natural objects.'[71]

This 'mood of indifference' has colored the whole of Christianized Western history, and paved the way to our present planetary circumstances. Of course, ideology, concept, and myth all inevitably shape our world-

[71]   Lynn White, Jr., 'The Historical Roots of Our Ecologic Crisis', in *Science 155* (1967), 1205.

view, and worldview shapes our ethics, our actions in the environments we inhabit. And the worldview of Western Christianity has long been, as White points out, one which imagines the human person as the true center of the cosmos. When we compare this with more ubiquitously represented worldviews and religious cosmologies—ones that imagine, for example, a mythic tree as the center of the cosmos—it is easy to envision how radically different patterns of thought and behavior might emerge from such divergent mythic foundations. A completely anthropocentric worldview seems bound to beget a world in which the non-human elements of Creation are marginalized, excluded from mythic narrative and ritual, and thereby in time beheld as incidental.

And thus we have made, and continue to make, ourselves quite alone in the world. This isolating mythic and philosophical orientation has come at an extremely high cost to us, and to all life on the Earth. Emerson summarized this rather desperate scenario in his aptly titled poem, *Blight*:

Our eyes are armed,
but we are strangers to the stars,
And strangers to the mystic beast and bird,
And strangers to the plant and to the mine;
The injured elements say, 'Not in us;'
And night and day, ocean and continent,
Fire, plant, and mineral say, 'Not in us,'
And haughtily return us stare for stare.
For we invade them impiously for gain;
We devastate them unreligiously,
And coldly ask their pottage, not their love.
Therefore they shove us from them, yield to us
Only what to our griping toil is due;
But the sweet affluence of love and song,
The rich results of the divine consents
Of man and earth, of world beloved and lover,
The nectar and ambrosia are withheld;

And in the midst of spoils and slaves, we thieves
And pirates of the universe, shut out
Daily to a more thin and outward rind,
Turn pale and starve.[72]

The foundational, historical aim of Rogation, as evinced in its anteced-ent, Robigalia, is to make prayerful request to an ensouled cosmos, ask-ing salvation from the pathogenic phenomenon of blight. For we who are ensconced in the cultural-religious milieu of contemporary Western societ-ies, the 'blight' that haunts us is less a disease of food-plants than a disease of the soul. The most dangerous pathogen we face is ultimately one of myth and ideology. I submit that this must now become a principal lens through which we view our circumstances as Christianized Western peoples, and as incarnate souls dwelling in human form on the living Earth.

Seen through that lens, Rogation is one small avenue of return to a world re-sacralized—and it must, indeed, be one small avenue among many, should we wish to accomplish any substantive change in our ideology and the world it's given rise to. This implies, and perhaps necessitates, a re-an-imation and re-enfranchisement of Nature, a re-sacralizing of non-human Creation in the language and practice of our sacral institutions—a thing our present myths and religiously conditioned worldviews will not freely give way to. Those same ideational constructs must therefore be made permeable to the fresh expanse of reconnection, of re-humation, of communion in and with the whole of Life. Each shift we make in our language and ritual is a small but courageous act of resistance against the corrosive elements of our materialistic and world-negating inheritance. It is, therefore, an act of love for Creation, and a resounding affirmation of divine values expressed in the eternal becoming of Nature.

Re-sacralization of the nonhuman world—bringing our plant and ani-mal siblings, and the Earth herself, back into the proverbial firelight—will require a difficult reexamination of our inherited Judaeo-Christian myths

---

[72]   Ralph Waldo Emerson, *Poems* (New York: Alfred A. Knopf, 2004), 46.

and assumptions, but the severity of our present ecologic crisis, from both a naturalistic and theological perspective, seems to demand such radical work; it seems, in fact, to render it an essential matter of justice. The question of whether or not we find the courage and creativity to seriously address the structural issues of mythic narrative and worldview that have led us down the perilous path of disenfranchisement and isolation is ultimately a moral question. Its implications speak not only to the sustainability of the Church as a socio-culturally and ecologically relevant institution, but also to its ability for genuine moral self-correction and intelligent revision in light of a divine vision of wholeness, of restitution and atonement. To orient ourselves otherwise is, to use Emerson's term, plainly unreligious.

With our gaze drawn firmly toward the promise of renewed linguistic, mythic, and institutional landscapes, I propose a collective faith-leap in search of new fields of wondering. Might we access the deepest fruits of our traditions through reflection on the truth of our intimate interdependence, our shared fate, our unshakable imbeddedness in and with the whole of Creation, in its metaphysical dimensions as much as its biological ones? As John O'Donohue once observed, 'Nature is the direct expression of the divine imagination. It is the most intimate reflection of God's sense of beauty. Nature is the mirror of the divine imagination and the mother of all sensuality; therefore it is unorthodox to understand spirit in terms of the invisible alone.'[73]

Philosophers of mind, cognitive scientists, and others are increasingly taking up the reins of *panpsychism,* the notion that all matter possesses some form of consciousness—at its core, a modern rendering of the oldest worldview known to humanity, *animism,* which describes the intuition and experience of a cosmos ensouled, a cosmos thoroughly conscious, pervasively alive. But leaving aside the infamous problems of defining consciousness, at a more readily accessed level of perception, Western science, since at least the middle of the last century, has understood in clear terms the totalizing

---

[73]   John O'Donohue, *Anam Cara: A Book of Celtic Wisdom* (New York: Harper Perennial, 1997), 50.

interdependence of all life on the Earth: 'Man is elementally indivisible from the biosphere. And this inseparability is only now beginning to become precisely clear to us. In reality, no living organism exists in a free state on the Earth. All of these organisms are inseparably and continuously connected—first and foremost by feeding and breathing—with their material-energetic environment.'[74]

The question must certainly come, then: Will Christian theologians—and the Church at large—find a way to fully re-join the circle of conscious participation in the great communion of Nature? Rogation is *in potentia* one minor porthole, one small sacred *ikon* leading out beyond the walls of our self-imposed limitations, our ossified dogmas and assumptions, our anthropocentric obsessions—: the 'Feast of Asking' as prayerful request for the natural world to re-embrace us, as petition for help in remembering what it's like to fully embrace the natural world in return.

An old British folktale, most commonly known as 'The Apple Tree Man', tells the story of a selfish younger brother who inherits the familial fortune and leaves his somewhat eccentric older brother in the cold, turning him out to live in a tiny shack at the periphery of the family farm, with no property and no real means to support himself. The elder brother, whose eccentricity derives from his remarkable love of non-human creatures, his unusual sensitivity, gentleness, and compassion, turns to tending a small grove of abandoned, withered Apple trees. In time, through loving connection with the trees, he restores them to full health and they begin to produce an abundance of fruit. The younger brother gets wind that there is treasure buried somewhere on the land, and plans to listen in on the farm animals on Christmas Eve (when it's said they might be heard to speak aloud in human language), in hopes of discovering where the treasure is hidden. He commands his older brother to come up to the farmhouse just before midnight to wake him, so that he might eavesdrop on the whisperings of those

---

[74]   Vladimir I. Vernadsky, 'The Biosphere and the Noösphere', George Vernadsky, trans., in *American Scientist Vol. 33, No. 1* (Research Triangle Park, NC: Sigma Xi, The Scientific Research Honor Society, January 1945).

in the barn. But the elder brother, having truly loved the animals and Apple trees alike, having treated them with gifts and hospitality like true friends, is told by the Apple trees where the treasure is. When the younger brother later comes down to the barn, at midnight, he hears from the animals that one who is worthy, who has rightfully honored the values of Nature and the reality of relational interdependence among all living things has been told the location of the treasure, while he, the younger brother, a 'greedy and unmannerly fool' has finally received his just reward.

This presciently instructional, ancient folkloric motif, which encourages precisely those worldview elements, those values, and those spiritual capacities we now so desperately need to reclaim, is expressed in a number of Western European folktales—and, indeed, in a host of traditional stories from indigenous cultures the world over. Unfortunately, we will not find such motifs in the Bible. And to fully bring the truth of this relational knowing into the framework of our ritual, our liturgical language, our sacral calendar, our song, and our story now stands ahead of us as likely the most pressing moral and spiritual task of our age. To re-enfranchise the world: that must become our sacred work.

As such, we will have to source the deep rooted, life giving tools needed to accomplish that work from outside the context of inherited Biblical literature and tradition—a fact that should not be seen to denigrate the latter, but rather to realistically and appropriately frame it, free of superstition and unhelpful attachment. The central invitation in this is to reimagine how we can and ought to curate our language, ritual, and narrative—to reclaim the full power and sanctity of our co-creative capacity.

One of my own practices, and a suggestion I offer the Church as a concrete and accessible way into a more holistic worldview, is to look to the wisdom of our pre-Christian Ancestors, and especially their legacy in myth and folklore (wherever those cultural streams happen to flow from, in each of us and in our communities of worship), and to integrate that wisdom into the inherited framework of Christian religiosity. Incorporate those narratives into the teaching and liturgical life of the Church. Incorporate, too, some of the ancient lifeways that historically held and contextualized those stories. And begin to put on the liberatory reclamation of orality as the primary methodology in the communal sharing of sacred story, moving away from the bizarre textual obsession that's hitherto tarnished the Christianized Western journey, away from the myopic exceptionalism that imagines Judaeo-Christian text and ideology as singularly noteworthy, uniquely divine, and uniquely beneficial for human cultures and societies. (As we have seen, such indefensible assumptions have in fact served to engender, mask, and perpetuate some of the most destructive ideas the world has so far witnessed.)

Holding the sacred gifts of pre-Christian traditions (and animistic traditions particularly) in dialogue and productive tension with established Church language and practice, making Church thought and ritual truly vulnerable to the revision it so desperately needs, we can see these two streams—the pre-Christian and the Christian—not as mutually exclusive, but as necessary partners in the needful work of legitimate, sustainable reformation. We can rediscover the ancient tales and lifeways as much needed avenues back to a world of animacy, a world reawakened in our conscious vision and experience—the Western vision and experience, for so long desperately impoverished. And we can gradually begin to see, then, the Christian narrative in its proper light: as myth, not history; as sacred story meant to illumine and inspire a spiritual process of individual and communal transformation, like the pre-Christian Mystery Traditions of Europe that preceded it. This lens, I would argue, is requisite for our forward movement, which, as T. S. Eliot once famously posited, we will find is in fact a movement back to where we started, to our deepest roots as human beings, as creatures of culture in pursuit of meaning and connection.

As the Church falls further toward the social margins, and its unintentionally isolating halls fall more and more silent—'A shape less recognizable each week, / A purpose more obscure'[75]—how might we come to understand our present situation not as curse, but rather as invitation, not

---

[75]   Philip Larkin, 'Church Going', in *Collected Poems* (New York: Farrar, Straus & Giroux, 1989), 97.

as closing down of witness and ministry, but rather as new beginning? As one revived focus-point for learning and exploration,—a microcosmic training ground—we might take up the relic of Rogation and breathe into it a new and ancient life. We might harvest therefrom a sincere and committed return to conscious awareness and celebration of our interdependence with the whole of Nature, and begin to practice seeing ourselves in continuous reciprocal relationship with a sacred and thoroughly animate Creation.

We would do well to recall along the way Lynn White's reminder that 'What we do about ecology depends on our ideas of the man-nature relationship. More science and more technology are not going to get us out of the present ecologic crisis until we find a new religion, or rethink our old one.'[76] To revise our religious dogma, our stories, and our perception of that relationship is a monumental and weighty endeavor, but one filled with gospel hope. Rather than resigning ourselves to being left behind by a culture in transition to rationalistic secularism, perhaps our task as the Church, our invitation—still largely unrealized—is to embrace a new expression of our historically crucial role in helping to reshape the underlying worldview of the dominant culture. Perhaps we can and should once more become sculptors of mythopoesy—but this time for the good of all living things, rather than to their detriment. This time shepherding a society tumbling toward exponential technological power with an exponentially eroding moral foundation: guiding it toward wholeness rather than isolation. Therein could lie the only potential relevance any longer left for us. And a potent and holy relevance it would be. The question is: Do we now possess the courage, creativity, and clarity of heart to accept that invitation, and to earnestly engage the processes of needful revisioning that such an acceptance would necessitate?

Whatever the fate of our institutions, the road ahead should lead us into thinking theologically and morally not just *for* the landscape, the plants and animals, but *with* them—an experience most of us in contemporary Western contexts can at this sad juncture scarcely any longer imagine. If

---

[76]   Lynn White, Jr., 'The Historical Roots of Our Ecologic Crisis', in *Science 155* (1967), 1206.

our clergy, our spiritual leaders and healers could once more become stewards and specialists of that sort of skill-set, then the way might in time be established to a more complete and effectual atonement, not only for us in the human community, but for Creation as a whole. And if our language and ritual in the Church could come to reflect those natural skills and values, then the needful changes would no doubt begin to unfold organically, and our witness could be one not of tired, outmoded rhetoric, but of lived transformation.

The basic principle underlying this vision of reform is, in its essence, a quintessentially 'orthodox' conception: that *all things* must ultimately be brought to salvation, to wholeness, together as a unified body. That, after all, is what atonement means in a properly incarnational understanding: 'at-one-ment', the bringing in, the enfranchisement, the 'wholing' of all God's creatures, of every soul, and of every manifest or material expression of the divine imagination. A truly holistic, incarnational vision of salvation—: a participatory salvation, found here and now, in reunion and reclamation, not in notions of a magically restored future effected by transcendent powers, or in trans-terrestrial realms of 'perfection' conceived by the least creative, least hopeful, and least naturally connected minds of Christian history.

May it be that we come to understand and honor the call, the invitation, and the acute needs of our time and socio-cultural position; that we come to understand and honor ourselves as true members of the great family of Nature, with eyes and hands and minds oriented to the life and well-being of all Creation on this holy and living Earth. And may we approach the work implied therein not unreligiously, but as travelers of true heart journeying to the depths of love and goodness in the divine dream of wholeness, asking not just once a year but always for the wisdom and will to return to our birthright as participants in a sacred and animate world, to move toward the Edenic promise of 'divine consents / Of man and earth, of world beloved and lover.'

Immram

The signs and signals ready themselves, and breath goes in and out of the body that is the world.

—*Brenda Hillman*

It is fatal to love a God who does not love you. A God specifically created to…enlarge the tribal borders of someone else. We have been beggars at the table of a religion that sanctioned our destruction. Our own religions denied, forgotten; our own ancestral connections to All Creation something of which we are ashamed. I maintain that we are empty, lonely, without our pagan-heathen ancestors; that we must lively them up within ourselves, and begin to see them as whole and necessary and correct.

—*Alice Walker*

It was surely for the scent of unmasked splendor that I walked one afternoon down the beach at Silver Strand. Musing on the Hawk of Achill, I moved through fierce wind over grassy bluffs and down into the wet white sand. Settling near a small band of rocks, I made my little gifts. Gifts to Sea, to spirits, Ancestors. A pinch of dried Lavender, of Juniper. Some Gaelic prayers and song.

A single Scald-Crow appeared from beyond the cliffs to my left, and circled directly over my head, almost too near for comfort, crying something immense into the cold Atlantic wind. A signal of acknowledgement, a message from the Otherworld. *Your voice has been heard. We are listening.* Or perhaps a harbinger of some strange revelation—a dark speech from beyond, about to break through into Middle World reality.

Who is it that hears? *They* hear, to be sure. Rarely do we here truly hear. Acknowledging their recognition of one who knows how to listen seems a very sensible thing—especially in a world that has largely forgotten them. Something even we who are here now in this incarnate form could easily relate to. All souls long to be known, to be heard.

I often wonder: What sort of thought and speech might be happening out there beyond the veil, unbeknownst to me, with regard to this tiny plot of experiential ground on which I presently stand?

I closed my eyes and sat there in the bright dark of internal stillness, in the forceful chorus of wind and wave.

It wasn't long before another broke in to the gray and solitary landscape. Coming with wind and wave. An exceedingly old and scraggly, near-toothless, white-bearded man, wearing a ragged, off-white tunic, his right arm crippled, carrying in his left hand a driftwood staff. Some part of me knew him, immediately recognized this strange apparition. Some part of me didn't believe it.

I'd heard folktale of the god of the Sea appearing on occasion as an old bearded man, usually to act the trickster, often seen walking the shores alone—seeking, perhaps, to teach a difficult lesson, or to work a bit of mischievous magic, steal the world abruptly out from under one's narrow, unsuspecting perception.

The stories cautioned me. The old man cackled roughly, quietly as he neared.

Are you he? Are you a god? What forms, what spaces does a god inhabit now, *can* a god inhabit now? Is a god also a soul, on the same kind of journey each other soul is on? Does a god also die?

I am that soul of which you speak.

Wasn't it so that the old gods dwelt no more in this Middle World? Some, I thought, had passed beyond its borders, taken on other births, other forms—some had gone into the Lower World, some the Upper World. According to some, become the people of the Sídhe, of the sacred mounds, the hollow hills.

I dwell in all worlds.

Of course, one imagines a soul of such power and wisdom could, even now in the dark night of the old gods, quite easily pass between. Though perhaps not as fully as before, perhaps more ethereal, more gossamer in his manifestation—less tangible, as if starved of our material gifts, of the tears and longings of this physical world that would otherwise make strong his shape.

Manannán, Son of Lir. Now grown so old, so ragged.

At your hearth, make a shrine to the Sea.

A bit of mischief, of cackling trickery. Wise old trickster. Dangerous sage.

The old gods were never safe. Potent, creative, wise, able to make whole—but never safe.

❧

Can we imagine the wonder of Conaire, as he awoke one morning at Tara with the mythic Crane Bag of Manannán hanging lightly around his neck, no rational explanation to hand?

Can we awaken with that same wonder, devoid of all recourse to rational, reductionistic excuses, so that we find at last we have no more defenses against the true magic, the miracle, the Beauty, and the impossible strangeness of being? With those false, egoic battlements dispensed of, we are vulnerable, then, to true vision—to the vision of Mag Mell, the red-flowered plain of Manannán's Otherworldly expanse. We are vulnerable to seeing with the eyes that gods see with.

As any good animist would know, such a sacred object as Manannán's Crane Bag, fashioned with prayer and magic from an animal's sacred skin, possesses a spirit of its own. And so the Bag may appear to whom it wishes, when it wishes—and perhaps to whom Manannán wishes. Who could really say? Formed by Manannán from the Crane-skin of Aoife, it is a sacred and totemic artwork, an object of the dreaming, imbued with ancient magic. Lugh of the Long Arm once carried it, and in his own time Finn is said to have won it.

This is how it came into being: Aoife, a woman of great beauty, was transformed into the shape of a Crane by the jealous sorceress Iuchra, for they both loved the warrior Ilbhreac. Iuchra imposed the magical *géis* that Aoife should dwell on the Earth in the form of a Crane for two hundred years. Aoife wandered in this form for some time, in grief and mourning, until finally she came to the Hearth of Manannán. Unable to return her to human form, Manannán welcomed and cared for her, until she died and her soul passed out of this world. From the skin of the dead Crane, Manannán then fashioned a fine leather pouch, which he deemed should hold, in honor of gentle Aoife, his most sacred and treasured possessions.

In it are thus to be found the potent magical amulets, the sacred power-objects of the Son of Lir. When the tide is in, the objects that the Bag contains are visible and their power may be drawn upon; when the tide is out, the Bag is seen by human eyes to be empty. And though it contains these great and holy objects, the Bag itself is said to be no larger than the hand of a man.

Lore varies somewhat on the identity of the sacred ìomhagain—power-objects, fetishes, magical idols which act as channels of connection to the powers of certain spirits, and effect certain changes in the manifest world—held by the Crane-skin of Aoife. They are variously given as: the shears of the King of Alba, the helmet of the King of Lochlan, the bones of Asail's Pig, the smith's hook and belt of Goibniu, and Manannán's shirt. Among them may also be Manannán's knife, and his hearth or household, a totemic bone of the great Whale spirit, and a magical belt of fish-skin.

Meeting him on the wide, turning Sea, Manannán Mac Lir sang to Bran Mac Febal these poetic quatrains:

Bran deems it a marvelous ocean, great of beauty,
in his coracle sailing on the clear blue sea,
while to me in my chariot from afar
'tis a flowery plain on which he rides.

What seems a clear sea
from the prowed skiff in which Bran sails,
is to me a happy plain, with profusion of flowers,
from the two-wheeled chariot in which I ride.

Bran sees the number of waves
beating over the clear blue ocean;
I myself see in Mag Mon
red-headed flowers without any flaw.

Sea-horses glisten in Summer
as far as Bran has stretched his glance;
rivers pour forth a stream of honey
in the land of Manannán Mac Lir.

The sheen of the main on which you ride,
the white hue of the sea on which you row:
Yellow and azure are spread there before me,
the Land is beautiful, and never rough.

Speckled Salmon leap from the womb
of the white sea on which you gaze:
They are calves, they are colored lambs,
dwelling in great affection, free from slaughter.

Though you only behold one chariot rider,
in Mag Mell of many flowers
numerous steeds ride o'er the Land,
though you yourself do not see them.

The size of the plain, the number of the host,
the colors which glisten in pure glory,
a fair stream of silver, cloths of gold
make welcome with all abundance.

A beautiful game of delights they play,
having drunk the luxurious wine of sense,
men and gentle women, under lovely bushes,
without sin, without any notion of crime.

Along the top of a wood has swum
your coracle across great ridges;
there dwells a wood of beautiful fruit
under the prow of your little skiff.

A wood with blossom and fruit,
on which is the vine's true fragrance;
a wood without decay, without defect,
on which are leaves of a golden hue.

We are from the beginning of Creation
without age, without consummation of Earth,
and hence we expect no frailty—

no sin has ever come to us.[77]

⟁

I will help you when you make the immram, when you make the journey over Otherworld seas.

As you helped Mac Cuill, bound and set adrift in his lonesome coracle, across to Inis Falga. As you guided Bran Mac Febal across the honeyed fields of Mag Mell.

And now being seen as you wish to be seen, being heard as you wish to be heard, what wisdom, what teaching, O Son of Sea, O Sage of Endless Journey, what council have you now to impart?

Hold in dearness, in poetic remembrance, in intimate nearness in the soul's fertile seat, the flow of Nature's movement—always the flow of seasons' change, of landscapes' change, the change of worlds, the turn of wave, of Earth and Sky and Sea. Let nothing become so congealed in you that you fall into delusion of thinking it fixed, immutable. Nothing is fixed, nothing immutable.

With his walking stick he drew in the wet sand between us a triskele—: a crude and more beautiful rendition of the form now pictured on the Manx national flag. *Ellan Vannin*: The Isle of Manannán.

And then a mist. Just that. Féth Fíada. No chariots on the waves, no white-billowed Horses. A great, forceful wind: a shaking and unraveling wind. A torn white tunic, a hobbling old man, fading back into vagueness of things just glimpsed, like the fraying remnants of a dream.

A plain of ocean lights, of wildflower blossoms. Blossoms on the wind like sparks, blowing outward into vision'ry expanse, beyond my seeing, passing by me like embers from a fire of field or forest—blowing upward somewhere in the vast, gray heavens.

⟁

---

[77]   From *The Voyage of Bran*; translation by the author, with inspiration from Kuno Meyer.

When the pool of the sacred Well at Colman's Cave, springing out from the raw limestone Earth, cradled by the ancient Hazel wood, drew me in and blessed me with dangerous blessings—blessings that shatter, like a Baptism of Bóann—I was brought empty-handed, then, empty-minded on hands and knees, to ask the breast of Anu, to ask the heart of felt Creation, and of her Source: the Mother we have called 'Divine Ground of Being' who birthed every searching expression of Beauty—with nothing to give but a few re-membered tales; old songs resurrected in the tongues of my Grandmothers; a pinch of wild herbs; dust of An Pucan Beireach, An Balgan-Buachair; a small, speckled stone from the foot of the ancient Hag's Seat.

And this the telling of its fruits.

Birdsong chorus from the mist of dream echoes through spiraled planes of being. A root and branch from the Land of Summer Stars; a joyous branch from the Tree of Worlds. From the steep, lush mountainside a chant of final letters, sounds of holy origins. Bees in fine array; Dandelion and Cranesbill. Marsh Orchid and Vetch in rare abundance. Spotted Orchids on the Heath. Helleborine and Cowslip. Nettle, Eyebright, and white-plumed Garlic. Ferns and Wild Thyme. Spring Gentians. Lone Hawthorns. Gray, gentle clouds and jeweled Sun. With gentleness unending, with divine hospitality. A fragrant honey—a wind of souls—a honeyed breeze of timeless breath.

These are my tidings from the brow of sweet Brigid, from the tongue of bright Ogma, from the heart of wild Macha, from the womb of holy Anu, from beneath fierce Badb's black-feathered cloak. These are my tidings from Colman's dark cell in the sacred wood of Fern and Hazel.

When I emerged into waking vision of that mythic clearing, I knew that all we needed or ever would need had already been given. There in that still, green shelter was all that was ever required for the way of transformation, for the taproot depth of atoning connection, for wisdom, for the path of truth. No more rituals, no institutions, no languages were any longer needed, or even desired. Everything one could ever require was already present, await-ing the arrival of our hearts, awaiting the arrival of our souls' clear seeing.

No other Sacrament will be necessary here; no liturgy shall break the vibrant stillness of this silent chancel, I quietly proclaimed. No more utterance of word, now that 'sight in you will be more visionary than vision.'[78]

To Bran Mac Febal and his bold companions, the bright, ethereal image of a woman, dressed in indescribable raiment, ever gives true counsel:

> Do not fall into idle slumber,
> nor let intoxication overcome you;
> begin now a voyage on the bright, clear sea,
> if you wish to reach the Land of Women.[79]

And thus will a few courageous souls embark, setting out on Otherworldly seas: pilgrims in search of mythic landscapes—in search of poetic Beauty—in search of the font, the undying source of wisdom.

---

[78]   John Moriarty, *Dreamtime* (Dublin: The Lilliput Press, 1994), 18.

[79]   From *The Voyage of Bran*; translation by the author, with inspiration from Kuno Meyer.

A Trinitary Vision

'The Trinity is like a mother's cloak wherein the child finds a home and lays its head on the maternal breast'. These words are from St. Mechtild of Magdeburg, written in the mid-thirteenth century. In the strange morass of images generally used by theologians and preachers to describe the Mystery of the Holy Trinity and Her internal dynamics, this image from St. Mechtild stands out to me as beautifully real, authentic, and true: the product of felt experience, the product of Mystery.

It reminds me as well of another maternal cloak: the cloak of Brigid. Holy Brigid, in her incarnation as Christian abbess in Ireland, sought to make her home at Kildare, which was a pre-Christian site long dedicated to Brigid as goddess. But when Holy Brigid of the mid-fifth century proposed to build a Christian monastery there, the King of Leinster refused to give her the land. After multiple requests and rejections, she finally went before him and asked if he would grant her as much land as her cloak would cover. Amused by the strange request, he granted it. But to his confoundment and wonder, when St. Brigid laid her cloak down on the Earth, it magically spread out and covered the whole of the Curragh Plain—roughly five thousand acres.

Like tree roots or fungal mycelia, Spirit always finds a way to break through into our myopic world and subvert the dominator agenda, to serve the will of truth and the work of vision. The wisdom of the divine feminine can never be suppressed for very long before it resurfaces. So Jesus proclaims: They will kill or suppress Her prophets, but 'Wisdom is justified of Her children'.

The understanding and experience of Trinity as feminine Reality, as shared with us by St. Mechtild, and implied as well in the story of Brigid's cloak—a Reality both tender and utterly subversive—is what we need to get back to. That's where we'll find our home again. And God knows we've had more than enough time of prodigal wandering in ignominy, with patriarchies and pogroms, materialisms, and dominator cultures.

Of course, the homecoming of our prodigal souls, of our errant cultures and religions, can never be merely a thing of ideation, concepts, and doctrines. It will have to be a process of active, lived experience. And no one is off the hook: every single one of us is responsible for whether we collectively get there or not.

Religion can pave the way of that homecoming, but not religion as we presently know it. It will have to be restored to something that's actually transformative at an existential level. Religion, properly grasped, serves one purpose only: it serves as a set of tools, of practices, to transform us from spiritual children into spiritual adults. And it must be restored to that singular purpose.

The child finds a home, finds comfort at the maternal breast, and is nourished, equipped, protected—but not to remain at the breast: never to remain merely comforted; never to remain static. As with everything in Nature, there's a process of dynamic growth associated with the soul's journey. It's the burden and the radiant task of that growth that's now placed on each of our souls with immense cosmic weight. Because it's not only the lives of our own souls at stake, but the sacred lives of countless other creatures on this living Earth as well.

So if a teaching or theological lens like the Trinity is to offer any enduring value for us, it will have to be in this way: within the frame of our own vocations, our own imminently needful work, both personal and collective.

It invites us, then, to see beyond the limiting and often destructive inclination toward binary thinking—which is thinking that everything is either one polar extreme or another, either fact or falsehood, historical or mythic, good or bad, real or unreal, black or white, and that everything can be neatly structured into rational, reductionist categories, and thereby grasped, contained, controlled. But binary vision is an impoverished vision. Trinitary vision, by contrast, is rich and expansive. Two is simply two: a polarity. But three is *all*, symbolically speaking, because three accounts for all that's unseen to us, all that lies outside the boundaries of our rational faculties. Three is 'both/and', rather than 'either/or'. And when we find ourselves caught in a polarized or binary construct, the invitation from Celtic wisdom is to seek the third, hidden thing, always already present but undiscovered, which will balance, synthesize, and resolve the dualistic tension.

An Mórrígan as *Anu*, *Macha*, and *Badb*. The ineffable Source as Creator, Sustainer, and Destroyer; Origin, Sanctifier, and Redeemer. Brigid as goddess, saint, and wet nurse to Christ; patroness of healers, smiths, and poets; mother of husbandry, fire, and sacred wells. No concept or dogma could ever explain the mystery of these truths. Only the heart, having gone to drink at the Well of Wisdom, could know them and access their deepest meanings. That's the kind of vision we'll have to reclaim if we want to redeem Western culture and religion. That's the kind of vision we'll each have to re-member.

The sacred experience of Trinity—and of *trinities*, as reflected perennially throughout the world of Nature—which is an insight from the Celts, by way of the great stream of Indo-European traditions, not an insight from Biblical text or from any branch of Judaic thought—could therefore be among the 'first principles' in our journey of spiritual reclamation and atonement.

To view the world through a lens of Trinity is to open ourselves again to one element of the deep ancestral wisdom that can redeem us. It's to open our hearts to an experience of homecoming—: the prodigal's return to a clear, visionary plain of bright being: of Mag Mell, spring blossom being, vast ocean being, dark-soiled forest being; of peace and restitution; of feminine wisdom; of divine values, which are the values of Nature; of real Beauty and interconnectedness in the endlessly diverse family of Creation.

Only in a culture and a religion that knows these truths, and facilitates the lived experience of them—which takes spiritual children and forms them into spiritual adults—can we find our way home again, and at last lay our weary heads once more on the maternal breast.

Pilgrim Travelers from
the Starry Road

All life is bound to individual carriers who realize it...every carrier is charged with an individual destiny and destination, and the realization of these alone makes sense of life.

—Carl Gustav Jung

Our birth is but a sleep and a forgetting: / The soul that rises with us, our life's star, / Hath had elsewhere its setting, / and cometh from afar: Not in entire forgetfulness, / And not in utter nakedness, / But trailing clouds of glory do we come...

—William Wordsworth

May I stay forever in the stream.

—Mary Oliver

We hardly dare to dream of how wild the perceptible reality in which we're embedded might actually be. We have distanced ourselves profoundly from the truth of the sacred, living

Earth on which we walk. We have come to systematically avoid real insight into the unseen layers of being that surround and inhabit us. Embedded in the very fabric of our normative socio-cultural conceits is a phobic avoidance of real initiation into spiritual adulthood, which means real vision and real trekking in the untamed landscapes that reside within us.

The Dream that continually dreams us is the Reality from which we've become most alienated—that Reality which imbues all living things with soul: stranger and more wondrous than we can suppose.

In the West we have become accustomed to a cultural climate that continuously seeks to repress or deny the unseeable dimensions of experience, the mysteries of Creation, holding us trapped in a perpetually deepening darkness, like an endless Good Friday. Cut off from wisdom-streams that would carry to us an experiential knowledge of the Dream, we have sold our souls to the false ideology of materialism and 'merely thisness', of anthropocentric reductionism.

The Edenic return we unconsciously long for and so desperately need is a resurrection to the truth of our own wildness, to the wildness of divinity, and to the depths of our own ancestral hearts, which preserve, as if in secret, the pregnant seed of our awakening; a rebirth of 'heightened receptivity to the meaningful solicitations—songs, cries, gestures—of a larger, more-than-human field…a world made up of multiple intelligences.'[80] It's a dawn that cannot be captured or contained by the eroding narratives of rationalistic, patriarchal dominion, which have strangled and determined Western destiny for many long, benighted centuries. True atonement for us must necessarily be a radiance that by its very nature defies and shatters the hard, oppressive shell of those aberrant narratives: a radical reclamation which exorcises the stories and assumptions that have shut down the Western mind and isolated it from the rest of Nature.

As children first learning to walk, we will have to find the ground again: the Divine Ground, the holy ground of the living Land, the ground of our own deep-rooted ancestral wisdoms. As T. S. Eliot once presciently observed,

---

[80] David Abram, 'The Ecology of Magic', in *Orion* 10: 3 (1991), 4.

'the end of all our exploring will be to arrive where we started and know the place for the first time.'[81]

In blood and bone of our nature, housed in flesh of living Earth; in sinew of our most chthonic inheritance; in secret breath of vail and mountain, fur and creek and feather—: only in and by and through these grace-filled truths can our atonement be known and co-actualized.

The invitation set before us, then, is to mine the depths below the roots of the great tree of our collective human experience, the chthonic strata of perennial indigenous wisdoms, using the tools of our own archaic cultural inheritance—whatever those might be for each of us. A sustainable shift of consciousness and perception is the only relevant path into the Otherworldly vision we are called to re-access. Pouring over tomes of textualized folkloric and mythic material is by itself insufficient to the task. To immerse in and reintegrate such materials into our lives once more as *living realities*, however, can usher us into a space of practicable and enduring value.

Might we learn to inhabit the deepwater consciousness preserved in our own genetic and epigenetic memory? Might we learn to inhabit the ancestral consciousness of the dawn-time of religious experience and its archaic cultural expressions—of the Europe of Lascaux and Altamira, of Newgrange and Loughcrew, of Uisneach and Anglesey?

Folk traditions—and particularly oral traditions of storytelling, poetry, and song—preserve much more of the archaic strata of human insight than we might be inclined to imagine. In spite of what our textually and technologically saturated minds are inclined to assume about the unreliability of organic memory and oral dispensation, oral traditions have preserved an astonishing amount of information accurately over vast stretches of time.

The archaic material preserved through centuries of oral tradition in Europe—much of it now held captive in textual form—is also preserved

---

[81]   T. S. Eliot, 'Four Quartets' in *Collected Poems, 1909-1962* (New York: Harcourt Brace & Company, 1963), 208.

in the genetic and epigenetic memory of those whose Ancestors anciently inhabited the European landscapes that gave rise to it. It is also preserved in the living Earth, from whom it initially came forth. These, I think, go a distance toward explaining why fairytales and myths often resonate so deeply in our hearts and our unconscious minds, even when our rational faculties would seek to dismiss them as childish, irrelevant, or mere entertainment. The ancient stories of our people and our ancestral Lands hold for us a proverbial golden key—: a key which can unlock the dry-well catacombs in the depths of our souls, where reside the dragons of our misguided attachments.

One of the great mistakes that folklorists have made in looking at traditional folktale as a genre is that they have more or less exclusively examined it through rationalistic lenses, which are completely counterintuitive to the art form itself. Such lenses cannot draw our vision with any notable degree of experiential value or accuracy into the depths of myth or fairytale. And the depths are precisely where we need to go.

Folklorist Max Lüthi proposes two determinative factors for the formation of folktale as an artistic genre. He states that the folktale is dependent, both in its origin and its form, on: (a) 'what type of person creates and cultivates it', and (b) 'the needs of the audience.'[82] A very safe, clinical proposition—dry as the Desert of Zin, the desert of our self-imposed exile. As in so many cases where two things are easily perceived, there is a hidden third thing yet to be revealed. I propose in this case to reveal that hidden third thing as *the landscape—both seen and unseen—on and from which the story is received and imparted.*

I mean here not simply to say that geography plays a formative thematic role in the creation of narrative (that is a somewhat trivial insight), but rather that, in the archaic worldview that gave rise to the folktale—that is, in an animistic worldview—the landscape itself is alive, and her gods and spirits, her sacred breathing body, both this-worldly and Otherworldly, are in one sense the true source of the most archaic motifs of myth and folktale.

---

[82] Max Lüthi, *The European Folktale: Form and Nature*, trans. John D. Niles (Bloomington, IN: Indiana University Press, 1982), 81.

Lüthi comes closer to the heart of the matter when he writes that the folktale 'in its own way…does give an answer to the burning questions of human existence, and this answer provides deep satisfaction.'[83] The reality, however, is that the folktale doesn't merely give *an* answer to existential questions, it gives many answers: properly received and embodied, it is something more akin to a sojourn through expansive natural vistas, through vast unconscious territories of ancient collective memory. 'The folktale… demands nothing. It does not interpret or explain; it merely observes and portrays.'[84] And the world it observes and portrays shows forth the archetypal truths, the patterns of human transformation, the interrelatedness of all things in Nature which are typically obscured from our perception. What it asks of us is to be as *it* is: to submit ourselves to a state of total receptivity, to be *natural* in the deepest sense, and to likewise refrain from interpreting or explaining: to simply *listen*, with the whole of our being.

It is therefore reasonable to say that simply telling and hearing the old tales again is among the most meaningful and life giving things that anyone now seeking legitimate, salvific transformation of consciousness and culture can do. For the Western heart and mind, the European folktale in particular holds a generous draught of the sophic, crystalline waters needed for atonement. This is as it would be in any cultural context: while there may of course be individual exceptions, as a general rule the myths of our own tribes tend to resonate most deeply with us because they carry countless generations of work and experience relevant to the particular makeup of our psyches, the landscapes from which our innate and inherited humanness has arisen and with which it has long had intimate discourse.

Those of us who come from cultures that have experienced a breakdown of oral tradition will inevitably find ourselves in the position of having to do some comparative analysis, putting threads of our folkloric inheritance next to similar threads from other cultures and attempting to discern what of our own inheritance is most ancient or most authentic—learning again how to

---

[83]   ibid., 82.

[84]   ibid., 85.

tune our ears to the ancient songs of the living Earth. There's a certain tension endemic to this scenario: it's not completely fair or accurate to do such comparative work expecting it to yield authentic information about a given cultural tradition. But the process of comparative study—at least in this scenario—can illumine dark corners of the landscapes no longer discernible to us, from which we're no longer able to make meaning, owing to the very long night of our forgetting. Regardless of methodology, we will have to move forward; we will have to determine how to authentically navigate the complexities of our cultural circumstances, continue to grow, transform, co-create new and ancient lifeways, new and ancient modes of communal experience. What feels most crucial now is rejoining the stream.

The critical thing here is experientially entering an archaic mode of consciousness, a mythically attuned mode of perception—: by putting on the kind of archaic awareness that birthed and maintained the natural values and experiences we should seek to re-access and reclaim. In that state of being—for example, in the mode of perception that wholly and non-analytically receives traditional folktale and myth in and from the living Land—there is actual clarity and insight, a direct link to archaic worldviews and value sets. The problem is that we are so deeply conditioned to negate that experience as a possibility. Particularly those of us who have labored in intellective work have been conditioned to believe the very concept (let alone the experience) of such a state to be somehow deficient, inadequate for forming any worldview or manner of life. But that is nothing more than a culturally constituted bias. There is no objective way to demonstrate the veracity of such an assumption.

This issue of culturally constituted biases becomes particularly relevant when we find ourselves contending with foundational assumptions that color everything we perceive and do—particularly if those assumptions are corrosive to the flow and the Beauty of Life. For example, our typically unexamined Western assumptions about the material nature of reality, about the soterical promise of 'progress', about the divinely mandated centrality of text in religious thought and discourse, about our (imagined) exceptional position in the world.

The contemporary Western world is at war with itself; it is as the duplic-itous king who tricked the little Hedgehog boy into believing he could have the king's beautiful daughter in marriage, while the real intention of the king was to exploit and marginalize him—and even to kill him, should he come to claim the promised prize. The king and his daughter were in the end both shamed and despised. In the boughs of the Juniper tree, a little bird sings out against our crimes—and especially against the violence we've done to the Land, to our Grandmothers and Grandfathers, to the wisdom of our deep ancestral inheritance.

Like distant echoes of our own collective voice, returning from land-scapes we no longer recall, our forsaken worldviews, our forgotten knowl-edge of the Mystery, may yet come back to us. That homecoming would be as the rekindling of a soterical flame, a hope-light sparked in the dark-ened cave of initiation. That would restore to us the possibility of a rad-ically alchemical form of life and community—a life lived once more in profound interbeing with the whole of Nature; it would be fuel for the fire of a Creation-centered, locally and ecologically minded socio-cultural revolution.

Thankfully, the neuroses of normative Western ideologies are now nearly spent. Too many generations have been wasted looking for salvation in all the wrong places, hoping and striving to make things somehow static, immovable, predictable, dead—imagining a God who bears all those quali-ties, and making an idol of that imagined God: one fashioned in the image of our own neurotic fears, our attachments, our grotesque materialism, our delusional visions of infinite material wealth and infinite technological prog-ress, and our insane rejection of the rest of Nature. That idol now dominates our thinking and our discourse, while we rape and pillage all that which is truly sacred, unwittingly manifesting all around us—in our religious, social, and political institutions—the icons of our pathology: windows into the depths of our profound mistakenness about life.

It's time for the light of our indigenous wisdoms to shine again, to illumine and burn away the delusional, Faustian wagers of our backwards worldviews, our childish, fear-based theologies, our materialistic obsessions. The world is ripe for our *aisling*, our dream-journey of remaking, our Otherworld homecoming. We begin where we are. But not reduced to the sad terms of our consciously inherited inclinations. Rather, with the fruits of our Great Valley Mother, our River Mother, the Land-born wisdoms of our Grandmothers—the ones we haven't yet come to understand again—firmly held in heart and hand.

Take the news to my people that our love has been drowned in the dark waves of the Sea.

A true transmutation of the present state of affairs toward a communion of and with natural values—toward Beauty, toward the immeasurably archaic wisdom of the Earth and her ineffable, originating Mother—will likewise mean a redemption of the misguided centuries of our collective past. Though in a sense the equation flows in both directions: 'It is time we had a Dreamtime past to which even now, being consecrated, we have sacred access.'[85]

Our holy excavation, our uncovering of the content and the context of our indigenous inheritance will itself become, then, a Sacrament. And Sacraments pierce the veil; properly grasped, they equip our souls and our communities for atonement. The stories of our Grandmothers will then live again as Sacrament.

The old tales surround me like a woolen cloak against prevailing winds; they speak in me like the forest itself speaks when in the midst of a wide-open dusk I wander and altogether forget my place in the society of noise; they breathe and burn in me, illumine darkened corners of my being, of the cosmos in the narrow light-shaft of incarnate perception.

Tabhair scéala ag mo mhuintir | Gur bádhadh mo mhíle stór

Let the night be white winds
of nearing, refuge
from wandering, shaking

85   John Moriarty, *Dreamtime* (Dublin: The Lilliput Press, 1994), 200.

out of the old
Hag's breacan,
brightest
of hidden flames,
covered sill,
three Crows of a morning's
stillness,
Foxes in the hillock's
deep den.

May it be called
ancestral learning,
fews of hidden
letters, signs
of fingers, window
of truth,
harp song of rest—

alight
with the herbs of homing,
soft dust
of far currents,
grey skies
of finding.

It took me many years to learn the simple truth that the chief responsibility of the poet, priest, healer, shaman—indeed, not only of these spiritual technologists, but of every true seeker after spiritual depth and wisdom—is to praise unceasingly the Beauty of Life. Not merely to praise in a perfunctory or obligatory manner, but rather to praise with all fullness, with lavishness, with extraordinary elegance, with a heart that seeks always to preserve the sanctity of Life, to preserve the aims and values of Creation. We might call this orientation of heart and soul *love*. Not love in a pedestrian or clichéd sense, but love with real stakes, love that knows sacrifice, and drinks of the complex totality of human existence. Praise of the Beauty and sanctity of that existence, respect for Life as a whole, honor of the entire Creation, and the unyielding will to preserve it, are all indispensable components of the deepest expressions of cosmic love. These are the things of true holiness, inasmuch as we can know and experience it in this life, in this incarnate human experience.

The cosmos moves unyieldingly toward ever deeper and more novel expressions and experiences of Beauty. An ecstatic creativity, moving out eternally across incomprehensible expanses,—plumb lining the possible depths of microcosmic interiority—toward a dynamic and always-as-of-yet-unknown vision of wholeness, of *at-one-ment*, relational knowing, diversity in unity, love and authenticity.

۞

True prayer is poetry, and every poetic creation is in some sense a prayer. Sacred, poetic speech is the root of all language, and therefore the root of the human person's ability to process and frame that which is sacred, to the extent that our limited capacities allow. We do justice only where we praise, Rilke observed. And poetic praise is intimately tied up with the attainment of wisdom—particularly in native Celtic traditions.

That this could be the essence of the whole pilgrim journey is a concept that once would have seemed to me too basic, perhaps even naive. It was in the throes of an initiatory crisis, after fully and realistically saying good-bye to this world, that the truth of the insight finally dawned in my heart. Which is to say, it wasn't until I faced head-on the deep grief of this existence, particularly the inevitability of death, and experienced it as the most intimate companion of Beauty,—until I felt with every fiber of my being the pain of being here and witnessing the ineffable radiance of this life, by way of the inevitable reality of losing it—that I came to see the real depth of this deceptively simple truth, and came to understand something of the existential stakes of Beauty.

The experience of the depth of real grief in the fabric of Creation—and in the human experience especially—though I had lived quite near to it for many years and in many different ways, came in its fully realized form through an experience that can only be described as a death and rebirth, an acute dis-membering and re-membering. It was in that depth of night that the reverberant glory of the cosmic becoming and the role of praise became unmistakably clear. As is always needful in deep waters, that glory was made manifest and known through direct experience, not through rationality or ideation; not as a concept, which by itself would be useless.

The mandate to praise is at the very heart of the archetypal shamanic vocation, the bardic-druidic vocation, the vocation of those who have felt called to be consecrated or set apart to pursue the hidden dimensions of existence, and to bring back to waking, manifest reality the healing fire of the Otherworld, in service of all life—to step into the stream of the eternal pilgrim project of wisdom: to spread and propagate Beauty and blessing like the scattering of wild seeds—to get down into the Earth, into the real grit of being, and to praise it abundantly, whatever the cost to oneself.

Living with poetic integrity means fully embracing the isness of this incarnate moment, with willingness to shatter all those false cultural constructs that would prevent one from doing so—all repressive, puritanical ideology, all world-denying ideology. The opportunity to breathe in the exquisite aromas of this embodied passage is perhaps the only verifiable miracle. Honoring that gift means honoring the diversity of creatures in this wondrous Creation, praising, blessing, and spreading Beauty wherever we go, furthering the cosmic Great Work.

As a set of ideas or theories, all of this is completely unimportant. As a lived experience, it is all there really is to life—: as Keats would have it, 'that is all / ye know on earth, and all ye need to know'. For as long as we're here, we're here to seek and experience the fullness of Beauty.

☙

Since experiencing the fullness of Beauty also means experiencing the fullness of grief, we as human beings—and especially as Westerners, who have too long suppressed or misdirected the authentic grief of our existential situation—must learn to weep. Our inability to do so makes us sick on every level of being—mentally, spiritually, and physically.

As Tz'utujil Mayan shaman and storyteller, Martín Prechtel, summarizes, 'When you're grieving for the thing you've got, it's called "praise". And when you're praising the thing you've lost, it's called "grief"'.[86] This really speaks to the heart of the matter, and neatly encapsulates the reason why both praise and grief, which are inextricably intertwined, together constitute the core foundation of the spiritual task. They are inherently interdependent: two faces of the same reality.

The French Existentialist writer, Albert Camus, put it this way: 'Beauty is unbearable: it drives us to despair, offering us for a moment a glimpse of an eternity that we should like to stretch out over the whole of time.'[87] Thence comes the grief inherent to authentic (i.e., awakened) being.

Beauty *must* shatter us if the stakes are high enough, if we're truly invested in Life. If we have truly been here, truly valued the astounding, ineffable qualities of being that surround us and interpenetrate us constantly (the whole reason, I believe, we come here to begin with, for why else would we want to subject ourselves to the suffering and insanity of incarnate existence in this world?), then we will be absolutely broken by the knowledge that we must inevitably leave it behind—indefinitely, so far as our rational faculties can comprehend.

This is not merely the natural human fear of death, which must be met and integrated (if not overcome) through the trials of initiatory experience and the cumulative wisdom of the spiritual quest. It is likewise a yet more foundational grief—and therefore praise—for the miraculous Beauty of the existence in which we mysteriously find ourselves.

---

[86] From an independently published audio recording of the talk, *On Grief and Praise* (location and date of recording unknown).

[87] Albert Camus, *Notebooks: 1935-1951*, Phillip M. Waller Thody and Justin O'Brien, trans. (Cambridge: DaCapo Press, 1998), 73.

'To have been this once, completely, even if only once: to have been at one with the Earth seems beyond undoing.'[88]

In terms specific to a pan-Celtic culture and worldview, the existential mandate to praise abundantly the true Beauty of Life describes well the heart of the vocation of the poet-seer or *fili*. The *fili* is one who is consecrated in part for the purpose of meeting the spiritual and communal need for eloquent praising and grieving. The central importance of this role in the culture and society of the tribe is one reason the *fili* must be prepared through a remarkable amount of training—: intensive mental and spiritual training, punctuated by self-shattering initiatory experiences, traditionally taking a minimum of twelve years (with an average of eight years for bards, twenty for druids).

To know intimately—and to honor, praise, and commune with—the Beauty of Creation, the manifold unseen powers of Nature, the Ancestors, the Earth as Mother of incarnate life, and the ineffable Source of All Being is the central sacred work which maintains human cultures and societies in harmony with the rest of the cosmos. Without the poetic and ritual work, the archaic, ancestrally disseminated sacral technologies necessary to maintain this harmony, culture erodes and human societies fall into decay.

This is no doubt one of many reasons why members of the druidic class (which included the *filidh*) were considered in ancient Celtic societies to be the most honored members of the social structure, even more so than kings or chieftains.[89] Druids and seers kept the fabric of society woven together, in harmony with the unseen world of spirit. They had to learn not only how to

---

[88]   Rainer Maria Rilke, *The Selected Poetry of Rainer Maria Rilke*, Stephen Mitchell, trans. (New York, Random House, 1982), 231.

[89]   It is fairly clear, in reflecting on the historical transformation of the druidic priestly class through the early years of Christianity in the Isles (especially as seen through the early medieval insular texts of Irish and Welsh origin), that the *filidh* or poet-seers played a decisive role in carrying the torch of earlier Celtic thought into the Christian era.

enter non-ordinary consciousness at will, to heal the soul, mind, and body, and to memorize and tell the histories and myths of the people, but also how to induce sleep, to induce weeping, and to induce joy—the latter two effected by praising or grieving with remarkable poetic skill.

In the collective mind of a shamanically oriented, animistic people group like the ancient Celts, there is nothing more demanding and nothing more sacred in human life than fulfilling this type of vocation, so the people who are called to such a path are accorded a special place of honor. This collective social honoring of the druidic class implies something significant about the Celtic peoples, because it marks what they have always valued most highly in their collective life.

Wisdom is the highest virtue and the principal aim of the pilgrim journey of spiritual development that each soul is eternally embarked upon. Wisdom means illumination, an increasingly totalizing alignment with Beauty, an understanding of and commitment to the values of Life, of Nature, which are also the ways of the Old Ones, the spirits, gods, and ancient Ancestors. Wisdom, thusly understood and embodied, keeps the human community in harmony with the great community of all beings. This is 'communion' in its fullest sense: *communitas*. Without it we wither and die. Therefore, those who embody this pursuit of wisdom and make it the central focus of their lives occupy a special place in the social strata.

This is certainly a dimension of ancient Celtic cultures we can learn a great deal from today. We exist now, in the contemporary Western world, in a milieu in which the dominant value system is utterly contrary to the pursuit of wisdom. We have created a world that is dis-spirited, de-souled, desacralized, hopelessly materialistic, crude, isolationist, and patently destructive. Rather than placing a high value on the pursuit and attainment of wisdom, spiritual depth, integrity, and eloquence, we hold up consumeristic obsessions, distraction from existential realities, material possessions, and money as supreme ideals.

It should not be difficult to imagine, then, how understanding what our ancient Ancestors valued and prioritized, and embracing those same values, integrating them into our way of being in the world, could completely transform our lives and our societies.

※

To be called to the life of a poet-seer—a healer, storyteller, diviner, carrier of ancestral knowledge, and pilgrim after wisdom—is to be called to a life of great sacrifice, as well as great depth and beauty. But all vocations, if they are true and authentic, are equal in value and sanctity. To attempt to put on a vocational mantle that is not one's own, to which one has not been genuinely called, is to miss the aim of the pilgrim journey. Community—well lived and properly cultivated—provides a natural context for the mutual discernment, training, and support of vocations, each and every one contributing to the good of the whole, which means not only the human community but the entire ecology to which the human community is connected. And the archaic technologies of initiation shape and support that crucial discernment.

What is most needful in community is a shared focus that places the sacred at the center of all endeavor, experiences it as integral to every aspect of human life, and embraces the archaic instinct to live in genuine love and reciprocal harmony with the whole of Nature. This is, in essence, what it means to be fully embodied and authentically human—: to honor the precious gifts of the Earth Mother, to co-create with Her as much Beauty as possible, and to live in elegance, in praise of Life. Once we learn again how to truly grieve, then we can begin re-learning what wisdom really is, both as individual souls and as a community of integrated spirituality: a cooperative collectivity in which the sacred unseen saturates and is interwoven with every aspect of human life, from the most minute to the most grand.

From a strange crystal curragh we stepped off into the misty West of this island world, stepped off as travelers from the great starry road. And we shall leave by the same mode of passage—like Connla, hand in hand with the Fairy Maiden, stepping out of this world onto the smooth, crystalline bough, stepping out of this world into the deathless lands of the Ancestors, into the Isles of the West, over the flowery Sea-Plains of Mannanán, stepping out of this world into eternality.

Or else by way of the great pale roots we'll go, the knotwork paths of Bíle, the Oaken Tree of Worlds. *Dair/Duir*—'Most exalted tree, highest of plants; craft of skilled artificer; most carved of craftsmanship'.[90]

Out into the night of ancient song, in pursuit of a soterical concrescence, into the strange, dark tundra and the brine-mist of the endless Quest, through the pillaged Wasteland of Modernity, through the catacombs of death, ear to the ground for a songline of truth held quiet in the soil, beneath the snow-covered duff, to proclaim the secret words of our long-forgotten tongue, to part the old hedge-rows, breaking into flower, to summon from sleep our Briar Rose.

Never *merely* a teller of tales, never *merely* a singer of songs. 'As poet and philosopher, I walk the path to Connla's Well. As poet and philosopher, it's my task to keep it open.'[91]

Some have suggested that the Celtic peoples had no true creation narratives. Looking at the insular mythic texts of Ireland and Wales, it's difficult not to notice the apparent lack of such cosmogonic tales. It's possible that the Christian monastic scribes who recorded the wisdom stories of the Celtic cultures simply omitted any trace of pre-Christian cosmogonic myth, in order to replace it with a Biblical one. To retroactively Christianize the myth and folklore of an ancient culture has unfortunately been a common practice throughout Christianized Western history. To be sure, Irish monastic scribes thought it needful to connect their own stories of origin to a foreign mythic lineage of Hebraic beginnings. Thus, for example, we are told in the *Lebor Gabála Érenn* that the first person to set foot on the Land of Ireland, *Cessair*, was a granddaughter of Noah.

---

[90] From *Auraicept na n-Éces*: the medieval Irish 'word ogams' for the letter *Dair* or *Duir*, 'Oak'.

[91] John Moriarty, *Dreamtime* (Dublin: The Lilliput Press, 1994), 195.

Cessair is accompanied in her landing by a host of women, by Fintan Mac Bóchra (her husband), and two other men. No one ultimately survives on the Isle but Fintan, who escapes the deluge of the great flood by shape-shifting into the form of a Salmon. Along with the Hawk of Achill, he subsequently appears as one of the two most ancient creatures in Ireland, having been alive there in various forms for roughly five-and-a-half thousand years. He relates the history of Ireland, though not from the true beginning, the cosmogonic beginning. The story of Fintan, while certainly rich with pre-Christian content, seems to contain no metaphysical speculation about a proper origin, about how life began.

One bit of possible evidence to the contrary is the presence of the flood motif in the story of Fintan. While this could of course be nothing more than the Christian scribe's attempt to connect the Irish people to Biblical narrative, we should also take into account the fact that the great flood is a fairly ubiquitous theme in creation myths the world over—and, as Peter Ellis points out, there is a possible parallel here with the Hindu creation myth in which the first man, Manu, is spared from the ravages of the flood and later gives thanks to Vishnu by means of a food sacrifice, from which his first daughter (and thereafter the rest of humanity) are born.[92] In the Irish tale, Fintan is not credited with giving rise to humanity—rather, he's a sort of detached observer who bears all the knowledge of what has unfolded, but remains a solitary figure while the various people groups come and go.

It is quite plausible that the Celts, like many other peoples, reflected the memory of an actual cataclysmic event in deep history—a great flood—in their creation myths. Mac Bóchra means 'Son of the Sea'. Some have speculated that Bóchra, being feminine, may be the name of an ancient female Sea spirit or goddess of primordial waters.

In a more deeply imaginal hour, we might muse on the resonance these watery motifs have with the ancient Eurasian Diver Myths, wherein an Otter or Seal (both sacred animals in Gaelic cultures) is asked by the Creator(s) to dive down into the depths of the uncreated abyss, and return with a bit of

---

[92] Peter Berresford Ellis, *The Druids*, (London: Constable and Co. Ltd, 1994), 116.

primordial Earth, from which may be fashioned Land for human beings to dwell on. Perhaps this was the task of the primordial Salmon, guardian of primeval wisdom.

Fintan was also known by an epithet that connects him to the seership tradition: Fintan the Wise. Indeed, the Old Irish root of the name Fintan (*Fin*) also means 'wisdom', and his transformational rebirth into the totemic figure of the Salmon, a key mythic image of the pursuit and attainment of wisdom in Irish tradition, is also significant. While he is not portrayed as a druid, per se, he is clearly a shamanic (and therefore druidic) figure: one who bears all wisdom and knowledge, and who possesses the classic shamanic ability of shapeshifting into the forms of various animals. We also see in this story evidence of the druidic doctrine of *metempsychosis*. This could point toward a druidic creation narrative that placed the druids themselves (or their proto-druidic, divinized spiritual Ancestors) at the beginning of things.

The apparent lack of a proper creation myth in Irish vernacular literature could certainly be the result of a self-consciously Christianized hand in the telling—that is, it could represent a whitewashing of authentic Celtic origin stories, now lost to us. Alternatively, the nature of the Fintan story in the *Lebor Gabála* and its placement 'in the beginning' could indicate that the ancient Irish in fact had no formalized cosmogonic myth, at least as commonly understood through the lenses of other cultures. This wouldn't necessarily mean that the pre-Christian Irish had no creation stories at all; but rather that their stories of cosmic and human origins were not of the variety we're accustomed to hearing in Western historical contexts. Or, it may be that, as Ellis posits, the Fintan tale merely wears a Christian veil, beneath which is an ancient Celtic creation narrative comparable to some found in other Indo-European environments.

Whatever the case, it might be helpful to reflect here on what Lynn White says of Graeco-Roman (and, by extension, more broadly Indo-European) conceptions of time and creation: 'While many of the world's mythologies provide stories of creation, Greco-Roman mythology was singularly incoherent in this respect. Like Aristotle, the intellectuals of the ancient West denied that the visible world had had a beginning. Indeed, *the idea of a beginning was impossible in the framework of their cyclical notion of time.* In sharp contrast, Christianity inherited from Judaism not only a concept of time as nonrepetitive and linear but also a striking story of creation.'[93]

If, as White suggests, a cyclical (or spiral) conception of time naturally inoculates the inclination to develop cosmogonic narratives, then the Celtic peoples would reasonably be expected to accompany their Indo-European cousins of the Mediterranean in feeling no need to create such myths. I would personally see this not as an 'incoherence', per se, but rather as a sensible orientation given the deep-rooted Celtic (and, presumably, pre-Celtic or Neolithic) inclination to view time through a lens of the continual recurrence of seasons, the turning and returning of heavenly bodies. The notion of Life or Nature in eternal movement, without beginning or end, also points rather elegantly to the Celtic notion of 'openness', the desire to dwell in liminality, in paradox, in the heart of the Mystery, without 'an irritable grasping at reason.' Indeed, the Judaeo-Christian mythic conception, along with its linear, finite approach to time—like the dualistic and anthropocentric ethos that underlies it, product of a harsh and arid landscape—stands in stark contrast to the Celtic approach; and, we might say, it betrays a neurotic need for 'closure', for surety, concreteness, measurement, control—: the perfect precursory foundation for the Western advent of rationalistic reductionism, and its hideous offspring, scientism.

❦

For the last lines of light:
coast barnwood,
Coyote Brush, Lavender,
a Crow call longing
through an un-
detectable distance.

---

[93]   Lynn White, Jr., 'The Historical Roots of Our Ecologic Crisis', in *Science 155* (1967), 1205. *Emphasis mine.*

Unkept memories assent
in spite of these
predictions, sojourns,
precipitate blooms,
elapse with coming rains—
in time each thing
carried back with the sea.

Julius Caesar records that the Gaulish druids maintained their people were all descended from the Celtic equivalent of the Roman god *Dis* (or *Dis Pater*). This could indicate at least one broad element of an ancient creation story, or at least an instance of tribal patronage, wherein certain tribes or people groups are thought to be descended from a specific divine or semi-divine Ancestor. Did the druids of Gaul teach that *all* people are descended from this Celtic 'Dis Pater', or would we be likely to find in Ireland and Scotland, for example, Celtic people groups claiming descent from an entirely different ancestral figure?

We know that Druidism was a common denominator throughout the Celtic countries, and can safely say it underwent its most crucial developments on and with a specific, singular landscape. Caesar states that those who wished to make a full and complete study of druidic wisdom traveled to Britain, the seat of Druidism, in order to do so. Probably this 'seat of Druidism' was the Welsh Isle of Anglesey, where later the British druids made their last great stand against the invading Romans.

We can assume, therefore, that whatever the druids' teachings on origins, those teachings were common, at least in general terms, to all Celtic peoples, all of whom were taught by druids formed in the same schools and probably in the same basic traditions. No doubt local coloring would have produced a diversity of interpretations and narrative frameworks for containing such teachings (as we see, for example, in the difference between the tale of Finn Mac Cumhaill and the Salmon of Wisdom in Ireland and its mythic relative in Wales, the tale of Gwion Bach). But if Caesar's information about the druidic teaching on human origins is accurate (and we have no compelling reason to suspect otherwise), it seems that the Celtic gods are also Ancestors—or at least this particular god, from whom some or all of the people are said to be descended.

In Irish and Welsh myth, deities are often portrayed as possessing distinctly human characteristics. While this is not unheard of in other indigenous traditions, it is certainly found in abundance in the insular Celtic traditions—and it can strike our contemporary Western sensibilities as odd or even repulsive. It can fan the flames of our desperately misguided atavism. But it can also make these strange gods and goddesses feel very close to us, very near at hand. If they are in one sense or another our Ancestors, then such nearness would not be without spiritual purpose or precedent.

Here the ancient stories and the landscapes that midwifed them must be heard. They are, in the final estimation, our only real teachers with regard to an ancestral metaphysic. The Land herself to teach us; our old ancestral tales to teach us; the Dreaming breath, an Otherworld wind, an Otherworld wave to teach us.

Where could we know something of Lugh if not at Uisneach? Where could we receive something of the mysteries of Anu if not encamped between her breasts in Kerry, knees in the stream, our postmodern angst, our restless and distracted minds surrendered like a sacrificial offering, flowing gradually down into the Clydagh? Where could we receive communion-knowledge of the ageless Hag who shaped the Earth, and therefore shaped our own fleshly forms, if not at Sliabh na Calliagh?

Caesar says that the 'chief god' of the Gauls, whom he identifies with Mercury and is almost certainly *Lugh* (*Lugus* on the Continent), is the 'inventor of all the arts', understood as a chief patron and divine Ancestor of artisans and craftspeople.[94] Craftspeople formed part of the second social tier or, 'class', in Celtic society, along with warriors—and in Irish myth, Lugh is not

---

[94]   As quoted in Philip Freeman, *War, Women, and Druids: Eyewitness Reports and Early Accounts of the Ancient Celts* (Austin, TX: University of Texas Press, 2002), 42.

only the master of all arts (*samildánach*, 'possessing many arts'), but also the great champion warrior and the keeper of the Spear of Lugh, one of the four talismanic treasures of the Tuatha Dé Danann. Whoever holds the Spear, it is said, cannot be defeated in battle. As patron of crafts and craftspeople, Lugh also became known and appealed to as patron of commerce, trade and travel, as Caesar further attests: 'the guide for every road and journey, and the most influential god in trade and moneymaking.'[95] Lugh is also known as Lámhfadha, 'of the long arm' or 'of the long hand', which may indicate solar attributes, or perhaps is simply a symbolic superlative to indicate the 'reach' of his skill with a sword, and more generally his mastery in the arts and in battle (both requiring strong, adept use of hand and arm).

It seems that some Celtic tribes (particularly in Ireland, as shown in the *Lebor Gabála*) claimed direct descent from divine ancestral figures, for example the Luigne of Counties Meath and Sligo, who claimed to be descendants of Lugh.

As also happened later with Finn, when Lugh was born, the king—who was his grandfather—ordered the infant to be cast into the Sea and drowned. The king in this case was Balor of the Baleful Eye, a tyrannical, one-eyed ruler of the Fomorians. A druidic prophecy had foretold that Balor would be struck down in battle by the hand of his own grandson. Lugh was rescued from the waves by an old *Ban-Draoi*, a female druid, a wise old woman of the wood, who saw that he was well raised and formed in the many sacred arts. Having mastered the skills of every class, Lugh gained entry into the halls of Nuadha, king of the Tuatha Dé Danann, and eventually met his grandfather in battle, where he indeed struck him dead by slinging a stone into his unveiled eye.

The Baleful Eye: the poisonous eye of tyrannical rule, of dominator culture, of greed, shameless materialism, treachery, reductionism, anti-feminin-

---

[95] ibid.

ity, anti-sacrality, isolation, unnatural worldview. The Baleful Eye, mounted like a jewel in the midst of our Hadrian's Wall.

Tá do shúile ag na péisti / 'S tá do bhéilin ag na portáin / 'S tá do dhá lamh gheala ghléigal

Darling Lugh in swaddling clothes, the eels have your eyes now, and the crabs have your little mouth. Old Woman of Wisdom, you too have been thrown to the waves—Fox Spirit Woman, the Sea holds captive your beautiful hands, your old sacred words.

Peter Berresford Ellis has attempted to reconstruct a general creation myth of the Gaelic peoples based on a comparative analysis of the extant insular material with what he sees as parallel Vedic sources, along with some personal intuition and a fair bit of poetic license.[96] He suggests in this new myth that *Danu* is the primordial Mother Goddess in the form of the 'Waters from Heaven'—a syncretistic reading I find unconvincing. These divine waters fertilize a previously barren landscape of primal chaos, and out of the newly fertilized soil comes forth the World Tree, *Bíle*, the sacred Oak. From *Bíle* then falls two acorns: from one is born the *Daghda*, and from the other *Brigid*. These two then couple and give birth to the rest of the gods (and, presumably, to humanity as well).

In my view, *Anu* is more properly the Source-Mother, the living Earth who births and nourishes all: 'Mother of the Irish Gods' (and therefore of the human tribes as well). And, as we have seen, it is likely a misdirected contrivance to force her into a cosmogonic narrative. Indeed, Strabo, a Classical witness to druidic teaching (drawing, perhaps, from Posidonius), reports a druidic doctrine that the universe, the physical Creation, is eternal, without discernible advent or end, but occasionally 'fire and water prevail', destroying the physical world(s), and giving way to the start of a new cosmic cycle. As Hilda Davidson points out, this is a teaching with clear parallels in

---

[96] cf. Peter Berresford Ellis, *The Chronicles of the Celts: New Tellings of their Myths and Legends* (New York: Carroll & Graf Publishers, Inc., 1999), 21-30.

Norse and Germanic worldviews.[97] The same general notion is also found in Vedic philosophy, and in certain schools of Stoicism.

Anu, the Great Mother, soul of the Earth, who seems to have been thought of in Gaelic contexts as the greatest divinity human beings and their cultures could realistically be in relationship with, would need no origin myth—and it may well be that the nagging need contemporary Westerners might feel to give Her one is foreign to the cultures that named and honored Her: a foreign impulse derived from our thorough (and now largely unconscious) conditioning to Judaeo-Christian norms of thought, grafted onto a context with which it ultimately cannot be reconciled. Again we encounter the likely possibility that reclaiming a genuinely Celtic worldview will first require of us an abandoning of the conditioned Near Eastern orientations that have haunted the Western cultural milieu since the coming of Christianity.

We should also point out that Brigid is described in the insular sources (e.g., in *Cormac's Glossary*) as a *daughter* of the Daghda, not as his consort. Ellis' narrative also conflates *Bíle*, the sacred Oak, the *axis mundi*, with the divine ancestral figure that Caesar conflated with the Roman *Dis Pater*. Others have also made this connection between *Bíle*, the primal World Tree which connects the three worlds, and a psychopompic god of the underworld, often connecting the Continental divine names *Bel* and *Belenus*, from Romano-Gaulish inscriptions, with *Bíle*. I find this to be implausible, firstly because the concept is unintuitive: in no other tradition that I know of is the World Tree itself personified as a human Ancestor (whether divine or otherwise); and secondly, because no folkloric, literary, visual representation, or direct etymological evidence exists that clearly links such figures with the World Tree.

The World Tree, *Bíle*, is the sacred center of the cosmos, not just in Celtic tradition, but in Nordic, Siberian, and other shamanistic traditions.

---

97   Hilda Roderick Ellis Davidson, *Myths and Symbols in Pagan Europe: Early Scandinavian and Celtic Religions* (Manchester: Manchester University Press, 1988), 188.

The Irish expressed this sacral designation of the World Tree in microcosm. Each tribe commonly had a small *bíle*, a symbolic incarnation of the Great Tree, which was held to be the sacred center of the tribal settlement—metaphorically, the heart of the people, the axis of the life of the tribe, and the symbolic connection with *Bíle*, the great primordial Oak (or sometimes Ash—for example as associated with Uisneach, the sacred Navel of Ériu), an open channel to the Otherworld, a sign of the pathway the druids and seers of each tribe would traverse in their visionary journeys or *immrama*.

Direct visionary experience has confirmed for me that in some way the journey out of incarnate existence in this world involves traveling through the roots or branches of a great tree. These roots and branches, I gather, belong to *Bíle*. The extremely vivid and powerful visionary experience that revealed this pathway of travel between worlds came to me in the throes of a 'near death' initiatory experience, independent of my intellective research and reflection on the subject.

In this sense, *Bíle* can rightly be associated with leading souls in and out of this world—though, in neither my direct personal experience nor in my research does this function seem to involve an anthropomorphic form.

The World Tree as pathway to the Otherworld, through the veil of death, will be familiar to students of shamanic history and technique. It is not uncommon for shamans in various cultures to travel on Otherworld journeys by way of the *axis mundi*, sometimes represented by the central house pole, above which may be found a smoke hole through which the spirit of the traveling shaman journeys outward toward the heavenly realms or to the unseen dimensions of this Middle World. The underworld realms would then be accessed by the roots of the Tree (or, more symbolically, by following the house pole underground).[98]

Life in this earthly realm may well have sprung in some fashion from the sacred, primordial Oak. The great human Ancestor, the 'father of humanity'

---

[98]   This is, of course, not the only model for Otherworld journey in shamanic practice—in some cases, for example, the shaman enters the underworld through a cave or other opening in the Earth.

is another matter. The Great Oak is our 'source' in the sense that it provides a pathway along which the eternal souls of mortal beings enter and exit this world.

۞

It seems that in Celtic cultures the primal druidic (or proto-druidic) Ancestors played a particularly significant role in the spiritual lives of the people. Ellis in fact gives evidence for this when he cites the story of Conlaí of Connacht, who once 'convened an assembly of druids at which a claim was made that they were creators of the world.'[99] The manner in which this anecdote comes down to us is no doubt colored by the Christian bias of medieval scribes, but I suspect it does contain a seed of truth—not that the druids claimed to literally be the fashioners of all Creation, but rather that their tradition (and therefore the archaic Celtic tradition) was, as Caesar indicates, that all the peoples of the tribes had descended from one primal divine Ancestor, and this Ancestor was also considered the first druid. In my estimation, this is the person of *Cernach* or *Dearg Corra*—*Cernunnos* in the Gallic context.

In the deep memory of many indigenous cultures, all conceivable human things—which is to say, the advent of culture and its associated traditions of knowledge—begin with the primal shamanic figure, the teller of tales, the originator of language and poetry, the first spiritual traveler: in a Celtic context, the first druid.

In the deep folk memory of the Irish, there also exists the concept of a primordial Grandmother figure who, in my reading, stands at the origin point of human culture and language. This figure is preserved in the insular poetic tradition, and is described only as 'the Grandmother who was at the beginning, who first ate of the (Otherworldly) apples'. This Grandmother whose proper name is unknown to us—perhaps because she herself represents the very dawn of language and therefore of naming, and so is herself remembered as being without personal name—is, we can presume,

---

[99]   Peter Berresford Ellis, *The Druids*, (London: Constable and Co. Ltd, 1994), 115.

the first partaker of the holy druidic Sacrament, the fruit of Wisdom, the (metaphorical) Salmon, the sacred Otherworldly food, the consumption of which confers all knowledge, but particularly direct, experiential knowledge of sacred things. Apples are one of several preeminent symbols of this veiled Sacrament in Celtic tradition. The veiled or hidden Sacrament is the mystical, Otherworldly food through which sacral knowledge—including language itself, which we can realistically assume would have been considered magical or miraculous from its inception—along with access to Otherworldly landscapes, power to heal, and all the vocational roles and activities that develop eventually into a sacral class, take birth in the human experience.

This Grandmother's age is compared in folk memory with that of *An Cailleach*. The ancient Hawk (or Crow) of Achill, after a poetic litany of age comparisons with the most ancient creatures—Hawk, Eagle, one-eyed Salmon (Fintan)—a motif also found in Welsh folklore (e.g., in the tale often known as 'The Long-Lived Ancestors'), finally proclaims to *An Cailleach*: 'I give you the branch (of victory)....You are as old as the old Grandmother, long ago, who (first) ate the Apples.'[100]

As *An Cailleach* is a deeply archaic image of the sacred landscape (perhaps inherited from the pre-Celtic Neolithic peoples of the Isles), naturally she is older than any creature, an esoteric knowing recalled metaphorically (and obliquely) in Irish folklore. But we find in this folk memory the evidence that there was once a human woman, a primevally ancient human Ancestor, who was credited with being the first to uncover or receive the gift of the veiled Sacrament, metaphorically rendered in this case as the Otherworldly Apples, and thus was the inaugurator of all sacred arts, of culture and language, and of the sacral tradition (i.e., Druidry), even if she is not technically remembered as the first druid, per se. She is the paver of the primordial path.

---

[100] Referenced by Eleanor Hull in *Folk-Lore*, 1932. cf. also: Caitlín and John Matthews, *The Encyclopaedia of Celtic Wisdom* (New York: Barnes & Noble Books, 1996), 84-85.

Matthew Fox notes that 'If we are to regain our lives, our spiritual roots that nourish us into growth, we must return to the pre-word times of original creation.'[101] Perhaps Fox simply points here to the necessity of returning, in spiritual practice, to a mode of perception that is in some sense effectively 'pre-linguistic' (that is, a transcendence of mental noise, allowing for a clearer perception of Reality). While that is true enough—and certainly representative of a needful experience—I think the implications are yet deeper than he likely imagined. It seems to me that the truly salvific task which lies before us now is to return not just to a temporary experience of 'pre-word times', but to a more pervasive and permanent experiential understanding of the font of wisdom which arose from that decisive and numinous event when the first human person—remembered in deep Gaelic memory as 'The Grandmother'—encountered the hidden Sacrament, a revelatory gift from the Otherworld. That is to say, we must return for answers, in search of wisdom, to the very source of all language, the source of all art and abstract thought and culture, to the dawn-time, to the experience of our ancient Grandmother, who first ate the Apples.

☙

To return for a moment to Ellis's reconstruction: I do find the broad, initial strokes of his vision to be sensible—which is to say, I concur that the ancient Celts (and their druids, more specifically) almost certainly held the ultimate origin of life to be a primordial Divine Mother. Based on the attestation of *Sanas Cormaic* ('Cormac's Glossary') and other insular Irish texts, however, at least in Ireland this Divine Mother was known as *An Mórrígan*, The Great Queen, a tri-form or trinitarian divinity, one of whose names was originally *Anu* (and likely not *Danu*).[102]

---

[101]   Matthew Fox, *Original Blessing* (New York: Jeremy P. Tarcher/Putnam, 1983), 37.

[102]   Though the words look similar, etymologically and historically speaking these two names do not seem to be co-equivalent or interchangeable. For a more nuanced discussion of this issue, cf. Sharon Paice MacLeod, *Celtic Cosmology and the Otherworld: Mythic Origins, Sovereignty and Liminality* (Jefferson, NC: McFarland & Co. Inc., 2018), Ch. 4.

Cormac states unequivocally that *Anu* is 'Mother of the Irish gods' (in Latin, *mater deorum hibernensium*).[103] Elsewhere we find clear evidence that *Anu* is one of the three names and aspects of *An Mórrígan*. The others are *Badb* (or *Badhbh*) and *Macha*.

What does a Mother like this one, Mother to the ancient gods, a *Mater Deorum Hibernensium*, mean for us now, here in the night of mechanistic depravation? How might She manifest to Her alienated people, the prodigal children of Her diaspora? As the *Logos-Sophia*, the guiding Voice? As Mother of hidden Sacraments? As great Initiatrix? As Earthly *telos*? As consciousness within the Land? To be sure, she is soul of the living Earth, as the mountains called her breasts in the West of Ireland boldly remind us.

However the Great Queen, in Her threefold form, has manifested in the currents of ancestral streams, the invitation and the obligation is now open before us to discover how She would like to manifest now, in the present current. What we seem to need now more than anything is a spiritual home-coming—a return to the Great Mother in all her aspects. And we will need a source-line, a midwife, a healer, a wise old Oak-dwelling druidess in the long, painful journey of our reclamation and resurrection.

In the Irish epic, *Cath Maige Tuired*, it is only when the Tuatha Dé Danann, by way of their king, An Daghda, join themselves in harmony with An Mórrígan that the battle against the moral depravity and toxicity of the Fomorians begins to turn in their favor. At Samhain, at the opening of the threshold between years and the threshold between worlds, An Daghda—god of storm and thunder, rain and therefore abundance—unites with An Mórrígan, above the River Uinius ('Ash Tree'). 'As a Goddess of Sovereignty, The Mórrígan's assistance, skill, magic, blessings and protection were

---

[103] cf. *Cormac's Glossary*, trans. John O'Donovan, ed. Whitley Stokes (Calcutta: O. T. Cutter & The Irish Archaeological and Celtic Society, 1868), 4.

required to ensure the victory and continuation of the tribe, and the prosperity of the land and its people, whether mortal or immortal.'[104]

Without abiding in union with the Sovereignty of the Land, without a direct life-line to the sacramental Beauty, power, and energy of Nature, the Life-corroding, dominator impulses in our psyches and our societies take hold and set up their tyrannical rule. They reject the feminine divine, they give way to matricide, exiling the Great Mother of the Land rather than uniting with her.

The very same battle goes on each year in us and in our cultures. At Samhain the ancient powers do their part, they pave the way for us, again and again, like a primeval cosmogonic ritual re-creating the circumstances that give life, that allow Life to flow forth in abundance. But we on the sad little isle of our alienation have utterly forgotten our part. We're no longer even aware of the union. We've forsaken the rituals and the lifeways, the sacred technologies, that once allowed us to participate in that unification, to re-member each year its significance. To re-member ourselves in that sacramental union.

The Baleful Eye, lifted against us by virtue of our own stupidity—like Tolkien's lidless 'Eye of Sauron'—poisons the waters, both literally and figuratively. It poisons the waters of our souls and minds, and will continue to do so until we come to our senses, take courage of heart, and, having relearned the needful sacramental skills, having reclaimed our sacred indigenous inheritance, can deal the blow that vanquishes its toxifying, dominator reign.

But first we must reunite with Sovereignty, with the spirit of the sacred Land, who is our Mother. Without first engaging that most needful task of unification, all our training and mastery and attunement of sacred skill will mean nothing. Until we get right with the Mother of Life and with Her Creation, we are impossibly lost at sea.

---

[104] Sharon Paice MacLeod, *Celtic Cosmology and the Otherworld: Mythic Origins, Sovereignty and Liminality* (Jefferson, NC: McFarland & Co. Inc., 2018), 115.

When we have thusly reunited with Her Body and restored ourselves to the sacred center—the cosmic center of Uisneach, the center that *can* hold, where the Tree of Worlds may again spread its mighty, sheltering limbs[105]— then the shining silver branch, taken from that sacred *Bíle*, with its blossoms of Hawthorn and Hazel and Apple—the branch of Otherworld music, of our cosmic lifeline—can be brought in from the hinterland dark.

And with it will come the wild-scented Fox pelt.

Let Trefuilngidh bring them both, walking tall enough to obscure the Sun. Let Fintan bring them, coming as Crow or Stag or Sage.

The true Sage returning would summon the Shining Ones back from hiding, would invoke once more the spirits of Nature, would call them back to their ancient dwellings.

I wonder: What songs might the maidens of our old sacred Springs sing to us now? What mythic histories might the Hawk of Achill now convey— wherever in the three worlds he is, whatever form he now inhabits?

In our desperate state of alienation, can we not—*must* we not—with a fitting flow of tears, ask:

Who now will augur the living world for us? Who will stand like Amergin White-Knee, one with the elements, consciously inseparable from the living Earth, and make peace with the three-formed Goddess of wisdom and battle, fertility and vision, Land and Life, Sovereignty and death? Who will speak on our behalf? Who will ask with authenticity about our strange affairs—about our pathways, straight or crooked, about the things we've left behind? Who will ask to reclaim our own holy wisdom, held in Land and

---

[105] W. B. Yeats, in his poem, *The Second Coming*, famously stated, 'Things fall apart; the centre cannot hold.' Certainly this proved to be true of modernity, and has remained true of all subsequent socio-cultural developments in the Western world. John Moriarty also made a poetic connection, in response to Yeats, between Uisneach—the sacred center of Éire and the cosmic axis of this middle world, where a great Ash *Bíle* once grew, and where stands the *Aill na Mireann*, the Stone of Divisions (i.e., the place from which the Provinces and the sacred cosmic Directions have been traced out)—and a 'centre that will hold.' cf. John Moriarty, *Dreamtime* (Dublin: The Lilliput Press, 1994), 95.

Sky and Sea, in Moon and Stone, Thunder and Wind, Oak and Hawthorn, Rain and Mist, Ash and Hazel—like a woolen cloak left safely stored but forgotten in an old Cedar chest?

And who, then, will mark and truly hear the answers—hear them with a heart that deeply listens? Who will translate the vatic words and visions, the wisdom-songs that come forth from those primordial wellsprings?

At Loughcrew, the stones hold deep-root memory. If one knows how to listen, one can hear them speak. One can hear them sing in forgotten tongues.

The Ancestors speak, too, in this place of holy remembrance. They give me songs—strange songs, unlike any others I know.

In the stones and in the wind and in the grass are whisperings of stories too sacred for English, for the language of industry, commodity, dominion.

I sit in the dark of the upper cairn. I've found the key and locked myself inside. Only a faint dusklight now illumines the entrance. I chant the strange songs I hear. I sing them back to the ones who gave them: back to the Ancestors. I sing them to the Earth.

Faintly I can see them, the Old Ones: moving slowly by firelight, in ritual procession. Here in the heart of the heart-chamber of Éire, in the cave of the heart, a root-stream runs. Stars in the darkness of Earth folding into timeless Sky; Seas in their measureless turning: the Otherworldly turning of original things.

Here no text, no Bible, no ideology can follow—: to the furthest vistas of interiority, landscapes beneath the hollow hills, horizons of Dreaming. To the sources of myths, of rivers, seas, and forests. To ritual nights so veiled as to be almost irretrievable, nearly blotted out from the fabric of our collective fate. Yet still they move: under the soul, in deep water currents: rivers beneath the ancient limestone.

In the Hag's Seat I sit and pray. The fierce wind makes me shelter underneath my coat and shawl. I gradually fall into dream. Suddenly I am entering the chthonic dark, through a long, narrow chamber leading down from the central shaft of the cairn. I am walking sightless, seeking only the opportunity to ask the right way forward, how to navigate the coming crises, whether I'm permitted to guide other souls along these pathways. Without the Old Woman's blessing, and the blessing of the Ancestors, I'd have no right and no power whatsoever to guide anyone else through these passages. I enter a cavern lit by a strange, Otherworldly light.

Seekers have been offering their gifts to me here for longer than any mind can fathom.

Wrapped in a *breacan* of ancient stillness, I stand there voicing my earthly questions.

Don't dare presume to reveal to others anything less than my utterly wild, unbounded nature. They will have to pass through midnight wilderness, through the trials of the old forests—not just of the Middle World in which your body now sits, but of this Underworld as well.

Increase in fire; increase in song; increase in vision.

A vision reflected in the dark surface of a Well: I'm running wild through the hills and fields, shedding my clothes, screaming a blood-curdling keen.

From this Well that stands in the midst of the cavern she instructs me to drink. The water burns as I swallow it down. Before I leave, I drink two more ladles, knowing the sacramental importance of three.

Then a rite—a rite of fire the Old Woman points to as somehow key for reweaving our severed relationship: the one between Her and us, between us and the ageless soul of the living Land.

She shapeshifts back and forth from black-veiled Hag to Raven.

Raven, soaring out from the pitch black of the cave, through the passage cairn to twilit sky over Sliabh na Calliagh, above the emerald plains of Meath.

A spiritual dictum claiming that the Source of Life is most adequately understood as Mother—perhaps in Her most cosmic essence incomprehensible, ineffable, but clearly embodied in the living Earth that sustains us, and knowable, relatable to us through that supernal, living icon—must have been the bedrock of spiritual experience for millions of human beings over millennia of time, until that intuitive knowledge and experience was subsumed under a tyranny of male-dominated cultural, political, and religious structures. When at last the alien warrior god came from the far deserts seeking dominion, was the groundwork already laid for his oppressive and autocratic rule?

God as Mother, the feminine divine, Source of our life, our sustenance, can be once more a source-doctrine, a homing star, a draught of healing waters, the beating heart of our work of reclamation.

It seems fitting that in Scottish Gaelic the word for 'mother' is also the root word for 'origin' and 'source'; the compound phrase, *màthair-adhbhar*, is defined in contemporary Gaelic dictionaries as, 'primary cause', 'origin', and 'source'.

One is tempted to view the Irish Gaelic colloquialism, *Tá Dia láidir agus máthair mhaith aige* ('God is strong and has a good mother'), through such a lens. While this could certainly be read in an exclusively Christian manner, i.e., as referring to Mary, mother of Christ the Incarnate God, it can also be equally read as a playfully subversive attestation to a more ancient understanding: that the Great Mother is the true Origin of Life as we know it. 'The God you name is strong, yes,' the phrase could be read to say, 'but standing behind him is a more ultimate source—as there is behind each and every child: a strong and loving Mother, to whom be the glory.'

Anu, the Earth Mother: Mother of all the gods.

'Because we no longer hear the voice of the feminine, we experience the state of spiritual impoverishment that is now endemic in Western civilization.'[106]

The Old Woman who haunts the forest of our ancient tales, and who haunts the hills and cairns of Loughcrew, desires to bring us in, back to the firelight of her hearth, to the den of her Wisdom.

---

[106]   Mara Freeman, *Grail Alchemy: Initiation in the Celtic Mystery Tradition* (Rochester: Destiny Books, 2014), 6.

It is not Jesus, or Moses, or Buddha, or Muhammed, or Zeus, or Zoroaster who stands guard at the sacred Well, ready to offer once more its holy and transformative waters to those who approach with proper reverence and respect. It is Badb, the Old Woman in the Land, Trickster Hag, Warrior Queen, Divine Sovereignty, one face of the Three-Formed Mother, source of our life, Weaver of the *breacan* of Beauty and wisdom.

🔱

Anam taisgealachd:[107]

'The cardinal teaching of the druids', Caesar confidently informs us, 'is that the soul does not perish, but after death passes from one body to another.'[108] The immortality and transmigration of the soul constitute the core metaphysical teachings of druidic religion.

In the Celtic heart and mind, the human person is understood most foundationally as spirit, a soul enfleshed on a pilgrim journey. This central druidic teaching did not change with the coming of Christianity to the Celtic countries, but was simply translated into language that fit the framework of the new faith.

Transmigration of the soul does not necessarily imply rebirth in a human body here on this Earth. In Gaelic thought, it is often assumed that there is an intermediary time in the Summerlands, in *Tír na nÓg*, the Land of Youth or Isle of the Blessed, where the soul takes pleasurable rest between incarnations. And death there in turn means rebirth in some other form. That form could be human, animal, plant, or something we can't presently conceive of, and could take place in any number of worlds.

Some Ancestors might remain in the Otherworld indefinitely, in one form or another, where they can be reached through prayer, shamanic trance and other ritual frameworks, by those of us now on an earthly pilgrimage.

---

[107] *Anam taisgealachd* means literally 'soul pilgrimage' and implies the journey of the soul not only in this particular incarnational moment, but through all eternity.

[108] As quoted in Philip Freeman, *War, Women, and Druids: Eyewitness Reports and Early Accounts of the Ancient Celts* (Austin, TX: University of Texas Press, 2002), 42.

In the Celtic mind there is no end to the pilgrim journey, the journey of the soul: there is no eventual absorption in the ineffable Origin (as in some forms of mystical Christianity or Hinduism), there is no ending of rebirth and snuffing out of human consciousness (as in Buddhism), and there is no realm where one dwells in a fixed state, either eternally rejoicing and praising God, or otherwise suffering eternal torment (as in Islam and most forms of contemporary Christianity). Rather, the soul journeys on indefinitely, experiencing, as Nature intends, an infinite and infinitely novel array of Beauty, an infinite diversity of experience—the soul experiencing the ever becoming, unending possibilities of Creation through an endless variety of forms and expressions. According to Welsh folklore, if the soul errs by failing to live in harmony with the values of Nature—that is, if it fails to increase in wisdom, and does ill to fellow creatures and Creation—it will be reborn in a form that is conducive to the specific learning and growth required of it at that stage of development.

The principal aim of the pilgrim journey, then, is to attain to greater and greater wisdom, inspiration, and illumination, and to grasp, experience, and praise the experiences of life more and more deeply.

Within the stream-course of that journey, one should also seek the nature of one's *dán*, a Gaelic word meaning: 'destiny', 'fate', 'gift', 'skill', 'art', 'faculty', 'vocation', 'poetic skill', and 'poem'. This is clearly a nuanced and culturally significant concept, but what it points to at the most foundational level is one's deepest nature and vocation as an individual soul: the thread of one's unique destiny, or the shape of what the divine milieu dreams for each of us as individual souls on an eternal journey of development and transformation. This applies both to the particular journey here in our present form on Earth, as well as to our spiritual journey as a whole, which is infinite in scope, not bound by time as we understand it.

It has been said that the old Gallic word for 'destiny' actually meant 'oath' or 'vow': quite apart from the fatalistic way we ordinarily understand 'destiny' in contemporary Western contexts, the ancient Celtic heart experienced it as an elective aim or guiding *telos*, made in freedom—probably an oath to the councils of Ancestors, to help actualize a particular sacred work.

The assumption underlying the concept of *dán* is that there is something unique about each soul, which the Source, the ineffable Weaver of Life, has dreamed or imagined. As with everything in Creation, that dream is fluid, living, and ongoing, not fixed or unchanging—though in each incarnation a certain set of qualities, taboos, and requirements shape the soul's work and experience, its lived pursuit of wisdom.

To discover something of the nature and depth of one's *dán*, both here on Earth in this incarnational moment and beyond,—both behind and ahead in the great stream of Being—and to shape one's life here accordingly, is thus a chief aim and responsibility of the spiritual life. To praise poetically the Beauty of Creation, to expand and co-create that Beauty—to honor and serve Life and to live as integral to it, in deep and harmonious relationship, for the good of all, toward the increase of wisdom and illumination for all—is in sum the chief aim of the soul's existence. And this is not really possible without being connected to and aligned with one's *dán*, for the *dán* determines *how* an individual is to uniquely serve the Creation—with what dimensions, what particular gifts, skills, works, and ways of being. Knowing and living in alignment with one's *dán* therefore means walking in optimal power and integrity. It means walking beautifully on the Earth.

The existential horizon stretches on forever, and we keep moving toward it, ideally learning, refining, becoming more connected, more transparent to the sacred—that is, wiser—as we go. To 'remain in the stream', as Mary Oliver puts it: that in itself is the aim, the *telos*. To remain in the eternal becoming of existence and to increase, praise, and grieve its Beauty. To experience, praise, and poetically honor the fullness of Life is itself the path of true sanctity.

In an ensouled cosmos, wherein the transmigration of souls is assumed, we might touch again and again the depth of sacred acquaintance, in many forms—human, animal, perhaps even plant, or in forms altogether non-corporeal. Souls once deeply acquainted might meet again after many long ages.

And the boundaries we assume between species are not, then, as clear or substantive as we imagine them to be. All souls in one great journey, one spiritual family, taking on many forms, through endless ages—through the temporary prevailing of fire and water.

Many variants of the old Irish tale of the Seal Wife or Merrow Wife are to be found in folk traditions the world over. In this perennial motif, a female animal takes on human form and temporarily becomes the wife of a human man. The marriage is happy and the woman is said to be an ideal companion—and, in many versions, an ideal mother. But inevitably something goes wrong: either the man becomes dissatisfied, or, more commonly in Celtic versions of the tale, the woman begins to long for her former home and community. And so she finds or takes up her animal skin and returns to Sea or Forest, to be again with her own kind, leaving the man and sometimes their children to fend for themselves, though not without heaviness of heart. A powerful and instructive example of this theme outside the Celtic milieu is the Inuit tale of the Fox Wife, told earlier in the present work. This undoubtedly ancient, perennial motif of animal spirits temporarily taking on human form carries many significant layers of meaning, and invites a number of compelling metaphysical questions.

One of those questions is whether the seeming divide between human and animal life is as much of a reality as we in contemporary, rationalistic cultures would ordinarily think. If the soul may be born into human or animal form, then whatever divide between us and our non-human brothers and sisters we imagine must be purely superficial. The deeply embedded tradition of shapeshifting in Celtic myth and folktale seems to affirm this.

There must also be a lesson for us in the recurring motif of alienation, of disenfranchisement, present in these tales. And particularly where the human man is the cause of these self-damning phenomena, as in the Inuit version of the tale, are we by implication not remiss in being left alone, abandoned by our non-human brothers and sisters? The story itself seems to ask of us: How long will the errant human children debase and abuse their fellow creatures, or simply ignore them, to their own physical and spiritual peril? And will those fellow creatures not rightly abandon them?

As Moriarty once said, we in contemporary Western cultures are utterly alone in our stories, because the Judaeo-Christian and scientistic myths that shape our cultures have no room for the souls of animals, for the spiritual presence of our nonhuman brothers and sisters.[109] Whether or not we are consciously aware of it, the fact is that in this aloneness we are radically bereft, robbed of many of the most precious and valuable gifts of being here. Moriarty suggested, by way of solution, that all our central conceits, including our mathematical equations and scientific formulas, should be written on the mythic Fox pelt.

At one time—certainly in mythic time, but also in ancient historical time—we lived much more closely with our animal kindred. And we were closer then to the truth of our own wild nature. What are the implications of us living now in a state of near-total divorce from our animal relations, which also necessarily means divorce from a huge part of ourselves? If we can objectify and utterly alienate animals, treating them as mere commodities— an attitude and behavior now normative in contemporary industrial and postindustrial societies—then we can and *are* objectifying and alienating an essential part of our own deepest nature. And we are certainly sinning against Beauty, harmony, and Life—against the values of Nature.

The results of such violent dissociation are clearly disastrous—spiritually, psychologically, and physically.

Might we encounter again here on this beautiful Earth our soul companions from long distant turns in the path? Like souls swimming in a vast cosmic sea, sometimes bumping into one another here in this Middle World, in this particular plane of existence, on this particular planet, as we navigate the vast starry roads. If we do happen to meet such fellow pilgrim souls here—souls we know well and would recognize in an instant by the deep, resonant signature they bear—in what forms will we re-encounter them? Might they invite us to re-member some forgotten profundity in our own hearts, to re-member the depth of our own souls?

---

[109] cf. John Moriarty, 'Seeking to Walk Beautifully on the Earth', from *One Evening in Eden* (Dublin: The Lilliput Press, 2007).

The human person, as an eternal spirit, briefly incarnate here on this earthly sojourn amidst an endless journey of experience, was in Irish tradition thought to contain three primary energy centers, described metaphorically as *cauldrons*. The cauldron is a potent symbol in Celtic spirituality, evoking deep memories of the divine feminine as source of all life and inspiration, as well as the wild Sky-Father's cauldron of endless natural grace, of undying sustenance.

The three Cauldrons in the human person were thought to correspond to different regions of the body: the first, the Cauldron of Warming, to the pelvic or stomach area; the second, the Cauldron of Motion (or Vocation), to the region of the heart; and the third, the Cauldron of Wisdom, to the head.

The legendary Welsh bard, *Taliesin*, tells us that the human person is made up of seven primary faculties, which he portrays with natural images: earth, fire, water, air, mist, flower, and southerly wind. Such poetic constructs should be considered within a framework of spiritual unfoldment. That is likely their origin and the primal intention underlying their appearance.

In Gaelic cosmology—particularly as expressed in Irish tradition—there are five sacred directions: West, North, East, South, and Center.

The sacred Center is the heart of the Land, metaphorically the heart of the human person, the core of the spiritual journey, the three-dimensional axis of reality. It is the place of Bíle, the Great Oak, the *axis mundi*. Before its base lies the sacred Well of Wisdom, and the Holy Grail with which one drinks from the life giving waters. There swims also the Salmon of Wisdom, fed by the sacred nuts of the nine Hazel trees which encompass the Well. Three times three, the sacred number. The Cauldron of Awen warmed by the breath of nine maidens.

A crucial and primary witness of the Celtic spirit is an unyielding emphasis on the sacrality of Nature, of Creation itself. This was retained well into the Christian era. Indeed, in many rural parts of the Celtic nations today it still persists. This core assumption and experience of the Celtic spirit implies that while we are indeed sojourners from the stars, we are also incarnational beings, beings partly constituted, here and now, by an animal form, a body-mind construct occupying particular time and space in the manifest physical world. And so it is not only with the human person, but with every being on the Earth—even those considered by contemporary, reductionist thinking to be 'inanimate'.

The divine can and does speak to us through all these ensouled beings that surround us in the natural world, through all the outward dimensions of our incarnate experience—so long as we know how to turn our hearts and listen. The matrix of these outward dimensions of our life here, which we might call the existential circumstances or 'facticity' of incarnation, are the will of Nature, and not an ontological accident. They indicate a deep current of purpose and intent within the warp and weft of Creation. All of Nature therefore acts as supernal icon for accessing the sacred.

The failure to understand the circumstances of our situatedness here in embodied human form as good and sacred is perhaps the principal sin of Modernity. Its roots lie in the corrosive heresies of Gnosticism, puritanism, philosophical materialism, and scientism. Yet more foundationally than this, they lie at the very core of Judaeo-Christian thought and myth, foreign in so many ways to the Europe that received them.

Adumbrations of a new and ancient map:

Is it really possible for contemporary Westerners to recapture or reconstitute something akin to a working map of the spiritual worldview and practices of their ancient, indigenous Ancestors (whoever they might happen to be)—to provide for themselves a stable, clear, and dynamic guiding framework through which to co-actualize a more life giving and sustainable way of life?

And could European-descended peoples actually reclaim their own indigenous traditions—as opposed to appropriating the indigenous customs of others in order to try to assuage a deep, unconscious (and genetically transmitted) grief over having violently severed themselves from their own roots? Could all of us living now in the Western world authentically and sustainably reclaim the archaic wisdom of our long-distant predecessors, to learn again how to live in harmony with the Earth and one another; to learn again how to truly know ourselves, in relation to where we come from—to the Ancestors, and to the living Land, our Mother; to reclaim an ancient wisdom and a body of techniques for knowing the sacred intimately in our everyday lives? Could we legitimately reclaim such wisdom now lost to us? And would it then be possible to integrate this wisdom effectively and authentically into a contemporary life in the Western world without unwittingly denigrating or trivializing it, and without lapsing into mere anachronism?

My own spiritual journey began, in early adolescence, as a sojourn deeply charged with these questions, and with a burning, grief-laden passion to answer them.

I've come to realize that the same process of discovery, thought, and practice implied in the aforementioned questions constitutes a road that my ancient Ancestors had to walk many generations before me, probably with the same general aims and concerns.

Such questions must have become pressing in their times and places with the introduction of Christianity to the Celtic nations. How to reconcile the old wisdom with the new? How to preserve the old traditions in an authentic way, while simultaneously acknowledging (and to some extent embracing) the sway of this new, foreign tradition that was sweeping over the whole of Europe, changing everything in its path? How to become Christians and still remain Celts, to adopt the practices and worldview assumptions of Christian wisdom without unwittingly putting their own cultural inheritance to death?

Theoretically, the way(s) of life produced by that process of wrestling, exploration, and integration—in all its beauty, grief, and complexity—is the life of what is commonly called the early Celtic Church (which existed as an autonomous cultural-religious milieu until the second half of the seventh century, though far beyond that retained much of its native color, insight, and essence).

At a certain point it became clear to me that the struggle I had been trying to work out for so long was in essence a microcosm of the struggle my ancestral cultures had navigated for hundreds of years. This was a profoundly transformative and liberating realization, and, in a way that perhaps can't entirely be articulated, broke open a new door in my interior life. It gave birth to the reconstructive and praxis-oriented spirituality explored in this book.

One of the primary problems with such endeavors, whatever their origin, arises when individuals lose touch with their dynamic and experimental quality—that is, with their nature as empirical explorations aimed at building an always provisional map on the grounds of direct experience, both individual and shared, personal and communal.

Wherever folks cling to the delusional notion that they have found all the answers, or the only true answers, and thus close down their ability to experience new and deeper layers of reality, there has been a dangerous lapse into ideological fundamentalism. Let the needful work be always provisional, always open, always living—an evolving adventure of exploration, which casts a new and ancient radiance on all it touches.

Truth, in the ultimate sense, lies beyond the scope of what we can measure; it dwells in the blessed realm of Mystery. It is only the symbolic, the poetic, the metaphoric, that can approximate a meaningful retelling of one's encounter with that Mystery, and it is only these things that can create a helpful framework for aiding others in accessing such experience themselves. Equipping folks for that experience—*their own direct experience* of the sacred—is the only justifiable aim of any spiritual project, any religious pursuit, structure, or institution.

Anything that negates or does not effectuate this most needful process should be rejected outright, because it is either manipulative and lacking integrity, or otherwise simply a distraction from what is actually pertinent, and therefore a waste of one's precious and fleeting time on this momentary earthly journey.

The intellectual is needful but only preparatory; it is not a valid end in itself, so far as the spiritual path is concerned. The poetic and the visionary must ultimately come to prominence and act as principal guide, where rationality can no longer illumine the path.

In the spiritual life, so often what is needful is for us to decisively reject our tendency to fall back on established assumptions or beliefs, particularly socially expected ones, and instead to privilege direct personal experience as the only ultimately valid means of understanding our existential situation. Our archaic Ancestors were quite familiar with this approach.

As pathways in pursuit of wisdom, indigenous Celtic worldviews and lifeways are inherently wedded to this assumption. This perspective, shared by many indigenous cultures, is no stranger to the fact that such pursuits require one to be firmly established in foundational first principles, particularly with regard to the metaphysical circumstances of the human experience. (When we speak of 'mysticism' or mystical pursuits, we simply mean an epistemological exploration that privileges the data of direct personal experience.) For indigenous peoples, what generally provides this framework is myth, and, more broadly, the inherited wisdom of the Ancestors.

In fact, among the most critical of first principles, held by all our ancient human Ancestors to be sacred and true, is the primacy of ancestral wisdom and witness, of the 'first ones'. This assumes that the spirits of those gone before us in this earthly pilgrimage are in some meaningful and at least occasionally detectible way present with us, present to our lives, invested in our journeys here (to one extent or another), desirous and capable of guiding us, not just in oral and written traditions passed down through the generations, but also by means of direct contact in the spiritual or 'Otherworld' realm, through ecstatic vision, dream, and inspiration. This is our collective inheritance, the shared experience of the Ancestors bequeathed to each and every one of us, whether we realize it or not.

The question, What is reality—and the more fundamental question, What is the consciousness that frames the question, What is reality?—has long haunted the endeavors of Western science and philosophy. But this is a decisively modern question. In the ancient world it would almost certainly have been general knowledge that one's cultural context provided, *in potentia*, inherited spiritual technologies one could learn and employ in order to attain to a clearer vision of reality (at least as experienced by members of that cultural group). Not everyone used these tools, of course—in fact, probably a minority of people did, and those were the priests, shamans, prophets, etc., whose voices were highly honored in archaic cultures. We can also assume that most or all of a given population in such cultural environments was at least broadly exposed to those technologies through the sacramental initiation into adulthood. In some living religious traditions, the knowledge and use of such technologies is still at least vaguely present.

In Christianity, however, most participants have absolutely no clue that such technologies ever existed within their own tradition, or otherwise they overtly mistrust and reject them. And for the few individuals who are aware that such things once existed and who desire to discover them, they are likely to have no one at hand to receive them from. And at any rate such seekers are sure to be disenchanted with the Church as it is commonly known and experienced.

As a result, those who feel called to seek spiritual insight are naturally drawn to where the spiritual technologies yet persist: namely, in non-Western spiritual traditions like Hinduism, or perhaps in Western occultism or Neo-Paganism, or in indigenous Central and South American spiritual traditions.

The problem that can arise for seekers who have gone to 'exotic' traditions in search of tools and answers is that they can easily find themselves in a psychologically and culturally foreign environment, which may not in the end be helpful with regard to their process of individuation and spiritual unfoldment.

The Western Christian ethos, broadly speaking, has become so fearful and reactionary, so watered down, so stripped of and alienated from its original intensity and purpose, that to be helpful at all to anyone who seeks to cultivate a legitimate and authentic spiritual life it must be radically transformed from the inside. And a transformation as radical as the one here needed is almost certainly one that no institutional Christian context would be willing to take on.

A large part of the problem with Western Christianity is language, because language shapes theology and practice—especially, in Christian environments, through ossified and dogmatic religious text. Such language, given the totalizing prominence it's been granted through the centuries of Western Christianity, inevitably shapes the inward orientation of its adherents. Most such adherents are so fearfully attached to their inherited linguistic constructs, and their resultant structures of belief, that they are simply unwilling to reimagine or reshape them. In one sense, fearful misgivings about this kind of reform are understandable and can be empathized with, because were we to replace all the problematical, ossified, and spiritually colonizing linguistic and dogmatic structures within the life and practice of the Church, the result would hardly be recognizable any longer as the Church. For many, particularly those who have spent their entire lives within such environments, this is a very frightening prospect.

But the fact remains that the language used in the Church to talk about God and the spiritual journey has become so denuded, so ineffectual, so placatory, so perverted and clichéd, that few want any longer to listen. Rightfully so.

Unfortunately, there is precious little in Western Christianity as we've inherited it that is any longer worth salvaging—because it has become so hopelessly denuded; because it has lost its transformative capacity, its wildness, and its spiritual technologies; because it has become, in large part, an internally confused and increasingly irrelevant institution that is more in the business of self-preservation for its own sake than in the business of actually 'equipping the saints' for the work of legitimate transformation.

This points to a pressing need now in the Western world to reach back toward much deeper and more life giving roots.

❦

To really access and draw from the deep heart of our humanness, direct experience of our origins—in the life and wisdom of the Ancestors, in the life of the living Earth, our Mother—is indispensable. And that requires of us a genuine transformation, effected through the committed and communally supported use of efficacious spiritual technologies.

A Well that we in the contemporary West don't often think to draw from is the Well of ancient ancestral witness—an endless source experiential wisdom handed down through thousands of years of indigenous tradition and practice. Those of us in the contemporary West who wish to access this deep well of wisdom, since the native oral traditions of most of our cultures have been broken, must look to disciplines like folkloristics and historical reconstruction. In this regard, the legitimate fruits of our rational pursuits must be put to good use—but never omitting or overshadowing the symbolic, the metaphoric, the mythic, the visionary.

❦

Within a traditional pan-Celtic worldview, perhaps the most foundational building block of the cosmic map is the Otherworld. The Otherworld is a conceptual and experiential realm, an unseen layer of reality overlying and interpenetrating our own perceptible reality: an interwoven, parallel continuum of spiritual or subtle landscapes, entities, and events. This Otherworld contains a tripartite cosmic structure of Upper World (or heavenly realm, associated with the Celtic element of Sky), Middle World (or earthly plane, associated with the Celtic element of Earth or Land), and Lower World (or underworld, associated with the Celtic element of Sea). All of these are connected by the central axis of the World Tree, *Bile*.

From the testimony of an eighth-century Irish manuscript related to the Fenian mythic cycle, we have a compelling and shamanically charged lens on the ancient Gaelic conception of the World Tree. In this mythic narrative, Finn Mac Cumhall, the great warrior-poet and prototype of the wisdom initiate, encounters a mysterious man sitting amongst the branches of a great tree. Perched on the man's right shoulder is a Blackbird, an ancient Celtic symbol of Otherworld travel. In his left hand he holds a vessel of white bronze, filled with water in which swims a Salmon, the superlative image of wisdom in Gaelic tradition (the cup or chalice being an icon of the Well of Wisdom, the Holy Grail). At the base of the tree stands a Stag.

Finn witnesses this figure seated in the great tree cracking open with his right hand the shells of hazelnuts—another poignant symbol of the attainment of wisdom in Gaelic tradition (nine Hazels surround the Well of Wisdom, and the Salmon of Wisdom eats the hazelnuts as they fall into the Well). Half of each nut the man in the tree eats himself, and the other half he offers to the Blackbird.

From within the vessel where swims the Salmon, he pulls an apple, a Celtic symbol of Otherworld voyage, sharing this with the Blackbird, too. And finally he raises the vessel to his lips and drinks, where the Salmon and Blackbird drink with him.[110] It is interesting to note that, in the old Welsh tale, *The Long-Lived Ancestors*, the first three most ancient animal totems or 'Ancestors' the Eagle applies to for knowledge are the Stag, the Salmon, and the Blackbird.

Sharon MacLeod observes of this image: 'The blackbird may symbolize the Upper World, the stag the Middle World, and the trout [or Salmon] the Lower World. This passage is reminiscent of traditional descriptions of the Norse World Tree, *Ygdrassil*. In the Norse texts, an eagle and a hawk rested in the uppermost branches of the tree, horned animals (goats and harts) leapt at the sides of the tree, and a serpent lay at the root of the tree. These animals seem to correspond with the three worlds (and with each other): Upper World (blackbird or eagle and hawk); Middle World (stag or deer and goats); and Lower World (salmon or serpent).'[111]

---

[110] cf. Anne Ross, *Pagan Celtic Britain* (Chicago: Academy Press, 1996), 421.

[111] Sharon Paice MacLeod, *Celtic Myth and Religion* (London: McFarland & Company, Inc., 2012), 67.

The significance of these sacred animals in Celtic tradition is attested throughout the insular literatures—for example, in this anonymously penned tenth-century Irish poem for Beltaine, the dawn of Summer:

The Blackbird sings a loud refrain—
to him the green wood is sacred inheritance.
The sorrowful, fearsome Sea now sleeps;
the speckled Salmon joyfully leaps.

The Sun smiles over every land—:
my parting from a brood of cares.
Hounds run and bark, the Stags now mate,
and Ravens flourish. Summer indeed has come![112]

The reality of the Otherworld is assumed in Celtic thought, and in a sense all other elements of the Celtic worldview flow from or into this shared experience. The druidic doctrines of rebirth and the immortality of the soul; the close proximity of the Ancestors and other spirits; the continual call to courage of heart, and to the pursuits of wisdom and Beauty rooted in a truly deep confidence regarding the eternal and interconnected life, nature, and *telos* of all souls—: each of these core elements of pan-Celtic thought find common concourse in a worldview that always assumes a vast portion of reality, of Nature, moves vibrant outside the bounds of ordinary human perception. One might therefore think of an understanding or intuitive experience of the Otherworld as a requisite starting point for any journey through Celtic spiritual landscapes.

Other shamanic cultures outside the Celtic milieu have their own equivalents of the Otherworld, such as the 'Dreamtime' of indigenous Australian cultures. This Aboriginal moniker is fitting, as the closest approximate experience we have to compare with the experience of entering the Otherworld is dreaming. In Tungusic and other Siberian cultures, as well as in Sámi and

---

[112] Translation by the author, with inspiration from Kuno Meyer.

other Finno-Ugric cultures, similar cosmologies are found. I think it is not unreasonable to say that this foundational worldview component, at least in broad terms, is perennial to indigenous cultures the world over, and is likely derived from a common, original shamanic experience at the dawn of human culture and language.

The Otherworld is, in one sense, a state of awareness, because it is through an altered state of consciousness (usually brought on by an acute perturbation of the ordinary mental state) that we access it. At the same time, it is also a definitive *place*, a cosmic layering of landscapes that exists apart from our own mental state, which we may touch or be touched by, but which is not dependent on our perception for its existence.

The Otherworld experience—that is, our directly accessing the unseen landscapes—is key to developing any map of reality rooted in native European traditions. Such an experience necessarily give birth to a particular understanding of the human person—namely, one in which the person is at the deepest level constituted by a soul, a spiritual essence which underlies the more apparent, outward elements. This soul, in Celtic conception, is unique and undying, and after the present earthly journey carries on its pilgrimage elsewhere.

As Terence McKenna, the late twentieth-century philosopher and ethnobotanist, once said: 'We are not primarily biological, with mind emerging as a kind of iridescence, a kind of epiphenomenon at the higher levels of organization of biology. We are hyperspatial objects of some sort that cast a shadow into matter. The shadow in matter is our physical organism. At death, the thing that casts the shadow withdraws, and metabolism ceases. Material form breaks down; it ceases to be a dissipative structure in a very localized area....But the form that ordered it is not affected. These declarative statements are made from the point of view of the shamanic tradition, which touches all higher religions.'[113]

This is almost certainly not exactly how the ancient Celts conceived of the soul and its afterlife journeys, but it nonetheless sheds a valuable light

---

[113] Terence McKenna, *The Archaic Revival* (New York: MJF Books, 1991), 91.

on the matter, and frames it in useful, contemporary language. However we
conceive of the nuances, the core Celtic teaching is that the soul is a distinct,
immortal entity which inhabits a physical body here (residing chiefly in the
head, which to the Celtic mind is the 'seat of the soul') for a time before
journeying on to another kind of body in another context elsewhere. The
Otherworld, or a particular location within it, such as the Irish *Tír na nÓg*
('Land of Youth') may provide a temporary resting place before the next
pilgrimage of the soul. The openness or ambiguity this view preserves is, I
think, as valuable as the metaphysical insight it offers.

This is not an understanding unique to the Celtic peoples, of course,
but is a worldview maintained by many animistic and shamanically oriented
indigenous cultures. It was novel and surprising to the ancient Greeks and
Romans, who found it to be noteworthy in its distinction from Classical
views. The Greeks, in fact, proposed the possibility that Pythagoras (who
taught a similar, though definitely not identical, doctrine) had either inherited his view from the druids or else the druids had somehow received
their doctrine from Pythagoras. This is no doubt spurious as an historical
claim, but it does show that the Greeks found druidic teachings to be quite
distinctive.

The basic doctrine of the soul as an individual and immortal entity is
part of what Aldous Huxley called the 'perennial philosophy'—a core element of human spiritual observation that has occurred in most cultural settings throughout the expanse of documented human history.[114] The concept
of the existence and eternality of the soul is a crucial part of our ancestral
inheritance as human beings, and a near universal truism amongst archaic
cultures.

The Celtic doctrine of transmigration in particular does have its own
unique dimensions, however, and, as noted above, happily leaves much to
mystery. It seems that one notion regarding the soul's migratory paths taught

---

[114] I should note that Huxley did not address this particular doctrine in his book of
the same name; rather, I am borrowing here his concept of a perennial set of archaic
spiritual teachings or observations found the world over, and applying it where I
think it is most clearly found: in shared, archaic experiences of shamanic origin.

by the druids is that when a soul is born or incarnated here, it has died to the Otherworld, and when it departs this Earthly plane it is then born again to the Otherworld planes. How long the soul resides in the Otherworld, then, or whether it is subsequently reborn into *this* world (or on this planet), as well as what physical form it takes on in subsequent incarnations, all seem to be questions to which the druids assigned no particular dogma. This is immensely practical and realistic.

These two foundational conceptions of soul and Otherworld are rich fruits of the tree of collective human experience, supported by thousands of generations of attestation born from the luminescence of vision, of ecstatic, altered perception.

The supreme experiencer in this case is the shaman: the one who crosses over to the Otherworld at will, who speaks directly with the Ancestors, and who brings back to the realm of ordinary perception a salvific and practical wisdom. For these foundational worldview components are fruits born specifically of the perennial shamanic vocation, which, as Mircea Eliade and others have observed, lies at the root of all religious and mythic exploration. To some degree all structured religious systems have at the baseline of their origin points these elements of archaic spiritual experience.

Shamanism—which Eliade famously dubbed 'the archaic techniques of ecstasy'—is the ur-spirituality of human history, the proto-religion *par excellence*. It is the most primary mode of spiritual exploration employed by human cultures in their collective infancy. Its root experiences may in fact have given rise to human culture.

Perhaps the most fundamental truth about shamanism is that it is a set of tools and shared, accumulated knowledge regarding access to the Otherworld via deliberately induced trance states: it implies a path of direct experience, not of belief or dogma. In this and other ways, its foundational principles are foreign indeed to the contemporary Western mind—even the so-called religious mind.

The human soul or spirit, in a shamanically shaped worldview, is an entity which has its original (and perhaps primary) existence somewhere apart from the physical form. The unseen essence of the human person bears an eternal signature.

The ancient Celts were so assured of this eternality that the Roman writer Valerius Maximus observed in the first century of the common era: 'It is said that they [the Gauls] lend to each other sums that are payable in the next world, so firmly are they convinced that the souls of men are immortal.'[115] This sure confidence in the eternal nature of the soul gives rise to two other crucial teachings of the druids: firstly, the critical importance of honoring the Ancestors and the wisdom they transmit to us; and secondly, the central place of courage as a moral ideal.

The traditional Celtic approach to honoring the Ancestors—and the central place this devotion occupied in ancient Celtic lifeways—was easily translated, with the coming of orthodox Christianity, into the cult of saints. The holy Ancestors (or Saints) are petitioned, praised, honored, and relied upon in daily life as critical sources of knowledge and wisdom. Particularly with regard to the divinized ancestral figures and gods, there is also a hope and expectation that their Otherworldly powers in healing, magic, self-actualization, and the vocational expressions with which they are each associated, can help us here and now in navigating and integrating the challenges and blessings of the earthly journey.

All the above traditions birthed in the Celtic mind an understanding of the human journey as pilgrimage. The theme of pilgrimage—both in the sense of the soul on pilgrimage here in this incarnate form, as well as in the related, microcosmic sense of journeys to sacred places to be taken within one's earthly life—has been an enduring theme throughout much of Celtic

---

[115] Valerius Maximus, *Factorum et Dictorum Libri*, II, 6, 10; quoted in Dáithi Ó HÓgain, *The Sacred Isles: Belief and Religion in Pre-Christian Ireland* (Woodbridge: The Boydell Press, 1999), 100.

cultural history. It foundationally shaped the unique indigenous expression of early Celtic Christianity. Probably the most well-known literary example of this is the popular medieval text, *The Voyage of St. Brendan*, a Christianized form of the much more ancient verse narrative, *The Voyage of Bran*.

In *The Voyage of Bran*, the pilgrim seeker, Bran Mac Febal, encounters the god of the Sea, Manannán Mac Lir, on the ocean west of Ireland. Manannán gives to Bran, in a kind of divine revelation, not texts or dogmas, commandments or instructions, but rather an invitation to a new mode of vision, a new spiritual clarity that illumines the miraculous nature of the world as it already is; and a magical branch from a tree—a silver branch that makes sweet, Otherworldly music and alters the consciousness of the one who holds it—to help facilitate that change of vision. In some versions of the tale, it is a mysterious woman from the mythical Isle of *Emain Albach*, also associated with Manannán, who gives to Bran the silver branch: a branch of the Apple trees which populate that mythic landscape of death-lessness and beauty. Some of these motifs are found in other Gaelic tales as well, such as the Irish story of *Connla and the Fairy Maiden*.

The magical branch of the Otherworldly Apple tree, symbolically connected with a long obscured druidic Sacrament, probably an entheogenic fungi or plant mixture, transforms Bran's perception so that he is able to see the deepest layer of things, to see the miraculous truth that is already surrounding him but ordinarily veiled or hidden from his perception. This is certainly one way of defining 'illumination' in the Gaelic tradition—a 'fire in the head', a transformed and inspired vision that leads one into wisdom.

Dogma and 'belief' here are completely irrelevant; the only thing that's relevant to the spiritual quest—which is, or should be, the central human quest—is direct, personal experience, from which arises clear vision and the attainment of Otherworldly knowledge. This much is clear from the surviving myths and folktales of the Celtic cultures. In a native Celtic approach to the religious quest, the pathway of transmutation—of coming into the 'heavenly state', to reference a much later but deeply embedded Christian notion—comes not through texts or beliefs, or through joining a particular community of faith, as it does in Judaeo-Christian religions, but rather through passing directly into a state of radically altered vision. This is a model that inherently rejects the agendas of control and spiritual colonialism, as well as the limiting, oppressive inclinations of institutional religious structures that propose to 'filter down' spiritual insight to believers. The Celtic model, as expressed in *The Voyage of Bran*, is one of deep relationship with Nature, who provides for the seeker all the tools he or she will need on the journey, and who rewards the seeker's courage with furtherance, protection, and support. It is an approach to the spiritual journey that privileges in a healthful way the direct experience of the individual pilgrim soul.

When Bran holds the white blossomed branch and it makes its beautiful, ethereal music, what previously appeared to him as merely an ocean becomes a verdant new landscape of forests and flowery plains. As the folks at *Bard Mythologies* rightly point out, much can be revealed about the Celtic way by reflecting on the difference between this revelation of divine encounter (which they call 'silver branch seeing') and that of the Hebrew tradition, wherein Moses encounters Yahweh, the god of war and thunder, and is given stone tablets containing mandatory commandments for right behavior, the violation of which is punishable by a horrendous death.[116]

The indigenous Celtic spiritual path, quite contrary to this text-based, Hebraic approach to life and religion, is one of natural mysticism, situated in a worldview that acknowledges and avails itself of Nature's grace and endemic sacrality. It is a characteristically *experiential* way which seeks to weave the soul more and more deeply into its own birthright in the fabric of Creation.

The Celtic way of wisdom is a personal—and communal—journey toward direct revelation, toward totalizing and integral encounter with the sacred, toward ever deeper and more novel expressions and experiences of Beauty. It is simultaneously focused on the numinous and immensely practical. It has nothing to do with adherence to any list of commandments or set of rules delivered by divine personae. In the native Celtic mind, no divine person—no soul inhabiting a divine incarnation—would ever seek

---

[116] cf. Bard Mythologies, at: http://www.bardmythologies.com

to deliver such a list, or to tyrannically and obsessively enforce its keeping, because true wisdom and illumination simply preclude such activities, which are inherently counter to the nature of sacrality and the flow of Life.

Though many Christians concerned with popular (and usually not very substantive) notions of 'Celtic Christian' spirituality would now rather avoid the fact, the truth is that there has always been an inherent tension in the notion of 'Celtic Christianity', because the elements of dogmatism, creedalism, and textual obsession that form much of the essence of the Abrahamic traditions could never be fully integrated with indigenous Celtic thought—and particularly the deep ancestral threads preserved in what we know of druidic philosophy (which, for example, negates the possibility of codifying any sacred teachings in textual form). The two religious perspectives,—the native Celtic and the Judaeo-Christian—along with the various underlying worldview dimensions they imply, are in most ways mutually exclusive. Animism, for instance, native to ancient Celtic thinking, finds no true, comfortable match with Biblical thinking. This means that for Christianity to exist in an indigenous Celtic context, both traditions must be, to one degree or another, bent to a new shape in order to accommodate one another. And that, of course, is what was done in the early centuries of Christianity in the Celtic nations, with concessions made on both sides. This characterizes the process of adoption in many contexts where Christian thinking has been overlaid onto indigenous, Earth-centered, animistic traditions. To the extent that this has been done in such a way that preserves in some degree of fullness the nuances of the pre-Christian traditions in question, it can at least be looked upon as a 'lesser of evils'—but, as I have argued previously—if Western Christian systems of thought and practice are to have any true relevance or express a degree of value that makes them worthy of preservation at all, it can only be as appropriately adapted dimensions of mythic structure, Sacrament, and liturgy held as secondary to reclaimed animistic wisdoms.

The 'openness' or liminality of image and experience in pursuit of the sacred, which are innate to Celtic thought and mythic narrative, point us back to the central value of direct personal experience and ongoing transformation along the soul's eternal quest for wisdom, awakening, and wholeness. The journey of life is seen as innately and necessarily dynamic. It is not linear but circular or spiral in shape, and no alignment with any external, self-made 'authority'—whether a text, a person, a god, or an ideology— could possibly confer authentic wisdom, which can only come from the lived experience of the soul's individual seeking and initiatory transformation. This stands in contradistinction to Judaeo-Christian traditions, which have gravely minimized if not outright rejected these crucial dimensions of human experience in favor of dogma, 'right belief', and obeisance to the presumed authority of 'revelatory' texts. A far cry, indeed, from all normative modes of Judaeo-Christian thought are the constant blurring of lines and boundaries, the eschewing of safe, clear-cut categories, the insistence on personal freedom, sovereignty, and courage in the quest of becoming, and the inherent resistance to closure which constitute some of the deepest, most profound gifts of native Celtic thought and custom.

True wisdom is always best facilitated through the non-prescriptive, precisely because it can only arise from direct, personal experience of the hidden or veiled dimensions of Being. And thus, as William Blake once observed, 'The wisest of the ancients considered what is not too explicit as the fittest for instruction, because it rouses the faculties to act.'[117] Symbol, metaphor, myth, and poetic speech—: these constitute the 'language of necessity' with reference to the project of passing on what has been experienced by those souls who have here devoted themselves to the pursuit of genuine transformation.

The invitation of Manannán to Bran is to look beneath the surface of ordinary perception to access a stratum of depth that is already present in Nature but typically hidden from the analytical mind, from the normative states of human consciousness.

The silver branch with its Apple blossom bells—its bells of sacramental, Otherworldly fruit—and its sweet, mystical music, its clear shamanic resonance and function, is the perfect symbol for the transformation of

---

[117] William Blake, *The Letters of William Blake*, ed. Archibald G. B. Russell (Edinburgh: Morrison & Gibb, Ltd., 1906), 61.

perception needed to legitimately access real wisdom, to encounter its Otherworldly sources. Not the measuring rod of scientific rationalism or the 'revealed' textual objects of the Abrahamic milieu, but the shamanic branch of hidden Sacrament, of the ecstatic, trance-induced passage of the soul between worlds—a branch from the Tree of Life.

Through the deeply interior, through the visionary, we access the unseen dimensions of Nature, the doorway to the Otherworld, which, if we are properly prepared to navigate the landscape, can open out into wide and beautiful vistas of inspiration, wisdom, and wholeness.

Time is a strange bedfellow. It appears as the ever-flowing boundary of our being here. *Panta rhei*, Heraclitus once proclaimed. 'All flows'. We can never stand twice in the same stream. *Potamoisi toisin autoisin embainousin, hetera kai hetera hudata epirrei*. Upon those who step into the same rivers, ever newer waters flow.

The world in which most of us presently live is a world driven by continual attempts to subvert or overcome the natural flow of time—to prevent the body from aging, to schedule every moment in the framework of a corrosive Protestant work ethic, and thus 'maximize productivity' (some of this neuroticism came also from the Benedictine obsession with programmed time). The anxiety which gives rise to such perilously demented endeavors is born of the materialistic and/or apocalyptic assumption that life itself is fleeting, momentary, and inherently charged with tension. 'Run the race', says the apostle Paul. That notion is utterly foreign to an indigenous worldview that is rooted to the natural cycles of Life, and certainly to the ancient traditions of Celtic wisdom. To be sure, we should savor the unique opportunities we presently have, here in whatever form we're in, but that should not be paired with anxiety, with a sense of 'racing the clock'. As we've already seen, in druidic teaching true courage arises from the experiential knowing that the present life is not a terminal affair, that the soul carries on indefinitely, through a measureless number of experiences.

The sheer speed at which we live in postindustrial Western cultures has become inhumane, and has further compounded our warped relationship to time, further distanced us from the natural world and from our own deepest selves. The natural rhythms of Land, Sky, and Sea, the graceful, simple, life giving time of the agricultural year, of village life lived in intimate proximity to the pulse of the sacred seasons, has been cast aside, traded for a high-speed, climate-controlled, processed prison of convenience and security. And this is an inherently unsustainable scenario.

The fear of time, and the fear of an imagined historical terminus, as found in Christian thought from its inception, is the result of a deep-seated neurosis, a form of Gnosticism (broadly speaking), an anti-natural world-view that mistrusts the flow and fabric of Creation. It is only such a world-view, deeply ill at ease with itself and with the facticity of our humanness, that could birth an ideological system like those generally found within the Abrahamic milieu—: a sickness of grandest proportion, utterly out of touch with the depths of Nature, afraid of Her necessary aspect of dissolution, and indicative of a cultural inclination toward pessimism, despair, self-loathing, and savagery.

It is not surprising that below all these neurotic modes of thinking, at the foundations of Judaeo-Christian metaphysics, we find a negation of the ongoing experience of the life of the soul, as well as the aberrant notion of an eventual resurrection of the *physical body* (preceded by a simple void of experience, a 'sleep in the Lord'). Tracing the advent of this profoundly pessimistic ideology, so atypical in the ancient world, is likely impossible; whether we attribute it to the harshness of the physical landscapes these cultures inhabited, or some other factor (or matrix of factors) is probably irrelevant. Regardless of the particularities of its origins, I think we must now do the very unpopular thing and call these modes of thought what they are: myopic, inhumane, paranoid, superstitious, and corrosive to Life, both human and otherwise.

We must call this spade a spade because the stakes are incredibly high; an entire planet is on the line, and we cannot afford to live any longer beneath the sway of such toxic ideation, which can only bring further endangerment to the holy fabric of Life here on the living Earth. And that ideation has tragically become an integral part of the Western inheritance, by virtue of the European acceptance of Judaeo-Christian norms. And the West has in recent centuries, through colonialism and a cut-throat capitalistic economic platform, exponentially infected the rest of the world with its ideologies and lifeways. The unholy marriage of violent, dehumanizing, and legalistic theologies with reductionistic materialism, Biblical literalism (and textual obsession more generally), the abandonment of an integral relationship with Nature, dominator egoism and its largely masculine agendas of control, a loss of real initiatory models, a loss of religious imagination and personal responsibility, and a misplaced emphasis on dogma and belief over direct, personal experience has birthed the socio-cultural circus in which we now presently find ourselves ensconced.

❦

The Ancestors, now outside 'the moving image of eternity', walking bare and free in the currents of endless unfoldment, remind us of the experiential truth, most often obtained through the ordeals of proper initiation, that consciousness, Life, and soul have no terminus.[118] The dead 'live now within a circle of eternity', wrote John O'Donohue. 'Within the circle, beginning and ending are sisters, and they belong within the shelter which the eternal offers of the unity of the year and the earth.'[119] Creation, Preservation, and Dissolution, seen everywhere in the iconographic beauty of the natural world, eternally in dialogue with one another, eternally following one another in the spiraling river of Being.

A core assumption of the pan-Celtic worldview is that the souls of the dead continue to be present with us, at least *in potentia*. This view affirms not only the ongoing life but also the inherent sacrality of the soul, and

---

[118] The dictum, *Time is the moving image of eternity*, is generally attributed to Plato, and occasionally to Plotinus.

[119] John O'Donohue, *Anam Cara: A Book of Celtic Wisdom* (New York: Harper Perennial, 1997), 227.

of those who have gone before us here in this earthly journey. The endless pilgrimage of life cycles ever onward, seeking new and refreshed modes of Beauty, wisdom, and experience. Nowhere in such a landscape could be located the sick, world-denying notions of 'original sin', 'total depravity', an inherent corruption in Nature or the human person. As Manannán so beautifully summarizes from his chariot on the sea: 'We are from the beginning of Creation / without age, without consummation of Earth, / and hence we expect no frailty— / no sin has ever come to us.'

The soul, the individual essence or 'conscious agent' within the human person, like the rest of Nature is always in flux, always in the stream of transformation. It does not cease from movement in order to reside perpetually in any fixed place or form. How dreadfully dull an existence that would be! The popular Christian notion of a static, never-changing God worshipped endlessly by unvarying 'saintly' souls trapped perpetually in one state of being and one locality, ceaselessly singing hymns of praise, is about as foreign to the ancient Celtic heart and mind and as distant from a genuinely connected spiritual sensibility as one could get—no less foreign, in fact, than the more archaic Abrahamic notion of a bodily resurrection. I'm certainly not the first to observe that were we to assume the reality of 'hell', such visions of the soul's future in paradise would in fact be good candidates for its description. And any god who would contrivedly engineer nightmare cosmic scenarios such as these would not only be murderously boring, monstrously egotistical, masochistic, and profoundly tedious, but also patently absurd. With regard to metaphysical absurdity, these visions of 'heaven' could perhaps be placed at equal measure with the legalistic doctrines of fatalism and eternal punishment attendant to the cult of the same Hebraic war god.

There is no life in such visions of death and divinity—no flow, no freedom, no Beauty. And if some version of either of the aforementioned visions of the afterlife propagated in Judaeo-Christian though is even roughly akin to the future state imagined by adherents of the Abrahamic faiths,—as the desired endgame for those who have done *well* in this present earthly life—

then it's frankly no wonder we've ended up with the disastrous cultures we have.

So to defy ideological routinization and the currents of the dominant culture, to Salmon our way free of the dismal tides of fundamentalism, dominator agendas, and Judaeo-Christian ideologies that have so long conditioned us, to gather all the strength of soul we have left in us, and at all costs to break free from the prisons of our collective making—: that must now be our principal task, our most pressing responsibility.

The Celtic metaphysical landscape is complex and many layered; there are rarely clear distinctions between and amongst spiritual beings, realms, and states of experience. In this poetic liminality the Celtic heart seems at home.

In any animistic understanding of the cosmos, all natural phenomena are imbued with spirit. Nature is ensouled. Existence is shot through with sacrality, with endlessly diverse, distinct spiritual agencies, each on their own journeys—: many stories within the greater Story. Though we now find ourselves to be deaf in a seemingly silent world of arbitrary materialistic phenomena, the ancestral wisdom of that communion, that endlessly vast tapestry of consciousnesses, of souls on the great Starry Road, cries out to us for reclamation. It cries out for a restoration of right relationship.

As Walter Wink has said, 'If Nature is dead, then there are no restraints on exploiting it for profits.'[120] That, in summary, is the horrendously moronic and desperate state of affairs we in the Western world—and in the Abrahamically conditioned world at large—have created. We are, one way or another, victims of a desperate reductionism—whether by scientism or religiosity: carriers of a materialistic cultural virus constituted by industrial expediency, arrogant rationalism, and fundamentalist religiosity. As this has inevitably come to shape our relationship with the Earth and with other cultures, we have gone decisively off the rails of Life. Whatever is not 'economically viable' or expedient is cast aside into the outer darkness of

---

[120] Walter Wink, *Unmasking the Powers* (Philadelphia: Fortress Press, 1986), 155.

isolation, and therefore destroyed. In the outer darkness there is no relationship; all legitimate communion has been banished. Our own souls have been banished and starved, alienated from the countless other souls that surround us. And this is a drastic problem, because relationship is the very essence of Creation, and therefore of wisdom. Without a conscious investment in the vast ecology of souls, without any conscious connection at all to the reality of interbeing, we can never grow in wisdom, and are likely to become—as indeed we have—destructive agents in a world perceived as fundamentally hostile.

Where, then, is the silver branch, the Otherworld branch brought to us by Trefuilngidh, by the mysterious woman of the Isle of Apples, by Manannán Mac Lir? A connection to the sacred world of the unseen, to the magic and transformative power hidden deep within the Land, as represented by that radiant branch, is our true soterical lifeline. It will have to be found again, reclaimed, taken in hand with deep humility, reverence, authenticity, and love.

Moriarty once observed that 'human beings have made themselves alone in their stories.'[121] We have lulled our children to sleep now for many generations with stories of our separateness from Nature. We have told ourselves horrific and isolating narratives rooted, however subtly, in a crypto-Gnostic rejection of the Mother. We have painted ourselves into a Creation no longer experienced as sacred, a Creation robbed of spirit, to be dominated and subdued by human agency—and thus we have cut ourselves off from our own life-source, like infants deprived of the nourishing breast.

'If you see something as less than it really is, you are sinning against it. If you see something only with an economic eye, you are sinning against it.'[122]

---

[121] John Moriarty, from the lecture, *Seeking to Walk Beautifully on the Earth* (Dublin: The Lilliput Press, 2007).
[122] ibid.

And so we might also describe the central calling of our time, in this hour of the world's deep night, as learning to dream once more with the Earth—as re-membering the true magic of Life.

> In the very earliest times,
> when both people and animals lived on Earth,
> a person could become an animal if he wanted to,
> and an animal could become a human being.
> Sometimes they were people
> and sometimes animals
> and there was no difference.
> All spoke the same language.
> That was the time when words were like magic.[123]

When words were still like magic: deep time of the first ones of sacred vision, of sacred art—of the Shining Ones of great Beauty.

Sàmhachd.
Crìonnachd.
Filidheachd.

Grace and peace to the five ancient roads; beauty in the three worlds; unending joy to the Old Ones on the flowered Plains of Honey, in the Land of Summer Stars.

May there be peace to the spirits of the sacred Land, and may the living Earth, our Mother, not give way beneath us. May there be peace to the spirits of the blessed Sky, and may the heavens not fall upon us. May there be peace to the spirits of the holy Sea, and may the waters not rise to overtake us.

---

[123] From an Inuit story, quoted by John Moriarty in *Turtle Was Gone a Long Time, Vol. 3.* cf. John Moriarty, *A Moriarty Reader* (Dublin: The Lilliput Press, 2013), 227-228.

St. Mochaoi and the
Bird of Heaven

O nce it happened that St. Mochaoi of Nendrum went into the forest to cut some timber for the building of a *dairthech*.[124] He had his bundle all prepared and was getting ready to hoist it up on his shoulder and start back toward the place where he had recently settled with one hundred and forty others for the purpose of establishing a monastic community. He decided, however, to wait for the those who had come to help him, who were off in different parts of the forest gathering their own bundles of wood.

As he sat there alone, waiting, he heard a bird singing very beautifully, and saw that it was perched on a nearby Hawthorn. This bird was more gorgeous than all the birds of the world, and his song was so haunting that it made St. Mochaoi weep.

Suddenly, the bird began to speak to him in words he could understand. 'You work hard, O cleric', said the bird. 'Such work is required of us in building a sanctuary of God', replied St. Mochaoi. Then he asked the bird: 'Who is it that now addresses me?' The bird replied, 'I am a messenger of God, a spirit from the heavens.' 'Why have you come?' asked Mochaoi. 'I've

---

[124] A *dairthech* ('oak house') was a small shrine or sanctuary constructed of Oak wood, which was common in early Christian Ireland, used primarily for private prayer.

been sent here by God to speak to you, and to sing to you for a while, with sweet music that might bring joy and peace to your heart.' 'That sounds wonderful', replied the saint with gratitude.

The bird then put his beak into the feathers of his wing, and began to sing again—the sweetest music one could imagine.

And for a long time St. Mochaoi sat there listening to this heavenly music, with his bundle of sticks by his side, in the midst of the forest. Tears streamed down his face from the beauty of it, and he lay down on the forest floor and closed his eyes to listen more deeply.

It seemed to him that only a single hour of the day had passed—and the wood in his bundle was no more withered than an hour would cause. When the bird-spirit bade him farewell, he arose with his bundle and walked back happily toward the monastery.

When he arrived, he saw a small oratory that had been erected by his people for the memory of his soul. He wondered at what in the world had happened. Then he went to the dwelling places, but all looked quite different, and none of the brothers and sisters knew at all who he was, until he related to them the story, and how he was cared for by the tender song of the bird. And they determined that in this world three hundred years had elapsed while he sat there in the forest, under the enchantment of the birdsong.

When the others heard this, and knew it in their hearts to be true, they knelt before him in awe. And they built, then, a wooden shrine from the sticks St. Mochaoi had carried; and afterwards they erected a church in that place.

Leaves from an Otherworld Tree

Interrelatedness is a common-sense observation...What's not common is the mind-body dualism that begins to come in with monotheism. And the alliance of monotheism with the formation of centralized governance and the national state, that's what's unnatural, and statistically in a minority on earth. The [most common] human experience has been an experience of Animism.

—Gary Snyder

It is only when we are aware of the earth and of the earth as poetry that we truly live.

—Henry Beston

The tools are there; the path is known; you simply have to turn your back on a culture that has gone sterile and dead, and get with the program of a living world and a re-empowerment of the imagination.

—Terence McKenna

Talk of this world—of our sterile and corrosive, ego-dominant culture—comes cheap. But speech that arises from the Otherworld Well, from the deep sensory streams flowing out of Fec's Pool, is transcendent of all worldly valuation: rarified and sacred by virtue of its natural birth, by virtue of its power to transform, to shape our observable reality. True speech means poetic speech, oracular speech. Thus, in ancient Gaelic tradition, law was poetry, and poetry was law.

Wisdom rarely speaks through establishment constructs, least of all those born of a culture built on exploitation and dominion. There is no horror like 'Manifest Destiny' or the Sand Creek Massacre that could ever be found in the heart and voice of Lady Wisdom. Her ways and the ways of this human-made world, this nightmare dominator landscape, are mutually exclusive. If something is not of the ways of this world, then it may be of the ways of the Otherworld. Wisdom gives of the Otherworld—Christ-Sophia, the *Logos*, speaks from the Otherworld Well, from the unseen, unquantifiable dimensions of Nature, 'not as [this] world gives.'[125]

A Mystery: Wisdom is Word, the voice of the living Earth. *Sophia* is *Logos*, and *Logos* is *Gaia*.

It's become quite popular in contemporary religious circles to speak of 'eco-theology' or 'green religion'. On the surface, at least, this is a good and meaningful development, because if we don't find our way back into a worldview that integrates and fully embraces the whole of Nature, then we're a dead species, set to spiral downward into ever deeper modes of destruction. It is crucial, however, that whatever work is done in this arena is deep-rooted and efficacious—qualities that have thus far been lacking in mainstream religious and cultural 'greening' efforts.

A hard truth that most interested parties will not wish to hear is that the only true 'eco-theology' is one that's rooted in animism. Without this archaic edge that opens out experientially into the dizzying vista of an end-

---

[125] John 14:25 (NRSV).

lessly diverse and thoroughly conscious metaphysical ecology, no reform of ideation or culture will be sufficient to retrain our hearts and minds, or correct the cataclysmic course we're presently on.

A return to a worldview and way of life deeply and authentically grounded in an integrative animistic understanding has the power to redeem the errant trajectory of our cultures and societies, our localized communities, our sciences, our religions. But animism scares the hell out of most Westerners, who have too long been steeped in world-denying, superstitious, and constipated modes of Abrahamic thought. These corrosive puritanical worldview elements color all our socio-cultural endeavors to one degree or another, regardless of how staunchly some individuals may have outwardly eschewed them. It is simply the water we swim in within the bounds of Western societies; we are all 'deeply conditioned by Christianity's anthropocentrism and irreverence toward nature.'[126]

It's thus a rather obvious conclusion that all normative Christian teaching and custom in the West is directly implicated in the present planetary cultural and ecologic crisis (in truth these two modes of crisis form a single matrix of interrelated factors), for the whole Christian construct as we've known it—socio-culturally, mythically, and religiously—is infected to the core with world-denying, dualistic ideology: ideology that negates the inherent sacrality and the values of Nature. Normative, establishment Christianity has from the start been rooted in worldview premises that necessarily undermine any real attempt at wholeness, any true embrace of Nature (both internal and external to the human person), any movement to reverse the course of our insanity and return to a sustainable way of walking on the Earth, rooted in Beauty, archaic wisdom and natural values. In other words, Christianity as we have known and inherited it cannot help us, as it forms a significant portion of the root of our sickness, and can therefore only deepen that sickness. Certain aesthetic, mythic, liturgical, and sacramental elements of Christianity can be salvaged or redeemed, but only if they are reshaped

---

[126] Bron Taylor, *Dark Green Religion: Nature Spirituality and the Planetary Future* (Berkeley: University of California Press, 2010), 11.

and/or radically recontextualized, placed in the larger framework of a deci-sively animistic worldview, in a context of oral tradition: in an environment that is concerned with hearing and heeding the true voice of Wisdom, the World Soul, and with learning to once more walk beautifully on Her sacred Body, the living Earth.

This puts us at a rather dangerous impasse, because of the thorough degree to which, either consciously or unconsciously, most Westerners are indoctrinated and conditioned with normative Christian assumptions, mak-ing them inherently resistant to real reform and to the needful task of archaic reclamation. How might this impasse be resolved? For most of us alive today it likely never will be, simply because most individuals in our present social context—particularly those of older generations—are far too comfortable in their current stations, and cannot be convinced of the brokenness of the systems they perceive have served them well for so long. There is still signifi-cant denial and repression of the cataclysmic destruction we have done, and continue to do, to ourselves and to the rest of the planet. As in an abusive interhuman relationship, some form of deep denial is required on the part of both abuser and abused for the pattern of violence to continue. The level of crisis that's needed to shake an apathetic and denial-ridden majority out of willful ignorance, stagnation, and criminal toxicity remains to be seen—and surely we will be shattered with collective pain and regret whenever that critical moment finally arrives on our doorstep.

But to us is given the present. And any way forward for those who are genuinely committed to a real and all-embracing atonement, to the co-actu-alizing of a 'heavenly kingdom' in our midst, to preserving the sacred Earth with which we're inextricably at one and embedded on this strange, myste-rious journey of souls, will have to be a way that intelligently and devoutly reclaims the deep, wild wisdom of our ancient Ancestors. That wisdom is, in short, the animistic wisdom of the dawn-time: the poetic Flower World knowledge of shamans and witches, fools and healers, mystics and sages, which was present from the first breaking-open of human spiritual percep-tion, and will always be present, at least in the Dreaming. This means a direct, experiential knowing of the diverse, all-encompassing ensoulment and inherent interconnectedness of all things in the natural world. To this we have recourse, and to this we are called, whether or not we realize it. The Horse goddess knocks at our door, with ever increasing intensity.

By contrast with the perennial, archaic wisdom of the ancients, what modern 'eco-theology' and related movements in the Abrahamic milieu have thus far primarily consisted of is a kind of agitated excavation: a sifting through the mire of text-based, establishment Judaeo-Christian assumptions and arti-facts, searching longingly—as if in a state of spiritual starvation—for any Nature-affirming crumb that might fall from the table of Biblical tradition: a scarce word or sentence here or there from the idolized, 'inerrant' textual corpus and the patriarchal images of divinity it enshrines, which might con-nect, however feebly or obliquely, to an ecologically minded awareness. Such a weak-hearted and ineffectual endeavor can never pass muster. So far as I can see, this strange, belabored process has yielded absolutely nothing of note—no 'fruits worthy of repentance,' no measurable value for the crucial project of reforming our minds, our hearts, our cultures, and our world. In fact, it seems to only deepen our shared state of crisis by perpetuating established patterns of denial regarding the severity of the situation and the responsibility our normative cultural-religious systems bear for it. And it sadly reifies the metaphysically bankrupt doctrine of inerrant and immov-able texts, immune from all sensible revision.

The 'greening' of the Abrahamic religions as we presently have them cannot bear transformative fruit because legitimate natural values and eco-logical awareness—by which I mean, in this case, a deeply felt and inte-grative experience of conscious interbeing—can never find shelter in an inherently world-denying ideology. Such efforts thus amount to little more than diddling: playing with the broken shards of a dysfunctional system that could never yield the visionary depth, the perceptive connectedness, or the spiritual potency now so desperately needed on this planet. Another danger-ous distraction from the real depth of calamity we're immersed in. And the straightforward fact is that we no longer have time for the luxury of diddling and denial; those days, though they were never truly justified, are now long behind us. The crisis is upon us in full force.

So the feeble efforts that have hitherto characterized Judaeo-Christian and other dominator responses to the planetary crises that envelop us—crises which those same dominator structures have largely created—can no longer be countenanced. Radical problems call for radical change. Setting aside the niceties of political correctness, which we likewise have no time to entertain, and seeking to assess the situation clearly, with as much freedom from cultural and religious bias as possible, one is inevitably confronted with the realization that without the courage to engage the needful level of foundational change in ourselves, in our worldviews, in our lifeways, and in our collective cultural styles, we are each implicated in the destruction of the Earth, and in the erosion of the dignity, health, and existential freedom of our children and grandchildren. None can bear the expense of skirting this issue, of giving in to fear about standing up and intelligently articulating the utter deficiency of the socio-cultural and religious norms in which we're immersed and by which the majority of us have been thoroughly conditioned, even when—or *especially* when—the rules of polite society dictate silence.

֎

There's an interesting little vision sequence in the otherwise dubious and often misappropriated Book of Revelation—poetic lines that might grant some true questions, give some true glances through a mythopoetic aperture into Creation's depths, where we don't ordinarily bear witness. Though almost certainly not intended by its author(s) to function in a capacity that inspires archaic modes of vision and spiritual pursuit, the passage in question nonetheless holds real potential in this regard—a potential that sounds forth like something dangerously akin to Otherworld speech: poetic speech that signals the genuine, the deep, the hidden, the needful: talk that isn't cheap, which defies institutional stagnation by pointing to mythic truths beyond it:

'Then the angel showed me the river of the water of life, bright as crystal, flowing from the throne of God, and…On either side of the river is the Tree of Life…and the leaves of the Tree are for the healing of the nations.'[127]

It is significant for our purposes here that the leaves of the Otherworld Tree perceived by the seer of this vision are prescribed for healing the nations. This is a poetic statement worth reflecting on: that the leaves of a mythic Tree which grows in the realms of the unseen could be true medicine for our ailing planet, our cultures and societies. Let us mark that it is not a program of 'leadership training' or a 'task force' birthed by institutional bureaucracies or any effort of governmental leadership suggested here for the task of collective healing, of making this ailing world whole, but rather leaves from an Otherworld Tree, which grows over the river of the water of life: a radically open, experiential, and visionary invitation to return to a world of magic, natural wisdom, poetic inspiration, and imagination.

These are deep, archaic images, and they're neither unique to Revelation nor original to Hebraic thought. Their mythic universality, in fact, bespeaks their transformative potential. Such potent mythic images, sufficiently grokked and integrated, naturally sow seeds of needful dissent—: dissent that invites us into deep waters; effectual waters; sacramental waters. Such images can be referenced and called forth in reflection not as artificial evidence of the non-existent 'greenness' of Judaeo-Christian worldviews, an excuse to carry on with our cultural-religious assumptions as-is, but rather as an indication of the kind of focus that is lacking in said worldviews—an exception highlighting the corrosive nature of the rule—thereby recommending the radical reformation or outright abandonment of those same worldview structures.

In many traditions—Norse, Celtic, Siberian, and others—there has long existed the notion of a Tree of Life, an *axis mundi* or Tree of Worlds. In Gaelic tradition we call it *Bile*: the central axis that upholds the three

---

[127] Rev. 22:1 (NRSV).

known worlds and bridges them. In front of this Tree of Life, flowing out from beneath its branches, is the Well of Wisdom. And from that Well of Wisdom flows all the Rivers of the Earth—perhaps most prominently the River Boyne in Ireland. The waters of Mother Bóann (from whose name the contemporary spelling of 'Boyne' is derived)—the waters of the White Cow Goddess, associated with ancient wisdom and with the secrets of visionary Sacraments held close by the poet-seers—are understood as Source: as the sanctifying waters of life that flow from the Otherworld font of wisdom into this world of incarnate perception.

Whatever cultural valence we apply to it, this Well of Wisdom is the spring of life, inspiration, and vision we must each learn to get back to. We are parched nearly to death—parched from a lack of connection to the source of real Beauty and depth in human experience. As such, we're into very serious territory if we attempt to follow these kinds of images back along their tributary paths, toward the Well that can sate our thirst—if we attempt to deeply encounter them and their implications by way of comparative mythology and religion, and, more fundamentally, by way of experiential development—free from the conditioned ideological frameworks that have normally held such imagistic transmissions captive in the nets of dominator ideas and institutions. These are the general makings of an appropriately radical reformation in our times, which could be described, at least in part, as a liberation of poetic speech, vision, and vocation.

Getting back to the Well of Wisdom implies real labor—*interior* labor: the sort that most will do anything to avoid, because it invariably leads to the dissolution of all previously held assumptions conditioned by the dominant culture. It necessarily dissolves delusion and denial. It is visionary work we are called to now, first and foremost: the hard, crucifying work of inner transformation, and, by extension, the transformation of our religions, myths, and worldviews. Without these foundational interior changes, none of the outward work we do will be fruitful or sustainable. And nothing else, it seems to me, can save the sinking ship we're on.

It is a great and true Mystery, a revelation that breaks us open, when we discover that Nature herself is alive, ensouled, intentional, profoundly conscious—that She is, in a deep and elusive sense, the *Logos*, the guiding terrestrial mind encountered by sages on the wild interior road of spiritual crisis and transmutation. Hers is the guiding voice that finally meets us in the depths of initiatory ecstasy, that longs to guide us again as a species, by way of our shamans, prophets, and healers, by way of the intimate knowing that sleeps in each of our hearts: to guide us again toward the Eden we forsook long ago in the Faustian bargain for power, control, material mastery, and the fleeting rush of egoic obsession.

When we meet that holy power, directly and personally; when we hear Her terrifying and resounding voice; when the Earth trembles beneath us with the potency of Her life force, Her totality, Her ego-shattering embrace, then at last we can know something of what the true heart of religion is and always has been: the heart of the Mysteries, of the many great myths of return, of the disciplines aimed at spiritual remembrance: our return to the sacred breast of the Mother, where we find true meaning, true belonging, true wisdom; where we are shown the reality of the soul and can shed the illusory fears related to bodily death, and to the death of the neurotic construct of ego.

It is in this sense that, as has been suggested by many commentators, authentic religion is at its core a process of learning to navigate the crisis of death—not only the inevitable death of the body, but the psycho-spiritual death of legitimate initiation or 'death before death'. The experience of learning to properly contextualize death, the learning of techniques for the soul's passage from this mortal existence, the acquisition of anxiety-dissolving habits and insights regarding the soul's immortal journey, do constitute a certain core, archaic framework on which rests the structures of the various mystical traditions. At the origin of this recurrent framework is the now untraceable ur-vision of the initial human breakthrough into radically altered consciousness, and the resultant revelation of the soul in connection with Source, with living Nature.

Perennial wisdom—perhaps unexpectedly for us in contemporary Western contexts—reveals the mysterious guiding voice variously theologized in the Christianized West as *Logos*, *Sophia*, or *Christos* to be intimately related, if not synonymous, with the living Earth, the Earth Mother or 'Gaian consciousness', who is spirit, soul, or *anima* of the planet.

Every ancient culture has developed and passed on its own way of relating to and expressing this ubiquitous and mysterious Presence, which in archaic contexts was much more foundational to the shared conception of felt reality than we in our intellectualized, abstracted, and disconnected modern religions can realistically imagine. We might liken the guiding voice of this Presence to the proposed 'Great Mother' figure of Old Europe, as imagined by Marija Gimbutas and others. In Gaelic and Breton Celtic cultural traditions, the planetary consciousness in question is known as *Anu* or *Ana*, later Christianized as St. Anne; She is *Tonantzin* or La Virgen de Guadalupe in Mazatec and other Mestizo cultures; *Sophia* and *María* in esoteric European Christianities; *Isanaklesh* in Apache tradition; *Eanan* in the Sami culture; *Jörd* in ancient Norse reckoning; *Gaia* in the Hellenistic milieu—to name just a few of Her cultural *personae*.

While our monotheistically conditioned minds seek to reach (if only conceptually) an 'ultimate' and transcendent divine personhood, the witness of the animistic cultures—which is to say, of all our ancient Ancestors—is that the principal guiding voice often encountered by mystics and shamans in the throes of spiritual ecstasy is in fact the voice of Mother Earth. It is not the voice of a remote, transcendent, and abstract masculine divinity who dwells in the heavens beyond this perceptible world, but rather of the ancient feminine power that lives beneath our feet and continuously births and sustains the structure of our incarnate reality.

This perennial guiding voice, heard by sages and shamanic travelers since the birth of human religious experience, could be approached as Nature, or more immanently as Mother Earth, the *anima mundi* or 'World Soul'. In either case, it is She who creates and guides as Source: a supreme but immanent divinity, 'Mother of the Gods'—and, in Gaelic tradition, first and primary among trinities: the ultimate we can know of divinity, of sacrality, here in this earthly, incarnate circumstance.[128] It is She to whom the ancient Sacraments give concourse, in order that the human person may hear, be shaped and guided by Her will. It is Her love and wisdom that ever seek to co-actualize with us, in harmonious partnership, the 'Kingdom' vision of Beauty, of Flower World life in conscious union or interbeing with all Creation, with the vast ecology of Spirit that contains, surrounds, and interpenetrates us.

It is not surprising, given the conditioned inclinations of the contemporary Western mind to seek an entirely trans-Earthly divinity, that even the 'Goddess movement', which arose largely from the Bay Area feminism of the 1970s and 80s, has tended to imagine and address 'The Goddess' in an essentially monotheistic fashion, rather than an animistic one, which, ironically, would much more accurately describe the worldviews of the ancient cultures that encountered and related to the presence of the Great Mother this movement claims to be recapturing). In keeping with the inherited Western tendencies toward an image of divinity that is personal, utterly transcendent and 'ultimate' (whatever that might signify), the Goddess movement has leaned toward simply replacing the masculine, monolithic

---

[128] It is worth mentioning here that a macrocosmic rendering of the trinitarian model of divinity, as found in Celtic, Vedic, and other Indo-European contexts prior to the birth of Christianity, may well have been abstractly conceived of by druidic philosophers as an indelible part of the fabric of the cosmos and its 'unoriginated origins'. Extrapolating from related Indo-European precedents, in a Celtic context we might imagine this Reality as the collection of eternal principles or 'movements' of Creation, Preservation, and Dissolution, which form or uphold the ineffable Ground of Being. This kind of theological construct, if it indeed existed in pre-Christian Celtic contexts (which seems reasonably likely, given the parallel Vedic conception as well as the influence Celtic thinking had on developing trinitarian theology via the Church in Gaul), would most likely have been anciently understood as impersonal and therefore not accessible through prayer and propitiation. This stands in distinction to *Anu*, the Earth Mother and 'Mother of the Gods' here discussed, who is a divine person, a soul, an entity with which other souls may—indeed, in our case as human beings, *must*—be in active relationship with. It is for this reason that I say the Earth Mother is the ultimate we can *know* of divinity, here in our present incarnate reality.

Judaeo-Christian (or, more broadly, Near Eastern) image of deity contrivedly enforced on the Western mind with a more tender feminine version of the same popularly imagined typology. As one might expect from an ancient aretalogy of Isis, for example, much of the language of the Goddess movement addresses the divine feminine as 'The One' or 'Eternal All'. To the extent that a reclamation of the divine feminine is drawing from genuinely archaic streams of wisdom, and thus finds its starting point completely outside the Abrahamic milieu, it must necessarily reflect a genuinely animistic worldview, not a monotheistic (or even henotheistic) one. In such an environment of archaic reclamation, the 'Great Goddess' would be known and envisioned as soul and power of the living Earth—what Terence McKenna referred to as 'the vegetable mind'.[129]

⸙

Combing the fabric of Western history in search of evidence for the felt experience of *Gaia-Sophia*, one might initially get the impression that such metaphysical insight has taken on the quality of a remote and arcane whisper, hidden and rarely felt or discussed since the dominance of the Eden myth and its attendant Judaeo-Christian trappings over indigenous European worldviews and lifeways. As Thomas Schipflinger states, the discovery of the World Soul in Western traditions seems to be 'the rediscovery of an obscure and ancient idea', and to some extent this is true, though the arcane thread of this perennial indigenous insight has in fact been woven through the whole of Western history, albeit in a veiled and often esoteric way.[130] Schipflinger further notes that 'in fact many significant thinkers throughout history spoke of the World Soul, which can be said to have been an important theme in the entire Western intellectual tradition.'[131] Once one

---

[129] Terence McKenna, *Food of the Gods: The Search for the Original Tree of Knowledge* (New York: Bantam, 1992), 93.

[130] Thomas Schipflinger, *Sophia-Maria: A Holistic Vision of Creation*, Trans. James Morgante (York Beach, ME: Samuel Weiser, Inc., 1998), 307.

[131] ibid.

knows what to look for, one begins to see the motif emerging in unexpected domains. Plato, for instance, on whose work it has often been said the rest of Western philosophy is merely a footnote, speaks of the world as 'a living being with soul and intelligence.'[132] The philosophical schools of the Stoics and the Neo-Platonists both carried on the archaic notion of the Earth as living and ensouled—though in some cases the 'World Soul' was abstracted to describe not only the Earth but the planets surrounding Her as well, and, more broadly, the whole of the perceptually discernible cosmos. This transcendent inclination gave way to the Renaissance Hermetic notion of *Natura* as Cosmic Mother or Soul of the Universe. Still, the foundation of all this speculation was the perennially felt (and heard) Presence of *Gaia*.

In the twentieth century, a few natural philosophers and scientific thinkers outside the mainstream like Gustav Fechner and James Lovelock returned to what we might call a more original expression of this notion of the World Soul: that the *anima mundi* is *Gaia*, the Earth Mother, the soul of the living Earth. The crucial framework missing from such theories is the animism that natively frames the archaic and perennial *experience* of that reality. Such direct, experiential encounter with the World Soul as Earth Mother does indeed seem scarcely attested in historical religious speculation throughout the history of Western cultures, but we can at least say that it has been felt and shared by a few intrepid explorers in our own time, Terence McKenna perhaps most notable among them. In the Gaelic stream of wisdom, a brilliant carrier of this insight into the living Mystery of the Earth was John Moriarty. In American literary culture, Gary Snyder, Thomas Berry, and Alice Walker have at least alluded strongly to the same living reality. Walker once wrote: 'In day-to-day life, I worship the Earth as God.'[133]

Part of the obscuration and suppression of the Gaian motif is certainly related to the fact that waking up to the hidden reality of the Great Mother comes only through direct experience—and usually (though not always)

---

[132] Plato, *Timaeus and Critias*, Trans. Desmond Lee (London: Penguin, 1986), 43.
[133] Alice Walker, *Anything We Love Can Be Saved: A writer's Activism* (New York: Random House, 1997), 9.

through an extreme form of experience known in anthropological theory as 'initiatory crisis': it cannot be grasped through reason alone. And, as is abundantly evident in dominant Western culture, we have since the dawn of modernity severely crippled our own capacity to grasp anything not reducible to the blunt measurements of reason. Without the sacred, initiatory conditions that reliably facilitate radical modes of conscious perception, the experience of liminality and communion felt by the initiated is bound to become a mere concept, and in time even the concept will fade from the collective awareness entirely. It is precisely these archaic, experiential factors that the reductionistic philosophical materialism of Christianized Western societies has negated and disallowed from sprouting into daylight. And it is these very same factors that we now need access to, more urgently than ever.

Experientially born insights of the kind in question, which are inherently esoteric and obscured to our rational faculties, are difficult to quantify and discuss; they are often private affairs, and have the dual qualities of profound intimacy and social vulnerability for those who experience them, particularly in the present dominant culture. This makes their appearance in public (or even private) discourse unlikely, even in those rare instances where the insight has been directly experienced. We do find the presence of the Gaian Mind preserved, however, in Western folklore and mythology. Schipflinger says of the Hellenistic mythos surrounding Gaia: '[She] was immeasurably wise and made Delphi Her sacred dwelling place. She spoke Her will in oracles through Her daughter Themis (which means righteousness, providence, and divine law). A python (symbolizing wisdom) guarded Gaia's Delphic Oracle and was used in communications (a patriarchal re-interpretation of the myth of Gaia later expropriated the Delphic Oracle to Apollo).'[134]

Here we encounter important symbolism linking Gaia with the archaic Earth Mother and Her Sacraments, including the ancient image of the serpent, long associated with Earth wisdom, initiatory rites, and the shamanic healing arts; an oracular practice linked to the guiding voice of the

---

[134]   ibid.

Great Mother; and a sacred place in the Earth through which that guiding voice speaks and through which Her presence may be accessed with special immediacy.

Such sacramental Mysteries can only be touched through direct, personal experience; no other method is capable of pulling back the veil that separates our deadened hearts and reductionistic minds from their life giving radiance. *Sacramentum*, from which we derive the English term 'sacrament', is in fact a Latin translation of the older Greek term, *mystērion*. The root of *mystērion* is *mystēs,* meaning, 'one who has been initiated', implying the experientially derived knowledge of initiates in the various Hellenic Mystery Cults (inclusive of early Christianity)—knowledge that initiates were sworn to hold in secret. Without the facilitative initiatory experience, a true Mystery makes little sense to the rational mind. But its intellective inaccessibility does not negate its truth-value; in fact, it only affirms it, once the necessary experiential data has been acquired and the matter is put into clear perspective by individual seekers who have indeed directly touched the *numinosum.*

The inability of the Western mind to naturally and intuitively access the Gaian Mystery is partly attributable to the fact that theology as a Christianized Western discipline has always sought what is *beyond* the Earth, in an endeavor of philosophical abstraction, whereas the indigenous witness points to Nature herself, to the soul of the ancient Earth Mother, as the principal voice of divinity—at least insofar as divinity is accessible to the human experience. As distinct from normative, popular Christian concepts of divinity, this immediate, living presence can be felt in concrete, sensory form and in the present moment. As McKenna observed, the experience of the Earth Mother as paramount divinity is primal and visionary in origin, 'coming at [our ancient Ancestors] out of the environment was a mind— not an abstract mind, not as we imagine God (an old man with a beard, an abstract principle, all this stuff), but actually a friend and a comfort: a feminine thing, not remote at all, not the creature of theology, but a creature of experience'.[135] This latter observation is key: not a creature of theology, but a creature of *direct experience*. The initial breaking-in of this mysterious mind, this guiding voice, in the landscape of human perception must have been as radical and formative an experience as humanity has ever known. It set in motion the eventual development of countless forms of religious speculation and artistic expression.

॰

At dusk I step into the empty, silent chapel of St. Jerome, on the sacred Land of the Taos Pueblo community of Northern New Mexico. The first thing I notice is the overtly indigenous expression of the sacred images behind the altar. The Virgin as Earth Mother, occupying the place of centrality, of highest honor, in the central niche of the make-shift retable, holding forth the blossoms of spring: Flower World Mother of the Kingdom already come. La Virgen de Guadalupe to Her right; the Celestial Mother to Her left, 'Queen of Heaven'. Corn stalks, beans, and other local, sacred plants, crucial to the life of this community for countless generations, frame the niches that contain these holy images of the feminine divine. Bowls of squash and corn and other fruits of the harvest, watched over by yet more images of Mary, the Mother of Earth and all her creatures.

It quickly dawns on me that in this holy place there is only one image of masculine divinity to be found at all: a statue of Jesus with arms outstretched in offering, off to the far right side of the altar, seemingly placed there as an afterthought. No masculine image holds a place of centrality at all in this sanctuary. The only other image of Jesus to be found in the entire chapel is a rather diminutive crucifix above the altar, showing Jesus as an indigenous man, his face an expression of peace and rootedness, not agony or the torture of sacrificial atonement. Smaller images of male and female saints—many of them indigenous—populate the shelves of the high altar below the primary images, a number of those representations also of Mary. Here the Earth Mother still reigns unequivocally.

---

[135] Terence McKenna, audio recording, lecture date and location unknown.

'At last, at last, the final illusion'; the sloughing off of colonial oppression and the needful subversion of attempted cultural genocide—like small plants breaking through concrete, a persistent survival of the representation of the Gaian mind herself; a bold and rooted revelation of indigenous wisdom shining unapologetically through the benighted shell of Western Christian inheritance. At last, the Earth Mother given once more her rightful place of honor: the feminine divine in the seat of prominence; the voice of the sacred, living Earth, guiding us back to oneness and cooperation with Her and with the whole of Creation. A living expression of the vision I received only three months prior at Teaghlach Einne in the far West of Ireland—this time not in Gaelic cultural terms, but Tewa Puebloan: an authentically integrated, living witness to the indigenous wisdom of their own holy Ancestors, whose spirits have inhabited this Land for centuries. The same thing we of European descent must learn to reclaim for ourselves, not in Puebloan language and imagery, but in language and imagery native to our own ancestral inheritance.

The reactionary bias from most Western Christians relating to indigenously framed expressions of Catholic Christianity (whether voiced or held quietly) is both ironic and appalling—firstly because fundamentalist critics generally have no understanding whatsoever of the things they're denouncing; and secondly because the very phenomenon they decry, i.e., the preservation of indigenous wisdom traditions under the guise of Christian religiosity, is probably the only real hope for redeeming the Christian religion.

The potential to reclaim an authentic, experiential knowledge of the divine feminine through images of Mary and/or Sophia (Holy Wisdom) is likely the only vein of real spiritual gold that Christianity still intrinsically holds. Its normative, male-dominator orientation and its world-denying, textually fixated ethos, rooted in corrosive Near Eastern myth and ideology, are completely devoid of value, spiritual substance, and redeemable cultural dimensions. The animistic worldview that is needed as an overlay to soterically transform Christianity is completely extrinsic to its nature; thus, Christianity must be radically reshaped. The mentality around establishment religion in the West has to fundamentally shift: the conditioned religious norms must be radically altered to accommodate and absorb indigenous wisdoms and natural values—not the other way around, as the normative approach has always been. As it turns out, Christians have had it backwards from the start. As they should have done from the start, beginning with the start of European conversion, the Mysteries of Christ will now have to authentically meet, accept, receive, and come (if they come at all) as a secondary, complimentary addition to pre-Christian, archaic wisdoms and values rooted in the living Land. Judaeo-Christian thought and custom can no longer be tolerated as a replacement for these latter wisdoms—which simply means the restoration of right balance in Western cultures and religious systems.

This witness of the feminine divine, and of the feminine divine as Mother Earth more specifically, does still live and breathe within the Christian tradition, but only in a veiled and subversive manner. The images of the Great Mother which continue to haunt the halls of the Western imagination can, in the right light, be seen to veil a memory of the ancient experience of the *Logos* or 'Word' as interiorly heard guiding voice, experienced and attested by Neo-Platonists, Hermetists, Alexandrian Jewish mystics, and others of the ancient world, known by shamans and ecstatic visionaries of the pre-Classical Western world and the non-Western world alike as spirit of the living Earth: Holy Wisdom as Gaia. That speech of divinity anxiously awaits the attendance of *our* ears—and our proper response, which is to magnify and maximize Her presence, at the deliberate expense of all inherited, text-based, male dominated, anti-natural, and world-denying ideologies, which have generally constituted Western religion from the start of the Christian period onward.

Fundamentalists, textually obsessed literalists, and cultic purists of all stripes within the Christian milieu will, of course, go to the grave clinging desperately to these toxic elements of their belief systems, thinking they hold something of supreme value, and assuming their corrosive ideological assumptions to have been delivered from on high, recorded indelibly in the 'inerrant' artifacts of Biblical witness. 'The Bible said it, I believe it, and that settles it' is the classic Protestant expression of this particular form of destructive human idiocy, though Catholic Christians certainly have their own versions of the same naivety.

Yet, in spite of all this, the Earth Goddess—and our primal, intuitive knowing of Her, which has accompanied us from the earliest instances of spiritual experience, from the first hearing of Her guiding voice in vision—lives on. Miraculously, poetically, fittingly, and justly She lives and moves in our midst, quietly planning, directing, and patiently awaiting our return to sanity, our return to Her life giving breast.

Perhaps it is Mary, in her various indigenously rooted guises,—whether native European or Native American—who best provides for us now in the West an image of the feminine divine fit for the great task of reformation and reclamation now before us. She is, after all, the only *living* and still dynamic image of the feminine divine that remains in the West, expressed in living cultural contexts. As such, her image and her name are accessible to the human heart and mind, in spite of the thoroughness of our Christian conditioning. So long as we are willing to remove those surface layers of Biblically bound notions that in many contexts still cling to the image, then the archetype can be transformative, and might well get us where we need to go in the desperately overdue project of reconnecting with the feminine divine as soul of the sacred Earth.

ༀ

On the drive back from New Mexico, in Southern Colorado, I spot what appears to be a shrine along the highway. As I pass, I see that it's marked with several wooden crosses and a host of prayer ties ('clootie ties', as we call them in Gaelic tradition). It's a place I know I've passed a dozen times, but never paid much attention to, assuming it was a small, private memorial established in memory of someone who had died there in a car accident (something commonly seen on highways throughout the Western United States). This time as I pass, however, something calls me rather profoundly to stop. I pull off the highway, park my car, and walk up the hillside to the shrine. What I find is quite astounding: much more powerful than anything

I would have expected. It is a sizable sandstone cave perched on top of a little ridge, surrounded by a host of smaller niches in the rock, all of which have been made to house statuary, candles, and offerings of various kinds. The cave seems to pulse with an ancient gravity: a sacred place for countless generations, long before the Christianized images which now adorn it were born in the religious mind.

I carefully edge my body under the barbed wire fence which separates the cave-shrine from the road. It is on this barbed wire that hundreds of clootie cloths have been tied. I ascend to the cave, which I then see is filled with statues, icons, candles, and prayer objects, placed identically to the way they would be in Ireland, with objects symbolically representing the prayer request of the one making the gift (eye glasses for eye ailments, shoes for foot ailments, hats or bandanas for mental dis-ease or problems of the head, etc.—a tradition attested in ancient Celtic practice from at least the Iron Age).

I note with joy and tender emotion—but certainly not surprise—that the predominant sacred image in this holy place is Our Lady of Guadalupe. Another Marian shrine I've been led to in this holy Southwestern pilgrimage. The Earth Mother appearing once more in her now favored expression for the peoples of the Americas: La Virgen de Guadalupe, Tonantzin, Our Great Mother, Sovereignty, Soul of the Living Earth.

After making some offerings and prayers, I turn to face across the highway and toward the vast landscape beyond, and am suddenly struck by the sight of the holy 'Spanish Peaks' (*Wahatoya* in the local native dialect of Ute, meaning 'Breasts of the Earth'). The breasts of the Great Mother dominating the landscape, directly in line of sight from the sacred cave-shrine. Clearly no arbitrary occurrence in the landscape, but an alignment that holds great power. This place must have been a sacred site from earliest times—: a truly elegant theophany. Sitting here in the cave, I sit in Her navel. Just as I've sat in Her navel at Uisneach, and felt Her breasts many miles away to the West in Kerry, so I sit in Her navel and gaze at Her sacred, life giving breasts here in the arid mountain landscape of Southern Colorado.

The Wahatoya and the Paps of Anu. Sts. Mary and Anna as Earth Mother, thinly veiled, preserving the heart of our deepest and most essential human heritage. The guiding voice of the Earth, the Gaian mind, 'Mother of the Gods', still whispering, still moving, still quietly directing the course of our collective life, trying desperately to wake us up, to help us retrace our steps and make once more the sacred connections, to correct the course of our perilous unraveling.

Like discovering a hidden secret, She has drawn me into intimate contact with the same kind of living wisdom I've known in Éire and in my own ancestral culture, but in this American landscape: a blessed sign of hope and renewal: a consciousness and devotion that preserves the archaic values of Nature and the Ancestors, subversively veiled under a beautifully unique, native expression of Catholic Christianity.

The world-embracing nature of animism, rooted in the shared experience of a continuous theophany or self-revelation of the Great Mother as living Earth, transmitted not in text but in spirit and vision, by way of oral tradition, Sacrament, ritual, and poetic speech: a perennial religious experience sharply contrasted with the fundamentally world-denying and text-obsessed 'revelation' of the Abrahamic faiths. True revelation will come not through texts and dominator structures, but from the leaves of an Otherworld tree: it will come through our re-attunement to the voice of Mother Earth, who longs to speak once more with and in and through us.

As Lynn White astutely observed in his 1967 article, *The Historical Roots of Our Ecologic Crisis*, according to the Judaeo-Christian ideology that has thoroughly infected the Western psyche, 'No item in the physical creation [has] any purpose save to serve man's purposes.' White goes on to state that, '[especially] in its Western form, Christianity is the most anthropocentric religion the world has seen…[having] not only established a dualism of man and nature but also insisted that it is God's will that man exploit nature for his proper ends.'[136] These observations should, at this stage in our collective history, highlight an obvious problem of critical import—a lethal problem, in fact, as the last fifty years or so since the publication of White's article have so unequivocally demonstrated.

We cannot afford to entertain such toxic, anthropocentric ideology, and nor can we afford to be trusting of easy prescriptions—particularly metaphysical or political ones, but also technological ones, since the latter represents for many the new soterical hope. The old hollow speech, however 'inspirational' it may seem, from pulpits or party platforms, should be excised with lethal precision; it should be actively revolted against, toppled, and replaced with something effectual, transformative, and life giving for human beings and the whole of Creation.

All religious rhetoric that keeps us bound to spiritually colonized and ecologically disconnected modes of thought and behavior—all rhetoric that keeps us isolated from our natural birthright of perpetual conscious interbeing, removed from a direct, felt connection with the living, speaking soul of the Earth—must be totally and systematically rejected, without equivocation or back-peddling, or a regression to the learned habits of apologetics, because those false modes of speech, of worldly speech, can only corrupt and further colonize the human soul.

This problem implicates the whole of Judaeo-Christian discourse, especially in its popular iterations, including that of the so-called 'liberal mainline churches' which increasingly bill themselves as 'green' or 'ecologically minded'. These latter attributions carry no spiritual weight within the context of the Abrahamic faiths, noble as the intentions behind their use in said contexts might be, because the very foundations of the Abrahamic faiths as they presently stand inherently negate the values implied in the process of '(re-)greening'. As such, theological attempts at integrative ecological awareness in these traditions remain feeble, shallow, and ineffectual, owing to the simple fact that they are still bound to the anthropocentric, textually

---

[136] Lynn White, Jr., 'The Historical Roots of Our Ecologic Crisis', in *Science 155* (1967), 1205.

obsessed, male-dominator assumptions of the Western Judaeo-Christian worldview, which is in essence a worldview of reductionistic materialism.

This falls desperately short of the needed return to an animistic consciousness, to a set of lifeways, religious frameworks, and experiences that transform the individual at a soul level, and uphold as universal ideals the furtherance of Beauty and the flourishing of all life on the planet in a state of interspecies *communitas*. As soon as the living Earth, our Mother, is robbed of soul, viewed and treated as object rather than sacred Person, then the path of heartlessness, disconnection, destruction, and horror has begun. For Westerners, that path was taken long ago—and the only move that can now correct our course is a totalizing cultural-religious revolution: a return to true, holistic *communitas*—a return to conscious participation in what Suquamish Chief Seattle called in Ted Perry's translation of his famous speech to Washington and the white settlers, 'the web of life': 'Man did not weave the web of life; he is merely a strand in it. Whatever he does to the web, he does to himself.'[137]

Communitas is atonement, and atonement is *communitas*. The term is generally used in anthropology and social philosophy to describe a structurally independent feeling of human bonding, unity, equality, and interconnection, usually facilitated by a shared initiatory experience: a common (if only temporary) experience of ego loss and liminality. I use the term here to mean all these things, but also something more: an ongoing experience, feeling, and conscious awareness of one's unity and interbeing not only with fellow humans in a particular cultural context, but with all living things in the vast web of Creation. In other words, an integrative and culturally nourished, lived experience of animism. I maintain that *communitas*, by this definition, is the only true salvation for the human species, and, given our now disproportionate ecological impact, for all species on the planet. Without this awareness, and without a framing cultural-religious style that honors these aims and actively orients toward them, all teaching, exhorta-

---

137   Chief Seattle, 'How Can One Sell the Air?' trans. Ted Perry, in *How Can One Sell the Air, Revised Edition* (Summertown, TN: Native Voices, 2005), 58.

tion, activism, and leadership—in any dimension of society—will inevitably fall short of the mark. Lacking the necessary rootedness, the depth of vision, the connection to non-human souls and to the sacred flow or *telos* of Nature herself, no reform can be optimally effective or sustainable.

Resultantly, so-called 'mystical teachers' and contemporary theologians still operating under terms of the safe, institutionally sanctioned constructs and assumptions of the residue of Western Christendom—the very ideological and institutional structure that has perpetuated such vacant, world-negating patterns—will have to be spit out as lukewarm, ineffectual, and ultimately part and parcel of the overarching problem that continues to haunt us as a species. The depth of transformation we need now can never come from such an arena. A willingness to upend, to scandalize, to risk careers and worldly forms of security is therefore absolutely requisite to adequately meet the challenges of our present global crisis, particularly for those attempting to effect change from inside the bounds of ossified institutional structures. A willingness to actually abandon the routinized ideologies we can clearly see now have not served us or the rest of Creation is among the first needful steps. Anything less than the full expression of this movement toward radical reformation, purgation, and reclamation now places itself in position to be hewn down and thrown on the burn-pile; to quote from Matthew's Gospel, 'Even now the axe is lying at the root of the tree; every tree therefore that does not bear good fruit is cut down and thrown into the fire.'[138]

We hold now all the information we need to grasp the nature and severity of our collective crisis, the historic missteps which gave rise to it, and the tools to cure it. All that we require is readily at hand. Our problem is not that we lack the necessary answers; it is simply that we lack the resolve and courage of heart to truly hear, receive, and efficaciously respond to the answers that sit before us. An efficacious response implies, of course, the difficult but absolutely needful work of disassemblage, and of intelligent rejection of cancerous dimensions in our inherited ideologies—as it were, a thorough pruning of the vine—followed closely by creative reclamation

---

[138] Matthew 3:10 (NRSV).

and restructuring. Ultimately, this is the work of Spirit, of Nature, of the everliving Mother, because it is the work of remembrance and redemption, of *return*—: to Life, to our rightful place as conscious participants in the vast ecology of souls.

❦

Talk of this world comes cheap: talk of those dressed for the feel-good party, phobically avoidant of the relational lapse that invisibly determines their reality. Real vision, by contrast, is the thing to be sought: soul-level experience, rooted in Beauty, rooted in the sacral, undying radiance of Nature. For that we'll have to be willing to put our hearts and souls and bodies on the line—: no longer guided by fear, but by courage of heart, by *Imbas*, by *Awen*, by divine inspiration, by the vision of a Mag Mell world that can and must be actualized here in our midst.

Walking out like an ancient sage from the Well of Wisdom, Christ, the embodiment of Wisdom, who is also the *Logos*, a *persona* or 'mask' of the sacred, living Earth and an icon of our own potential transformation in Her Beauty, shatters all the assumptions of this world, and proposes the notion of consciously entering a renewed Creation. The only real question, then, is the existential one: Will you put yourself on the line? Will you strive, and will you make yourself vulnerable to being shattered? If you do, then as John Moriarty once wrote, 'sight in you will be more visionary than vision.'[139] Then you will really live. Then we as a people will really live.

The wisdom of the Otherworld Tree, of Connla's Well, of the Mag Mell Flower World that always awaits the ascent of our hearts and the participatory co-actualization of our heads and hands, is, at its core, a return to the voice and vision and Presence of the living Earth, the World Soul. May a taste of Her life giving waters be on our tongues, and haunt our souls until at last we have no more defense against the sacred call to be broken, to be remade, to step into the radiance of Creation renewed on this living Earth, on the Body of our ancient Mother.

---

[139] John Moriarty, *Dreamtime* (Dublin: The Lilliput Press, 1994), 18.

Mythos and the
Sacrament of Nature

My own suspicion is that the universe is not only queerer than we suppose, but queerer than we *can* suppose. I have read and heard many attempts at a systematic account of it, from materialism and theosophy to the Christian system or that of Kant, and I have always felt that they were much too simple. I suspect that there are more things in heaven and earth than are dreamed of, or can be dreamed of, in any philosophy.

—J. B. S. Haldane

Eternal Wisdom builds; may I become Her palace, for She has found in me, and I in Her, all peace.

—Angelus Silesius

The universe is the primary revelation of the divine, the primary scripture, the primary locus of divine-human communion.

—Thomas Berry

It may be that some little root of the sacred tree still lives. Nourish it, then, that it may leaf and bloom and fill with singing birds.

—*Black Elk*

Wilderness is the native landscape of Spirit. There we must go to meet truth, with reciprocity once more our watchword: a word on the tongues of our open hearts and a breath on the palms of our outstretched hands.

Nature is the first and primary Sacrament. At Her breast we receive our deepest nourishment. At Her feet we recall our eldest stories, receive our truest hints of meaning. From Her *theophany*, Her self-revelation, we receive all genuine wisdom. And She rewards the courage of all pilgrim souls who are willing to make the needful sacrifices to access that wisdom's source: the Otherworld Well of mythopoesy and vision.

John Muir once wrote, 'Wonderful how completely everything in wild nature fits into us, as if truly part and parent of us. The sun shines not on us but in us. The rivers flow not past, but through us.…The trees wave and flowers bloom in our bodies as well as our souls, and every bird song, wind song, and tremendous storm song of the rocks in the heart of the mountains is our song, our very own, and sings our love.'[140]

Among the ancient traditions of the Ancestral Puebloans of the American Southwest there existed a spiritual concept known as *The Flower World*. The Flower World is, firstly, the typically invisible spiritual dimension which overlays the visible world in which we dwell. It is the realm in which gods, ancestral spirits, and spirits of the natural world reside: very near to us, and in fact an integral part of the landscapes that surround us on the Earth, an 'overlay', generally invisible to human eyes. In this sense, it is very much

---

[140] John Muir, 'Mountain Thoughts', in *John of the Mountains: The Unpublished Journals of John Muir*, Ed. Linnie Marsh Wolfe (Boston: Houghton Mifflin Co., 1938), 92.

akin to the Celtic conception of the Otherworld, of the Gaelic 'Mag Mell', poetically depicted, for example, in Manannán Mac Lir's oceanic plain of endless flowers.

The Flower World is also a world of supernal Beauty, of divine virtue, a kind of 'heavenly kingdom', which exists within and all around us—rather like Jesus' Kingdom of Heaven, especially as portrayed in The Gospel of Thomas. Like the Kingdom, the Flower World only exists for human beings *in potentia*, and therefore requires our participation to be co-actualized with Spirit as a living reality in this manifest, visible realm of ordinary perception. That means cleansing of the senses, spiritual purgation and interior trans-formation, to have the eyes and ears that see and hear Otherworld truths; it means being awakened to visionary capacity; and it also means hands-on practices in the realm of manifest things.

Thus, in Ancestral Puebloan conception, all sacred work is necessarily the work of Beauty: to bring through from the Otherworld to this world—and with that Otherworld to continuously co-create—an expression of the cosmic will toward Beauty in diverse and endless becoming. In other words, through our participation with the spirit world, this earthly, sensorily per-ceptible Middle World realm can be transformed into an idyllic or heavenly place and state of being.

The Flower World is traditionally symbolized with brightly colored blossoms, birds, and insects, flowing waters, and rain clouds—in general, by the lush and endlessly diverse Beauty, novelty, and abundance of Nature. According to ancient Pueblo wisdom, the Flower World must be actively expressed in human society, ideally made manifest by the whole community, each through their various gifts and vocations—though this sacred work of co-actualization with Spirit falls especially within the domain of the sacral functionaries: poet-seers, shamans, priests, musicians, artists, and artisans. Co-actualization with the spiritual dimensions of Nature occurs through conscious human agency, intentional human alignment with the values of Life, which are the values of Beauty. In particular, this is achieved by focus-ing in daily life on expressions of the beautiful, the good, and the true, which implies a fully integrated religious sensibility: sacred music, visual art, beautiful natural decor, prayer and ritual, communal ceremony, storytelling, and fellowship: surrounding oneself with and making oneself an open channel for the Beauty of Spirit, of the living Earth, and of the Otherworld.

Life in The Flower World means life in harmony with the flow of Nature: a life of abundance that arises from being aligned with Her central *telos*. Life in the Flower World means Otherworld-connected, Mag Mell life, Kingdom of Heaven life. The Flower World is mythically, spiritually, and conceptually aligned with these other ancient visions: with the Thomasine Kingdom of Heaven, and the Gaelic Mag Mell. One might say, in fact, that these are different cultural lenses on the same felt and intuited reality: a reality not only hoped for, but in a meaningful sense already extant, glimpsed by the poet-seers, prophets, visionaries, and shamanic functionaries of every culture from time immemorial.

Jesus said: If your leaders say to you, 'Look, the Flower World is in heaven,' then the birds of heaven will precede you. If they say to you, 'It is in the sea,' then the fish of the sea will precede you. But rather, the Flower World is within you, and it is all around you.[141]

European-descended cultures and their religious practices have become astoundingly stagnant, bereft of imagination, disconnected from real Beauty. We have too long dreamt our mechanistic dreams of greed and domination, and so have lost touch with Spirit.

What does it mean that the Christian mythos as we presently have it gives no meaningful place to plants and animals, to rainclouds and birds, to rivers and seas? What does it mean that the Christian mythos is so completely and myopically anthropocentric? What does it mean that it is almost utterly devoid of the elegance and mystery of Nature, that it bypasses these crucial elements of the Creation in order to play out an isolated narrative of, by, and for the narrow alleyways of human intellective speculation? A strange and troubling fate, to be sure.

---

[141] Adapted from *The Gospel of Thomas*, Saying 3a. Translation by the author.

Any story that's aimed at (and arises from) the human spirit should smell of the wet forest floor, taste of the briny ocean breeze, touch the listening ear with hushed sounds of archaic mysteries too old to place in time. If it wishes to hit its mark, realistically it cannot be devoid of such elements because the soul incarnate in this world, and in this human form, cannot be separated from the memory and experience of the living Earth. These natural gifts have always constituted a kind of primordial, symbolic language of the soul. And the moment we exile them, we're out to sea with no sail and no oars.

The windows of our churches are cluttered with human images: overpopulated, like the world itself, with *homo sapiēns* (or, perhaps more appropriately, *homo insipiēns*)—and a disproportionately male rendition of the human form at that. It is precisely the disenfranchised, human-afflicted world of natural landscape, of non-human life, that our windows keep at bay by an oversaturated and overdesigned veil of neurotic self-obsession. They aim to cast an illusion of some fantastical heavenly abode, wherein the toxic, misguided agendas of an anthropocentric dominator culture rule eternal. The perfect image, in fact, of hell.

The windows we need in our sanctuaries are those that flow with and are transparent to the supernal iconography of Nature. The anthropocentric veils will need to be shattered to let in the light of truth: the light of the Mother, which will illumine the darkened corners of our blindness and our destructive self-obsession.

The whole Hebraic mythos, along with the Christian one that emerged from it, by way of conscious omission reduces the natural world outside the human person to a collection of more or less incidental factors. We could say that in these particular worldviews the human person replaces the original *axis mundi*, the World Tree, and is elevated to such a high status that the rest of Creation effectively disappears from focus. This in fact leaves the human being in a benighted state of existential isolation—: the inevitable result of carrying stories that fear, mistrust, and reject the non-human worlds of

Nature. This orientation makes the Judaeo-Christian mythic structures—along with other related traditions of Near Eastern origin—a strange aberration in the history of human cultures.

The rejection of Nature and Her omission from our religious narratives is, from the standpoint of any ancient indigenous worldview, a catastrophic betrayal of truth and morality. Its disastrous consequences are visible all around us in contemporary, industrialized societies. This betrayal of our deepest roots as human creatures has greatly aided the production of the mechanistic, consumerist, and reductionist cultural norms we are now enslaved to in the West. It has resigned the rest of Creation to the fate of being mere resource for human consumption and commodification.

Thus, Thomas Berry proclaimed that our task in contemporary Western societies is 'to convert religion to the world rather than convert the world to religion.'[142]

We should seriously reflect on the conceptual differences between a worldview that imagines a sacred tree at the center of its cosmos, and one that imagines a human being—and in particular a *male* human being—as the cosmic axis. Consider a religious milieu that continuously reifies its own myopic assumptions through representational isolation, excluding the whole of Nature beyond the human realm, as compared to one that embraces animals and plants and landscapes as allies, religious icons, and fellow members of the great spiritual family of Life. We should be mindful of the radically different cultures that inevitably arise from these respective frameworks of myth and religiosity.

Our myths, our stories, shape our reality, whether or not we're consciously aware of that fact. We therefore have an immense responsibility to curate those myths carefully and intelligently. This is not only good psycho-spiritual hygiene, but it is an ethical responsibility by virtue of the potent effect our stories have not just on the well-being of our human children, but on that of the entire planet and all its inhabitants.

---

[142]   Thomas Berry, *The Sacred Universe* (New York: Columbia University Press, 2009), 12.

The common stories we've adopted, however strangely or contrivedly, in the Western world have come to us in a state of severe and inherent deficiency, because they are stories that fear and reject Nature, that fear and reject the feminine divine. They are stories that elevate the human being falsely above the rest of Creation, but simultaneously (and ironically) propose that the human person is inherently flawed or evil; stories that misguidedly suggest the destiny of the human soul lies somehow beyond the rest of Nature. These stories were propagated by Western power structures to neatly bolster and perpetuate their dominator agendas, political habits, and hierarchies, to fulfill the sadistic fantasies of self-loathing eunuchs masquerading as mystics, intellectuals, and theologians. They have led us nowhere but to psychological, spiritual, moral, and ecologic ruin. The Western purchase of these destructive ideologies has also meant the loss of real Western cultural traditions—: the near total destruction of indigenous European cultures, leaving contemporary, European-descended Westerners culturally orphaned and essentially bereft of real values, gullibly convinced by the hollow promises of materialism.

The whole variegated umbrella of Judaeo-Christian myth, as adopted and perpetuated throughout the Western world, must therefore be thoroughly reshaped, or otherwise discarded. In order to be worthy of preservation, it will have to be altered so completely as to actually reflect the truths and values of Nature. Particularly in its normative combination with other equally atrocious ideas like philosophical materialism, this framework of religious thought is toxic to the world, an affront to Life and to the Source of Life. It is, by its delusional anthropocentrism and its rejection of the inherent goodness, sanctity, and ensoulment of Creation, contributing to the destruction of life on this planet, rather than to its flourishing and atonement.

As Berry notes: 'The only real society is the complete society of the natural world. We are awkward at this manner of thinking because our religious as well as our humanist traditions carry a certain antagonism toward the natural world. But now the refusal of human beings to become intimate members of the community of the earth is leading to their own destruction.'[143]

This antagonism toward the natural world lies at the very foundation of Judaeo-Christian mythic structures: it begins in Genesis, where an animal is said to be responsible for the 'fall', error, and transposed guilt of human beings; where human beings are instructed to dominate, rule, or 'subdue' the Earth; and the human person is expelled from the proverbial Garden, the Edenic state of oneness with the rest of Nature, cut off from the Tree of Life (an icon of the *axis mundi*, the World Tree) and the fruit of the Tree of Knowledge which grants all wisdom (perhaps representative of an entheogenic plant Sacrament). All these motifs are symbolic of humanity's radical, artificial, and, according to the conceits of the myth, *God-induced* severance from the dynamic, living communion of Nature. This severance from the life giving essence of the World Tree, and the deliberate expunging of animals and plants from the mythic imagination, means that the human being is not only left in existential isolation, but neurotically elevated in his own arrogance to a place of cosmic centrality: a truly disastrous, aberrant, and delusional event in the mythic and imaginal landscape.

If viewed through an indigenous lens, and reimagined with the right theological nuance, the Cross as Tree on which the embodiment of Wisdom, the Christ-Shaman, is symbolically hanged to model the perennial path of initiatory transformation in communion with the Three Worlds, might redeem the mythic errancy of the Genesis narrative and its subsequent Judaeo-Christian readings and extrapolations (e.g., Augustine's criminally vile theology of original sin). This would require, however, a radical shift of the entire mythic base of Western Christianity.

An American Indian proverb (of unknown tribal origin) says, 'Regard the Sky as your Father, the Earth as your Mother, and all that lives as your Brother and Sister.' Wisdom we also once knew. And a stark contrast to Abrahamic myth—and Christian theology more specifically—which we in

---

[143] Thomas Berry, 'Our Children: Their Future' in *The Little Magazine, Vol. 1, No. 10* (Rochester, VT: Bear & Co.), 8.

the West have foolishly adopted, and by which we've effectively sold ourselves down the river of spiritual depravation, isolation, and delusion. Myth, textual inheritance, and ideology that colonize the soul and render it unfree. Until we arise from this nightmare of dominator, patriarchal agendas, grotesque materialism, reductionistic thought, and egoic isolationism—a nightmare foisted onto us by the political-religious structures of control—there will be no discernible way forward for us into a way of life that honors the truth and authenticity of our individuality as human persons, as well as our profound interbeing within the whole of Creation.

⸙

A real cultural change in our time therefore firstly demands a totalizing transformation of perception: a radical shift from a way of being in which we treat Nature as a hostile force to be dominated and subdued, and the natural world around us a collection of potential resources to be exploited for our idiotic material ends, to a way of being in which we experience Nature as a loving Mother, and see ourselves as continuously immersed in an ensouled Creation populated by non-human entities that desire to be in harmony and cooperative relationship with us. But alongside this foundational shift in how we exist in the world as incarnate beings, our stories and myths must fundamentally change. In fact, one cannot be truly and sustainably changed without the other. Our narratives must change to reflect the truths and values of the indigenous witness, the truths of Nature, the truths of the inherent sanctity of Life, our deepest human heritage. And this means co-actualizing a kind of mythopoetic revolution.

The roots of that mythopoetic revolution must necessarily be experiential; mere ideation will never yield the needful fruits. Reclaimed ancestral lifeways, folk traditions, models of community, languages, stories and storytelling practices, spiritual disciplines, rituals, Sacraments, and robustly framed initiatory ordeals—: only through such re-membering can we find our way back to a path of sanity and wholeness.

'If the Christian story—or any story—wishes to be the great story, it must literally include everything', John Moriarty once said.[144] If that Christian story is to be preserved at all (and I make no assumption that it should be), then some definitive re-writing—or rather, *re-speaking*—long overdue at any rate, will be requisite. Not a casual or haphazard re-speaking, but a re-speaking from poetic and prophetic depth: from direct experience of the sacred, of the wisdom that always waits in the unseen dimensions of the wondrously ensouled tapestry of Nature—: a re-speaking from the ancient Well of Wisdom. For 'to know, and to continue to know, that any well we dip our buckets into is Nectan's Well is why we are a people.'[145]

In the realm of myth and archetype, the now dominant images of divinity as commonly expressed through inherited Abrahamic religious models are not only insufficient for the task of theological description and sense-making, but also largely unintuitive—and, with reference to our present ecologic crisis, immoral. For the heart and mind that abides in intimate connection with the living Land, with the wilds of Earth, the courses of rivers, mountains, and white-waved seas, it seems nearly impossible to find a resonant thread of poetic truth and spiritual applicability in those hostile and barren images—images which, granted, emerged from a culture forced to navigate a hostile and barren desert landscape. (A strange marriage, indeed, for the European psyche with its vastly different experiences and symbol-sets.) Were one to be very generous with regard to this matter, one might say that somewhere, at some point in time, the warring, authoritarian, xenophobic, patriarchal, and life negating images that come with the Abrahamic faiths served a useful end—a proposition I personally reject—but even if we accepted this point, as Heinrich Heine once said of religion more broadly, 'When daylight comes…it is foolish to use blind old men as guides'.

---

[144] John Moriarty, 'Seeking to Walk Beautifully on the Earth', from *One Evening in Eden* (Dublin: The Lilliput Press, 2007).

[145] John Moriarty, *Dreamtime* (Dublin: The Lilliput Press, 1994), 18.

By contrast to the standard Abrahamic images of divinity, the wide host of ancient European icons and expressions of holiness—for example, the wild and unbounded, threefold goddess of Earth and Sovereignty so central to ancient Gaelic religion, or the three Norns and knowledge-seeking Odin (self-sacrificed to uncover the secret language of Nature), so central to ancestral Norse religion—seem to offer not only greater resonance with the European psyche, but also much deeper insight into the truths of Creation. For one on the path of rewilding and indigenous reclamation, the rather tired and dry, imbalanced images of wrathful judge, regal lord alighted on the high throne of heaven, or distant clockmaker, are simply devoid of any helpful content.

I would go so far as to contend that when deeply examined in the light of Nature, and in the light of legitimate, direct spiritual experience of sufficient depth as to be transformative, these Abrahamic images of divinity in fact become self-evidently absurd. When the individual soul is immersed in the natural light of Creation, it becomes increasingly difficult to discern how one could encounter such imagery and feel that it reflects anything at all about the ways of Life, of Nature, or how it could ever function adequately as a set of explanatory archetypes for the sacred.

I think it can be fairly stated that the imperial, legalistic, and warring god in question is merely a god of dominator politics, of territorial feud, of weaponry and conquest—in other words, of the presumptive endeavors of imbalanced and egoically obsessed men. But that god cannot be the god of Creation, of the wildness of Nature, of birth and death, of trees and birds and rivers and cattle, of oceans and cairns and windswept fields. The Source of these things, the 'God of Life', can only be an incomprehensibly wild and ineffable Mystery. She is best described, I think, with the ancient symbols found in a number of Indo-European cultures—and most prominently in Celtic cultures—that show three dimensions of form in one cohesive whole, endlessly following one another in motion; or, perhaps, somewhat differently and of course by imperfect analogy, through comparison with the internal dynamics of the threefold Earth Mother in Gaelic conception: always embracing of Her children, but also untamable; sometimes a Trickster, a

Hag or Witch in the mythic wood; a wild Mare, an ancient Initiatrix. Or perhaps even as a Crone of fierce winter weather, surging seas, and darkened forests, who is also shaper of the Land and guardian of animals, whose age cannot be fathomed and whose truest nature, so mysterious as to strike the ordinary human heart with terror, can never be unveiled.

For hearts that wish to draw nearer to that Mystery, particularly in the context of reclaimed indigenous Western traditions, the Gaelic cultural milieu is rich with language, story, and symbol much more befitting the task of poetically and mythically framing divine movements, natures, and origins, insofar as such an endeavor is possible. (Indeed, all the old European traditions are rich with such language and imagery.) The normative Christian inheritance is, by contrast, tragically bereft of adequate mythic and metaphoric tools. While a few blessed mystics here and there have managed to break free of that prison of unbefitting language and imagery, their impact on the institutional structures of the Church, even collectively, has never been anywhere near potent enough to shift the course of the dominator hierarchy, to dam up its force, or to reshape its core assumptions, aims, or methods. The selective, revisionist approach now popular among liberal Christian, wherein such minor saintly witnesses are strongly highlighted while the rest of the whole atrocious structure that surrounds them is ignored or excused, is totally insufficient to the needful task of clarity, courage, reason, and spiritual liberation.

Since that core structure, and the language and imagery that has long been used to bolster and to justify it, has causally given way, over centuries of accretion and misdirection, to the totalizing socio-cultural and ecologic crisis in which we are now imbedded, the issue of divine imagery and related mythic narrative is something which cannot be dismissed as a marginal curiosity or relegated to the narrow halls of academics. Rather, it has become for us a matter of life and death. Our collective cultural and religious errors will have to be remedied—at the very foundation—thoroughly and quickly, if we wish to save ourselves from the sinking ship of Western endeavor. The ship itself—that is, the totality of the inherited assumptions and cultural habits of dominant Western culture—cannot be salvaged, and nor should it be. But our souls can be saved if we're willing to close the book on centuries of colonialism (interior and otherwise), reductionism, materialism, fundamentalism, and the whole lot of Western Judaeo-Christian idiocies, and to seek instead the waters of Life from the grandmothers of our forgotten indigenous inheritance, from their source at the Otherworld Well.

❦

I am aware that many of the foregoing words will be difficult for some to hear, and impossible for others. In some will cry out the aching question: Is there nothing redemptive to be salvaged from the centuries-long endeavor of Western Christendom? I will not deny that there are profound threads of light and witness woven into that dreadful milieu. There are, in fact, even a few precious strands of Creation-affirming theology, to be found among the saints of Catholic Christian tradition. Could we not, for instance, take refuge in the life and witness of a Hildegard of Bingen or a Francis of Assisi? I suggest that only if the whole foundation were rebuilt around such figures could any significant portion of normative, institutional Christianity be salvaged.

Beginning with Lynn White's writing on ecology and Western religion in the late 1960's, it's been popular for progressive Christians to imagine Francis of Assisi—that 'second Christ', as he's often been called by Roman Catholics—as a potentially salvific image with the power to somehow correct the wrong turns of Christian religion. Many have suggested that Francis beheld clearly the luminous theophany of the divine in all Creation, and is therefore a suitable model for Christian reform. Though I do think it is fair to say that Francis likely does—or did at one time—represent another possible path for the Church, my reservations already given on this manner of selective revision still stand. The fact is that, even if we agreed such a path were there in potential, it was a path not taken by the Church or by any notable number of its adherents—even Franciscans (perhaps *especially* Franciscans). We must be careful of romanticizing, and be mindful of the fact that Francis himself—along with his disciples—practiced a great deal of destructive medieval piety and superstition, and held many cultural assumptions (including, perhaps ironically, crypto-Gnostic ones), which would at all costs have to be thoroughly rejected by any sane, clear, and intelligent person of our own time and place.

Symbolically, there is a certain radiant and persistent depth in the stories of this holy Brother, who knew himself as sibling to Sun, Moon, Stars, animals, plants, and the sacred Earth herself—but alone that image and its attendant narratives simply don't draw enough water.

As I sit here writing, among the shelves in a Benedictine library in the Eastern Rocky Mountains, my eyes suddenly fall on a statue of St. Francis, carved by hand long ago from some gloriously twisted and cracked old limb of Piñon Pine or Cedar. Its beauty for a moment shakes me.

I think of Tacitus writing hyperbolically of the druidic holy groves in Gaul, reporting that they were populated with 'stark, gloomy, and crude images carved in wood'. This stark, crude icon of Francis seems it would be right at home in an ancient Nemeton, a sacred grove of the druids. Perhaps beside an image of holy Brìghde, 'crudely' carved with spring's solar cross and flame. Perhaps near an image of the antlered Cernunnos, seated in cross-legged position, surrounded by Stag and Boar, Crow and Serpent. An image of the Adder, the sacred Serpent, keeper of the hidden knowledge of plants, who brought the clear sight of wisdom to Eve in the Garden, who instructed wise Glaukos in the ways of overcoming death, who gifted the three miraculous leaves of resurrection to a young and unsuspecting prince, who brought to the Upper Amazon the sacred knowledge of Yagé.

The saint stands with arms outstretched in welcome to all Creation, as if greeting every living thing; as if proclaiming his own distant version of the Lakota phrase, 'All my relations'. His eyes are closed in meditation. His habit is simple, and so at one with the tree from which it was rendered it seems to disappear back into its source, into the very bosom of Nature.

Yes, perhaps there is yet some hope of redemption in the Christian inheritance—a starting point, at least. Provided, of course, that this witness of Francis—not of the Francis of history, but of *this* particular Francis, crudely carved in twisted Pine or Cedar, eyes closed, arms outstretched to the Mother, arms outstretched in praise of all Creation—were actually lived, actually followed to its furthest theological and experiential conclusion, and all ideology and practice within the institution that defied or undermined that purpose were expelled. Alas, the odds seem hopelessly remote. The force of the long-imbedded, woeful current seems far too strong to accept a Gospel so true as that, to accept the depth and authenticity of the sacred grove.

Notwithstanding, this diminutive little man, this simple and unlikely sage—or at least the image of him which now descends so gently on my disaffected heart—seems truly Son to the Mother of Life: a faithful Son set adrift in a world of treacherous betrayal.

At his feet the birds gather, to hear the song he sings of their eternal Mother. Soul to soul, in thanks and praise toward one indefinable Mystery.

⟡

The choice regarding what myths and what theologies we'll live by is ours and ours alone. To say that the choice belonged instead to one specific and culturally constituted conception of divinity in a long distant time, in a hopelessly foreign landscape, is both an evasion and an excuse. It is also an absurdity.

What kinds of myths can we—or the Earth on which we dwell—now afford to entertain? The question cries out from stream and forest and vale; it cries out to us in hope of a sensible, serious, and committed answer.

⟡

Reclaiming the sanctity of Creation requires a decisive rejection of the many generations of total disenfranchisement the natural world has experienced at the hand of the dominant Western ethos, along with every instance and mode of language, every ideology that could still be used to fuel that immoral marginalization. It requires the telling of a new and ancient story of and for the whole of Nature—a story that must be our own, whoever we are and from whatever landscapes our people descend: a story with fingers in the rich, dark loam: a story with deep-Earth roots.

To continue telling ourselves and our children renditions of a sinister Judaeo-Christian narrative of creation, fall, and 'redemption' seems an idea too heavily weighed down with danger. In fact, it feels deeply and horrifically irresponsible. If these narratives are to be told in Western societies at all, they can only be rightly told as myths of marginal and tertiary interest: stories far lesser in importance to our own indigenous stories. Telling them orally, and not from text, might well address the problem, were it done with true art and commitment, for then the stories would organically reshape themselves in service of the needs of our time, and, ideally, the needs of Nature. Either way, we will have to learn to hold again, and to carry and speak with beauty, our own native stories of Creation, of divinity, of wisdom—stories of the sacred that have never disenfranchised Nature, but offered an understanding of human life as inextricably interdependent with Her and all Her creatures.

Beholding the desperate need of all living creatures and stirring up our courage of heart and soul, might we move now once more toward the ancient, life giving stories native to our ancestral soils? Might we move our hearts a bit nearer to the root-branch embrace of their potent, imagistic revelations, a bit nearer to their mysterious waters? Not just in the occasional telling, but perpetually, as integral to our everyday experience. Let us sink our spines and knees and souls far down into the living Earth from which those sacred tales once rose, and ourselves be radiantly retold by them.

'Would the Mother of us all receive me again as one of her children? Would the winds with wandering voices be, as before, the evangelists of her love?'[146]

---

[146] A. E., *The Candle of Vision: Inner Worlds of the Imagination* (Dorset: Prism Press, 1990), 1.

What happens when we lose the soul of things; when we lose hold of the Mystery and eschew the magical; when we throw in our lot with a trivial, surface-oriented vision of life? We die. Because our very life has its origins in the unseen, in the hidden depths of reality, in the Mystery. That is the Well from which our souls must drink. And if we cut ourselves off from that Well, we sever the core of our own roots, and inevitably wither and perish. Of course, we *are* withering and perishing—as individuals, as a culture, as a society.

Depression, anxiety, fear, confusion, loss of meaning, the paradox of hyper-connected isolation, unsustainable consumption, shameless materialism, lack of real depth or direction in life: these are the hallmarks of American culture now in the twenty-first century. And the most common solution on offer? A deadening of the senses, by whatever means available.

If our souls are imprisoned sparks of light, destined for heaven or hell, and the manifest world in which we now live is either antagonistic or irrelevant—or, if we and the rest of the world constitute a mere collection of inert material forms with no underlying essence—then how does any of this really matter in the long run? Both of these positions, painted here in very broad strokes, represent the two most dominant worldviews of our time. They are, I contend, not only hollow but sinister and false, incapable of helping us toward the shaping of a better world.

In spite of what's often assumed in both of these basic worldviews (e.g., in scientism and philosophical materialism, or in the world-denying cult of popular Christianity), our sensory experiences aren't corrupt or incidental; nor are the experiences of our interior landscapes, of dream or ecstasis. To the contrary, in fact, those experiences allow us to come intimately near to what is sacred—assuming we possess the needful tools, the needful clarity of vision.

Once the Irish hero, Cormac, set off on a journey, sailing West over the ocean, determined to find the Otherworldly Isles. On the way he encountered the Sea god, Manannán, who offered to guide him on his quest.

After many long days on the wide, surging Sea, with Manannán offering the way-pointing signs, Cormac finally arrived in the Land of the Ever-Young. He disembarked from his coracle and set his feet on the Otherworldly shore. The first thing he noticed on that mysterious Isle was a radiant pool, emerging from a great spring; and flowing out from the Well were five streams, each of which seemed to flow on forever, disappearing beyond the horizon.

Cormac asked Manannán the meaning of this Well with five streams flowing from it. And Manannán replied, 'The five streams are the senses. Everyone drinks from the five streams. But only mystics, poets, and those with the gift of vision drink from the five streams as well as their source: from the Well of Wisdom itself.'

These five sensory streams, tributaries of possible experience, symbolically flow from the source of all wisdom, the Otherworld Well of Segais. And to drink from the source means, in one valence, to have followed the five steams back to their Otherworldly genesis. But the senses continually carry depth and wisdom forth to our hearts. At some typically untapped level of consciousness, they are there all the time in fullness of ripe expression, waiting for us to behold and receive their fruits. Tom Cowan notes: 'the information that comes through our senses comes with otherworldly wisdom from the Land of Truth. Physical reality is not just physical, it is spiritual; it comes from a place of truth, wisdom, and sacred knowledge.'[147] Just as myth is never *merely* myth, so matter is never merely matter, and the sensory capacity of the human person is likewise never reducible to 'mere' physicality. The phenomenological power and potential of our sensory capacities, both physical and spiritual, constitute in themselves a kind of Sacrament. And the widening of the aperture of that potential can open us to the principal *Mysterium*, which is that of Nature; which is Beauty,

---

[147] Tom Cowan, *Yearning for the Wind: Celtic Reflections on Nature and the Soul* (Novato, CA: New World Library, 2003), 16

truth, marked by the sojourn out of time. To alter our state of consciousness—through contemplation, meditation, or dreamwork; through the long
pilgrim's journey; through ritual engagement with the hidden fruits of the
'Tree of Knowledge'—: such is the ancient and long attested methodology.

And what, then, if we deliberately dull these portals of wisdom—if, in
attempting to cope with our state of crisis, our reality of spiritual enslavement, we choose those 'medicines' that negate the true potential of our being,
our humanness? If it is through those apertures that the possibility of real
communion with the sacred is opened to us, then denying them, ignoring
them, or willfully obfuscating their power cannot be less than blatant sin.

What a far cry this view of the human person from those of the villainous
cults that have come to dominate Western consciousness—a consciousness
that allows itself to be daily debased by inane, grotesque, and trivial distractions. Distractions that destroy true clarity of sight, negate all broadening of
consciousness, erode the will to set out on the true quest of humanness, the
initiatory quest of transformation. A treachery and a scandal.

The place from which to set forth on that journey—that journey in
search of the Well and its holy Matron; in search of the clear, salvific vision;
in search of Manannán's honeyed plains; of the Flower World of Endless
Youth; the Otherworld source of Wisdom and Beauty—is not some distant
or exotic landscape. When at last the mind is free to set out, the place of
initial embarkment will be found beneath the middle of your ribcage, and
slightly to the left. Then the true source of Life and wisdom, whether sought
by Earth or Sea, will await you at the Tree of Worlds, where sits the hooded
man, sharing sacred food with the animal souls who guard with him the
ways of Otherworldly passage. The cup he holds is the Grail, an icon and a
chalice for the sophic waters of the Well that never runs dry.

The true quest always begins from that interior shore, with the eyes and
ears of the heart: eyes and ears that are open, cleansed, freed from the bur-
dens of unhelpful conditioning, and thus prepared to encounter the Grail,
to know and to trust the right questions to ask in response. In wholeheart-
edly traversing the wild landscapes within us and within the natural world
we inhabit—traversing them in spirit, with courage and with all the senses

engaged, with reverence and a commitment to real reciprocity, with intent to encounter unseen dimensions, to undergo trial and be transformed—we are brought into conscious interbeing and dynamic relationality with the revelatory, theophanic gifts of Nature, with the living Earth, our Mother, and with the great family of souls, in this world and the Other.

The deepest answers we seek are five short steps from our front door. Maybe fewer. That's the true Gospel, the 'Good News' about us and our facticity as incarnate souls here on the living Earth. With courage to reclaim our authenticity, our ancestral inheritance, our wildness, our humanity and depth of soul, the Wasteland can be healed, atoned. Then the spirits of the sacred springs, the maidens of the holy wells raped and left for dead by the false kings and prophets of a dominator agenda, might bestow on us the pardon and the blessing that we don't deserve, and reveal in us once more a Flower World Kingdom, a Kingdom of Logres, a wild and sovereign Land redeemed: a heaven in which we will then finally see we always already dwell.

The Woman of the Sea

One Midsummer's night, a young man was walking by the Sea. He had been all day in the fields, and was come down to the shore to cool himself after a hard day's labor. The Moon was full and the wind was blowing fresh off the water.

As he came to the shore he saw the sand shining white in the moonlight, and on it the Sea People were dancing. He had never before glimpsed them, for in most times they show themselves as Seals. But on this night, because it was Midsummer and a Full Moon, they were dancing for joy. Here and there he saw dark patches where they had flung down their Seal skins, though they themselves were clear as the Moon itself, and they cast no shadow.

He crept a little nearer to see them more closely, and his own shadow went before him. Of a sudden, one of the Sea People happened to dance upon it, and immediately the dance was broken. They looked about and saw him, and with a cry they fled to their Seal skins and dove into the waves.

But one of the Sea Folk ran back and forth on the sands, wringing her hands as if she had lost something. The young man looked about and saw before him, covered by his own shadow, a patch of darkness. It was a Seal's skin. Quickly he threw it behind a rock and watched to see what the Sea Woman would do.

She ran down to the edge of the Sea with her feet in the foam and cried out to her people to wait for her, but they had already gone too far to hear.

The moonlight shone on her, and the young man thought she was the love-liest creature he had ever seen. Then she began to weep softly to herself and the sound of it was so heartbreaking that soon the young man could bear it no longer. He stood up and went down to her.

'What have you lost, dear Woman of the Sea?' he asked her. She turned at the sound of his voice and looked at him, terrified. For a moment he thought she was going to dive into the Sea, but she came a step nearer and held out her hands to him.

'Sir', she said, 'Please return it to me and I and my people will give you the treasures of the Sea.' Her voice was like the waves singing in a shell.

'I would rather have you than all the treasures of the Sea', said the young man. And although she hid her face in her hands and fell again to crying, more hopeless than before, he was not moved.

'It's my wife you shall be', he said. 'Come with me now to the priest, and we'll go home to our own house, and it's yourself shall be mistress of all I have. It's warm you'll be in the long winter nights, sitting at your own hearthstone and the peat burning red, instead of swimming in the cold green Sea.'

She tried to tell him of the bottom of the Sea where there comes neither snow nor darkness of night and the waves are as warm as a river in summer, but he would not listen. Then he threw his cloak around her and lifted her in his arms and they were married in the priest's house.

He brought her home to his little thatched cottage and into the kitchen with its earthen floor, and set her down before the hearth in the red glow of the peat. She cried out when she saw the fire, for she thought it was a strange crimson jewel.

'Have you anything as bonny as that in the Sea?' he asked her, kneeling down beside her. 'No', she replied, so faintly that he could scarcely hear her. 'I know not what there is in the Sea', he said, 'but there is nothing on Land as bonny as you.' For the first time she ceased her crying and sat looking into the heart of the fire. It was the first thing that made her forget, even for a moment, the Sea which was her home.

All the days she was in the young man's house she never lost the wonder of the fire, and it was the first thing she brought her children to see when they were born. For she had three children in the fourteen years she lived with him. She was as good a wife as any man could hope for, and she baked fine bread and spun the wool for the fleece of his Shetland Sheep.

He never mentioned the Seal's skin to her, nor she to him, and he thought she was content, for he loved her dearly, and she was happy with her children. Once, when he was ploughing on the headland above the bay, he looked down and saw her standing on the rocks and crying in a mournful voice to a great Seal in the water. He said nothing to her when he came home, for he thought it no wonder that she would be lonely for the sight of her own people. As for the Seal's skin, he had hidden it well.

There came a September evening when she was busy in the house, and the children playing hide-and-seek among the stacks in the gloaming. Suddenly she heard them shouting and went out to them. 'What have you found?' she asked. The children came running to her. 'It looks like a big Cat', they said, 'but it is softer than a Cat. Look!' She looked and saw there, hidden under last year's hay, her old Seal skin.

She gazed at it, and for a long time she stood still. It was warm dusk and the air was amber with the afterglow of sunset. The children had run away again, and their voices among the stacks sounded like the voices of birds. The Hens were on the roost, and now and then one of them clucked in its sleep. The air was full of little friendly noises from the sleepy talk of the Swallows who were nested beneath the thatch. The door was open and the warm smell of baking bread flowed out to meet her.

She turned to go in, but just then a small breath of wind rustled over the stacks and she stopped dead again. It brought a sound she had heard so long that she never seemed to hear it at all. It was the Sea whispering down on the sand. Far out on the rocks the great waves broke, and close in over the sand the little waves rolled and went racing back.

She took up the Seal's skin and went swiftly down the path that led to the shore. The children saw her and cried to her to wait for them, but she did not hear them. She was just out of sight when their father came in from the byre and they ran to tell him. 'Which road did she take?' said he. 'The low road to the Sea', they answered, but already he was running down to the shore. The children tried to follow him, but their voices died away behind him, so fast did he run.

As he ran across the hard sands, he saw his wife dive into the Ocean, to join the great Seal who was waiting for her. He gave a loud cry to stop her. For a moment she rested on the surface of the Sea, and she cried with her voice that was like the waves singing in a shell, 'Fare ye well, my dear, and all good befall you, for you were a good man to me.'

Then she dove down to the hidden places that lie at the bottom of the Sea.

For a long time her husband watched for her to come back to him and the children—but she came no more.[148]

---

[148] Adapted from the version recorded by Helen Waddell in *The Princess Splendour and Other Stories* (London: Prentice Hall Press, 1969), published also in *Folk-Tales of the British Isles*, ed. Kevin Crossley-Holland (London: Faber and Faber, 1986).

A Light in the Darkness:
Redemptive Story and the
Call to Transformation

T*he light shines in the darkness, and the darkness did not overcome it.*[149]

I wonder if the person who first penned those words in the Gospel of John was aware of how deep rooted and universal their meaning was, how they reflected a perennial motif probably as old as story itself.

For a while now I've been gradually awakening to the fact that what really interests people,—what most people really want to hear—is a good story. Not theology, not poetics or poetic speech, not folkloristics, not ancient history, not mysticism—not even literary theory (I know—I'm aghast at that, too!). All these things are personal passions, and integral parts of my own vocation, but the fact is that they don't afford a lot of traction with most folks, and don't hold their attention for very long—probably because people generally feel such endeavors aren't relatable to their most immediate needs and concerns. I certainly don't fault anyone for that.

Whatever the historical, socio-cultural, and/or evolutionary reasons might be, the reality is that we're deeply wired for story in a way we're not

---

[149] John 1:5 (NRSV).

wired for other endeavors of the mind. Story is somehow a uniquely innate part of our humanness—like a primal language we instinctively know and respond to. 'Narration is as much a part of human nature as breath and the circulation of the blood', wrote A. S. Byatt.[150]

And a really good story is one that has something salvific to say, one that draws us in by reflecting our own personal journeys, our human struggles. It shows us how the meager, the oppressed, and the unlikely can conquer all odds and come out on top. It inspires us to feel that we too can overcome the challenges of environment and personal limitation and discover the light of real transformation: the Solstice light, the Christmas light, light of the incarnate Sun: the fire that always remains burning beneath the heavy shroud of despair.

The significance of a great story is that it not only tells us something about ourselves, but, more importantly, invites us into a deeper way of life, a transformed way of being in the world. And a story is ultimately of little value if we don't accept that invitation.

Writing expert Lisa Cron says, 'A story is how what happens affects someone who is trying to achieve what turns out to be a difficult goal, and how he or she changes as a result.'[151] That's what draws us in; that's where the deep relevance blossoms.

The motif of the undying light—reflected, for example, in the Christian tradition of the Incarnation, remembered and celebrated especially during the festal days of Christmas—has an incredibly transformative power if we open ourselves to the deepest truths it conveys. Chief among them: that the light—in Christian tradition, Christ the Divine Word and Wisdom of God—must be born *in each of us*. Then—and only then—does the story really come alive.

I would argue that our ability to enter into the story, not just imaginally but as participants in a lived, real-world expression that leads to our

---

[150] A. S. Byatt, *On Histories and Stories: Selected Essays* (Cambridge, MA: Harvard University Press, 2002), 166.

[151] Lisa Cron, *Wired for Story* (Berkeley: Ten Speed Press, 2012), 11.

own transformation, is the proving ground of a story's depth and utility. It's also the proving ground of our own spiritual depth and acuity, our spiritual maturity—and sadly we're living in probably the most spiritually immature era the world has ever known, because the bulk of adult human beings, especially in the West, are in essence uninitiated children: they have never undergone the ancient, perennial process of being formed into spiritual adults, with knowledge of their own deepest nature and vocation, their role in society, their connection to the Ancestors and the world of spirit.

It's on that proving ground of participation where we either accept the invitation to action or deny it, either become a meaningful part of the story or remain mere spectators. It's there the hope we long for and find within the story either ignites us to fruitful transformation, or becomes just another form of entertainment.

And, in spite of popular assumption, deep story is not about entertainment—or diversion. Not remotely. In the words of Mircea Eliade, 'If it represents an amusement or an escape, it does so only for the banalized consciousness, and particularly for that of modern man.'[152] This is because the modern human person is generally one who has been disconnected from his or her true origins, from the sacred Land, from the old ancestral stories and the spiritual technologies they preserve, from a worldview that grasps the holism or interconnection of all things—which is to say, one who is uninitiated.

If we look closely, we find that most of the symbolism found in religious stories and myths, whatever their cultural origin, is in some way related to one foundational pursuit: our deeply human need to find hope in the face of adversity, to be transformed *by* that adversity, and on the other side to meet once more the warmth and illumination of the life giving Sun, when it seems the dark cold of winter has forever taken hold. All of this flows into what Eliade called the *exemplary initiation scenario*, a perennial, archaic process of spiritual initiation or awakening, the basic model of which is

---

[152] Mircea Eliade, *Myth and Reality* (San Francisco: Harper & Row Publishers, Inc., 1963), 202.

preserved in many ancient myths and folktales—for example, in many European fairytales.

The fact that this process is so universal tells me that Wisdom has been speaking to us for a very long time. She's been speaking to us in every human culture, every spiritual tradition, from the very beginning. To me that seems only logical. Though too often in the Abrahamic faiths this fact is overlooked.

I'd like to share an indigenous story from the Northwestern lands of North America. It's a story of Divine Wisdom at work in the world; it's a story of the birth of a holy child who brings salvation to all people—though it's not a Christian story. It's a story of Raven, one of my dearest Otherworld friends. May the Ancestors of those whose cultures first received this tale bless me now to offer it here.

Once upon a time, long, long ago, the world was in darkness. When the sky above the Earth was clear, a little light from the stars shone through, but when it was cloudy there was only the pitch-black of night.

Raven was troubled by this. He saw that this was a problem for all creatures.

Now, he knew that the light was being held by a selfish old chief in the heavens, in the world above, and he decided to do something about it. So he flew high up until he reached the opening in the heavens and entered there the Upper World.

He came to the old chief's lodge, and just as he approached, he saw the chief's daughter going out to a nearby stream to fetch water. So Raven transformed himself into a tiny leaf of Cedar, and floated on the water. And when the chief's daughter went to draw water from the stream, she drew up the Cedar leaf and, not seeing it, drank it down.

Shortly after this, the young woman became pregnant, and though they knew not how, the chief and his wife were happy, and the chief prepared a special place in the lodge for his new grandchild.

Nine months later the baby was born—a boy—and they received him with great joy. What they didn't know was that the boy was Raven in disguise. The chief and his wife cared for the boy lovingly, but it seemed the child was often very unhappy; for he would cry continually. They realized after a time that he was crying for a box with two other boxes inside it; this was the box in which the chief kept the light hidden away. He kept it on a high shelf on the wall, wrapped in skins.

The chief adored his grandson so much, and thought, 'What harm could it be to let him play a little with the box?' And as the boy would not stop crying for it, he took the box down off the wall and gave it to him, placing it by the fireside where he could play with it.

Now, as soon as the boy put his hands to the box, he quickly opened the first to uncover the second, and the second to uncover the third, and opening the third box he took out the radiant ball of light. Immediately he transformed himself back into the form of a Raven and flew off with the light in his beak.

The chief was in a rage at having thusly been tricked, and he tried to enlist all his warriors and all the hosts of the Upper World to help him pursue Raven to take back the light. But it was too late, for it was but moments till Raven was through the veil and back in this Middle World, and he released the light into the sky. And that light became the Sun, and the world was then no longer in darkness.

The old chief looked down and saw for the first time how beautiful the world was, and he saw for the first time his daughter's face illumined, and saw that she was more beautiful than he ever imagined, and he could not long remain angry, for his mind and his eyes had been illumined, too, and his heart was transformed.

❦

A salvific tale of the finding and restoration of light, of the birth of the redeeming light in this world, reminding us of the one thing our hearts and souls most long for.

The theme of the restoration of light is found in nearly all mythic traditions. In the West we're perhaps most familiar with it in the form of the Christmas story, though it's to some degree been buried there under many other layers of accrued Christian symbolism.

In recent years it's become fashionable to state that all such solar or celestial mythic symbolism is reducible to early cultures' awed observance of heavenly movements. Underlying this is the tacit assumption that such things demonstrate the 'falsity' of mythic systems or else render them merely material in origin. But environmental observations and metaphysical ones are by no means mutually exclusive, and nor does one in any way disprove or trivialize the other; it's only the 'banalized consciousness' of mechanistic thinking which assumes they must.

Such an overly simplistic view robs our ancient Ancestors of the credit they deserve for deep, nuanced, metaphorical and poetic thought; and it also shuts down our possibilities for foundational transformation here and now, both individual and collective. To close down the symbolic and reduce it to mechanistic physical phenomena seems to me a foolish and overly linear approach: yet another telling expression of materialistic reductionism, which we desperately need to grow out of. To be sure, such growth would be one of many resultant gifts of the transition from spiritual adolescence to spiritual adulthood.

Perhaps what makes the Christmas story, or any expression of the same basic motif, so powerful and enduring is precisely that it reflects a much more ancient and universal narrative structure. In other words, its roots have always been there. Whatever the earliest expressions of that theme, they may well have arisen from a deep recognition that what was observed in the outer world reflected similar processes in the deep interior of human consciousness, and such profoundly beautiful symmetry—taken as evidence of the true glory and mystery of the cosmos—certainly deserves to be celebrated, relived again and again in story and ritual. We might call that mode of devotion an organic unfolding of *wisdom*. Perhaps Divine Wisdom herself has been telling this story in our hearts and minds from the dawn of human language. That, I think, is a wondrous possibility.

At Newgrange,—the passage tomb built more than five thousand years ago in the Boyne River Valley of Ireland—on the morning of the Winter Solstice, just a few days before Christmas, the Sun shines directly through a portal above the doorway, illuminating the interior chamber with a shaft of radiant light and reminding us that the flame of life ever endures: even in death, even in the deepest dark of Winter.

Somewhere in mythic time, in the early eons of Creation, Raven the great trickster is born as a little child and rescues the light of the Sun from a selfish old chief, hanging it in the heavens so we're no longer bound to a life lived in darkness.

At Bethlehem, under the incessant strains of oppression, God's Holy Wisdom becomes incarnate in the form of a tiny child: a ray of light, of hope breaking into a benighted world: the birth of the Son, also symbolically the return of the Sun at Midwinter. And so the altars in our churches look expectantly toward the East.

One motif, expressed in a variety of forms over many thousands of years, inviting us to actualize in ourselves and in our societies the principles of light: of nourishment, growth, transformation, of cultures that celebrate, support, and align with the values of Nature, of Life. But culturally, spiritually, ecologically, we live now in a world more benighted than that of our ancient Ancestors. We still need desperately—perhaps now more than ever—the hope of the atoning light. We still long to huddle together against the frightful cold, at the hearthfire of spirit, of *communitas*, and hear a great, redemptive story. And by that redemptive firelight, the life giving Sun is born again, even if only for a moment's time—: it's born again in us.

One of the things that inhibits this revelatory process in us is that we seem to have lost the ability to truly hear and embody deep story, in our conscious minds and hearts, in our rituals, in our self-conception, in our way of being in the world. Perhaps it's our continuous immersion in environments of endless distraction; perhaps it's our digital devices; perhaps it's the centuries we've spent losing our oral traditions and instead becoming dependent on text; perhaps it's our loss of the art of deep listening. Likely it's all of the above.

I wonder: Could hearing once more a story of the undefeated light, in whatever form it's come to us—once more in the right glint of flame, together in the bonds of community—: could it rekindle in us that lost and precious art? Could it stir our hearts to transformative action? Could it awaken in our genetic memory the impulse to seek the old ways of initiation, that we might truly be changed? Maybe if we sat together as we used to, as a village community, round the warming glow of hearth and kettle, and heard it as our Ancestors heard it in times of old. Then maybe—just maybe…

That's my enduring hope. It may be a fool's hope; but these ancient stories tell us that a fool's hope wins in the end. And somehow in my bones I know it to be true. 'For the wisdom of this world is foolishness to God….[and] God chose what is foolish in the world to shame the wise; God chose what is weak in the world to shame the strong; God chose what is low and despised in the world, things that are not, to reduce to nothing things that are.'[153]

The lowly, the foolish, the unexpected—the trickster, the prophet, the wildman, the witch in the wood, the shaman: figures who have always carried the light of Wisdom in this world, and have been persecuted or marginalized for doing so.

We already hold the stories our hearts most long for—the stories those souls have passed on to us. We've held them from the start. The question is: What will we do with them? How will we respond to the invitation they continually extend to us each time we hear them or hear a derivative motif?

It's true enough that 'unwittingly, and indeed believing that he is merely amusing himself or escaping, the man of the modern societies still benefits from the imaginary initiation supplied by tales.'[154] But in the end it's not enough to feel inspired for a moment or two, or to unconsciously benefit from our inherited ancient stories without a meaningful and *participatory*

---

[153] 1 Cor. 3:19; 1: 27-28 (NRSV).

[154] Mircea Eliade, *Myth and Reality* (San Francisco: Harper & Row Publishers, Inc., 1963), 202.

connection to them; we have to take up our own part in the narrative. As the Gospels would have it, we have to take up our cross and follow the way of transformation—to be the hero or heroine who endures the necessary trials, and then helps restore the life giving light to a darkened world. In European folktale, as in most indigenous traditions, that needful process is preserved in the form of the initiatory journey, which takes us from spiritual adolescence to spiritual adulthood.

Not only the tales we still sometimes tell, but *the whole of Creation* models that way for us. It's in the very Sun, in the cycle of seasons, woven into the fabric of Life. Will we finally wake up and follow it?

May the birth of the light—and the stories that remind us of it—truly come alive in us, kindle in us the fire of Spirit that can save this world from the darkness of materialism, disconnection, triviality, and degradation. May the light shine always. May it shine especially in your hearts and souls, dear readers: in your seeing and in your hearing, in your speech and in your every step on this sacred, living Earth. May the darkness never overcome it.

The Raven's Bread

Where is the Life we have lost in living? / Where is the wisdom we have lost in knowledge? / Where is the knowledge we have lost in information?

—*T. S. Eliot*

Three Ravens dance around me in an empty drugstore parking lot. Ravens have always seemed to visit me in threes. On this particular afternoon in the high mountain desert of the American Southwest, they stir and caw and whirl about, beaks open wide, as if in re-creation of some deeply archaic ritual.

I stop off into an art store to buy some pens. As I leave the shop, walking down a barren alleyway, the Ravens fly overhead, now noticeably calmer, with an air of quiet celebration. I notice that one of them carries in his mouth a large, circular piece of bread.

The Raven's Bread. I laugh to myself as they gather on a high rooftop above to enjoy their feast, giving no indication that they might be willing to share.[155]

---

[155] The Raven's Bread is an ancient folkloric motif: a cross-cultural image signifying the divine, sacramental food which the gods (or God) provide for the spiritual

There's a state of being that's free from the neurotic structures of conditioned ideation: an internal state of freedom from the ravages of dogma, from myopic self-obsession, from the noise of ceaseless thought, and the illusion that one's personhood is synonymous with those reflexive mental constructs. A state free even of 'God', of all preconceived and inherited notions of what is sacred. This is the state of conscious awareness in which all real transformation begins. To enter into felt communion with the Mystery, ideology must first be cast aside.

As human beings, our knowledge is provisional at best. The admission of this fact, had we the courage and humility to truly embrace it, would itself completely transform the landscape of dominant Western culture. So many of our cultural pathologies are rooted, either directly or indirectly, in the egoic hubris that the cosmos at large is essentially knowable, transparent to the faculties of reason. Scientism and the 'revealed' Abrahamic religions both assert this in their own ways. Either the fullness of truth is revealed in some magical text, or will yet be revealed in the all-potent light of rational deduction. With respect to this travesty of human self-reflection, the aim of *kenosis*, of 'self-emptying', strongly recommends itself.

Once a university professor in Japan went to see Nan-in, a great Zen master. The master served tea. He poured the professor's cup until it was full, but then kept pouring until tea was running out all over the table. The professor was dumbfounded watching this, and finally after a few moments shouted in frustration, 'It is overfull! The cup will hold no more!' Nan-in finally stopped pouring and said, 'Like this cup, you are full of your own

---

seeker while in the depths of fasting and transformative ordeal in the wilderness. In iconography, the Raven's Bread is usually depicted as circular, like a Eucharistic host or the circular cap of a mushroom. I contend that, like the Salmon of Wisdom or the sacred brew of *Awen* in the Cauldron of Cerridwen, it is an image simultaneously concealing and revealing the 'heavenly bread' in its most archaic sense: as the veiled entheogenic Sacrament of Eurasian shamanistic traditions.

ideas, opinions, and speculations. How can I show you Zen unless you first empty your cup?'[156]

The sacred gifts of inspiration and wisdom, the 'fire in the head', cannot come without a total shift of perception, and that shift cannot take place without deep interior stillness, which is firstly manifest as freedom from the prison of ideology and assumption.

A return to the unbounded truth in Nature presents itself as the prime prescription.

Alan Watts, once an Anglican priest, reflects on the differences between Far Eastern and Western religious sensibilities:

'It is fascinating for us to consider that [Far Eastern works of sacred art] are not just what we would call landscape paintings, because they are also icons, a kind of religious or philosophical painting. In the West, when we think of iconographic or religious paintings, we are accustomed to pictures of divine human figures and of angels and saints. When the mind of the Far East expresses its religious feeling, however, it finds appropriate imagery in the objects of nature.... The contrast in these two forms of expression arises as a result of the sensation that the human being is not someone who stands apart from nature and looks at it from the outside, but instead is an integral part of it. Instead of dominating nature, human beings fit right into it and feel perfectly at home.... The problem is that we have been brought up in a religious and philosophical tradition that, to a great extent, has taught us to mistrust the nature that surrounds us, and to mistrust ourselves as well.'[157]

No matter how we might be inclined to frame it, the reality is that our recent forebears have handed on to us an untenable situation: a world which now stands at a critical and quite possibly lethal precipice, beyond the 'tipping point' of a planetary ecologic crisis. By unquestionably accepting the 'sins of the fathers' as right and good, by accepting the mistrusting philosophical and religious thinking Watts refers to, and rationalizing or

---

[156] Adapted from 'A Cup of Tea' in *Zen Flesh, Zen Bones* (Tokyo: Tuttle Publishing, 1985), 19.

[157] Alan Watts, *What is Tao?* (Novato, CA: New World Library, 2000), 24-25.

ignoring its repressive, puritanical evils, happily receiving and handing on the Faustian deal of Judaeo-Christian anthropocentrism, they have left us out to dry. Those same recent forebears ignorantly invested their faith, their lives, their precious time, their ill-equipped hearts and minds in the hollow promise of salvation through dominion and material wealth, through the expedient destruction of the natural world. And thusly they handed on to us, their children and grandchildren, a way of certain death: a lifestyle and religious sensibility that are patently unsustainable, spiritually ineffectual, devoid of real magic, of Beauty, of Life.

❧

As Tolstoy famously asked in 1886, *What now is to be done* (or, *What, then, must we do*)? This is a question which begs to be asked with an immensely seriousness mind, with openness of heart, and with careful attention to history.

When the fathers are corrupt, one astutely seeks the help of the grand-fathers—or, better yet, the grandmothers. Wisdom asks us to reach back to a time before the 'Fall' of Western cultures, and there seek the values and guidance we need, the knowledge that can save us; to intelligently re-integrate those true human values, those values of Nature (without giving way to the pitfalls of anachronism or unquestioning traditionalism) into the way we live and move in the world.

Terence McKenna called this 'a return to archaic values'. We might also call it a return to good sense. To restore ourselves to real 'sensibility' means, as David Abram puts it, being rooted in a 'phenomenology that takes seriously our immediate sensory experience', which necessarily implies a 'wrecking' of the falsely contrived, conditioned ideologies of dominion, human exceptionalism, grotesque materialism, cancerous disconnection from the rest of Nature and from the consequences of our unnatural thought and practice—all of which have for centuries constituted the foundation of Western endeavor.[158]

Our calling now is with the long and difficult processes of de-conditioning and re-membrance, unlearning and return—: processes that require a culturally supported system of authentic initiation. They will further require the wisdom of the Ancestors, an orientation away from text, back to natural symbol and orality, back to sacred song—which is to say, to the sacred songs of Nature, of Her eternal dynamism and Beauty: songs that in truth still live in us, even though we have, at least in our conscious perception, distanced ourselves so thoroughly from their melodies.

The great story is never finished; its delicate weaving carries on without ceasing. It is, after all, an eternal story, in which the cosmic impulse toward Beauty and atonement is always operative, and, wherever suppressed, finds ways to subversively break through the proverbial concrete used to pave away its truths, its undying hopes, its radiance. Nature is the great Weaver, like the three Fates seated beneath the Tree of Worlds. But we, too, are called to be weavers, to participate in the unfolding of this grand and mysterious narrative, in a way that truly honors the whole cosmic family of souls.

And so our work goes on. The Earth Mother plants Her astounding, pregnant, and poetic seeds. She forever calls us back to awareness, back to wholeness, back to Her life giving breast.

The lost, hidden Sacrament of Celtic traditions—the Salmon of Wisdom, the Raven's Bread—resurfaces like Otter in an ancient Diver Myth. So long as she evades commodification—so long as she avoids the sinister hands of exploitation—a host of wondrous gifts could lie ahead.

Moriarty's poetic vision of the Otter spirit stepping into an old country church, carrying a fistful of soil and placing it on the altar, is an icon of the only hopeful and redemptive vision left for Western religion; indeed, for the

---

[158] David Abram, *The Spell of the Sensuous* (New York: Vintage Books/Random House, 1997), 48.

Western world at large—: an icon of ancestral reclamation, of re-member-ing. The rightful restitution of the truth and presence and values of Nature to the cold and desolate chambers of our empty churches. The rightful con-clusion to our prodigal wandering. Our homecoming to the house of the ancient Mother, to the ways of Beauty and the wisdom of the Old Ones. 'I sat there in what Heidegger has called the age of the world's night, and prayed that there would once again be ground that would ground us.'[159]

That is my prayer also. The return to ground, to soil, to roots, to spir-itual reciprocity with the living Earth, and with the great communion of souls. The return to ourselves: to what it really means to be alive in this puzzling form, to walk here conscious, self-aware, among the spirits of Land and Sky and Sea. Our return to wholeness. The Fox Spirit Woman at last courted back to our lonely hut.

The Logres road is long and hard. But as long as Life persists, the work of Beauty never ends—so hope never really dies, no matter how bleak things become.

In spite of our abuses, the stream flows ever onward.

We each have precious gifts to give this ailing world; our job is to discover those gifts, to faithfully and uncompromisingly actualize them with every ounce of strength and vitality we possess, in service of the cause of Life.

May our way be always a way of communion, of Beauty and atonement, of oneness with the living Earth, our Mother. May we learn once more to be sources of healing and blessing and truth to all living beings.

May we be as a radiant word among letters, gifted with courage, with a keen protection of heart. May we see with the eyes of Otherworldly vision, and walk the floral Plains of Honey. May the undying light of wisdom, which burns in the depths of Nectan's Well, and on the hearthstones of our ancient Ancestors, shine evermore in our hearts, in our minds, and in our souls.

---

[159] John Moriarty, *A Moriarty Reader: Preparing for Early Spring* (Dublin: The Lilliput Press, 2013), 224.

Gathering Mistletoe:
A Dialogical Epilogue

Humanity's last and highest leave-taking
is leaving God for God.

—*Eckhart of Hochheim*

T he following conversation took place in December 2019, in the Eastern Rocky Mountains of Colorado. Answers were given by Brendan Ellis Williams, with questions posed by Patrick Dobbins. The aim of this dialogue was to address some key questions related to the preceding text, and to establish for the reader some foundational premises that might give fuller context to statements and assumptions made in the primary body of the work.

Q: You speak a lot about the problems of contemporary Western cultures and societies, about us being disconnected from the rest of Nature, 'severed from our roots', and these are ideas that you've explored in a nuanced way here. But if you had to succinctly summarize the central problem, how would you describe it?

A: I think we could summarily say that in some sense it all comes down to story. What kinds of stories are we telling ourselves and one another—about us, about the planet, about Life itself—and are those stories life giving, oriented toward Beauty, reflective of the relational truth of inter-being, and therefore redemptive? Or are they world-denying, repressive, puritanical, materialistic, reductionistic, and therefore destructive to Life?

The bulk of what's generally called 'Western Civilization' has been built primarily on stories from the latter category. We've been living with those stories for centuries, and it's created a nightmare landscape of disconnection, isolation, and dissociation; it's created a dominant culture in which we continually tell ourselves that we're the masters of Nature, somehow set above the rest of Creation, and so we can and should exploit that Creation to our own benefit, with little regard for consequence. In my view, probably the most egregious expression of this ideology in the West has been the crypto-Gnostic puritanical Christianity that's so long sullied the water we swim in. That ideology asserts, in essence, that Nature outside the human person is neither ensouled nor sacred, and therefore dispensable, to be plundered and discarded as we see fit, with absolutely no ultimate consequence, in what Lynn White called 'a mood of indifference'; and that the human person is by nature inherently flawed, hopelessly broken from the start, and yet simultaneously the absolute center of the cosmos and the only creature that in the end really matters. Contemporary Evangelicalism is an especially neurotic, delusional, uncritical, and dangerous excretion of that basic worldview, which we see is very much active and still asserting cultural-political influence today. But this kind of world-negating ideology is also, somewhat ironically, the underlying foundation of secular rationalism and reductionistic materialism.

Corrosive stories—and particularly religious narratives spun by imbalanced and psychologically disturbed pseudo-theologians—have shaped the fabric of our worldview assumptions and therefore our cultures and societies. So the kinds of stories we tell ourselves is a matter of profound import, and we need to wake up and begin to account for that fact, so that we can be more conscious and more responsible in curating the narratives that might help birth a future we actually want to live in, rather than a nightmare we want to escape.

Q: You frequently use the phrase, 'conscious interbeing'. Could you summarize what you mean by that?

A: An old teacher of mine once said, 'If you observe clearly, you will see that everything in Nature is perfectly at ease with itself, perfectly at peace with its own being, with its own work in the world—everything except we human beings, who are never at ease, always restless.' Most beings in the natural world, so far as we can tell, live innately in that state of basic harmony and intuitive relationality—in a kind of 'vocational ease' wherein they can simply be what they are and do what they do, without second guessing themselves or their circumstances, without getting caught up in egoic machinations and agendas. We might therefore say that these non-human creatures live in a state of '*un*conscious interbeing', whereas we, on the other hand, with our particular mental faculties, our conditioning, our lifestyle, and our present worldview assumptions, must deliberately cultivate that state of perceived interbeing and harmony with the rest of the natural world, if we wish to experience it. It doesn't come naturally to us anymore.

It seems to me that one of the principal reasons for this is that in our stories and religions we've forgotten—or, in many cases, consciously rejected—the already always present reality of our interbeing with the rest of Nature. Obviously our capacity for rational inquiry and self-reflective thought make us different than other animals, and that introduces a host of complicating factors in itself, but we can choose the kinds of narratives that frame our perception and worldview, and therefore our actions. The destructive stories we've been telling ourselves have caused us to forget who we really are, how to be at ease in the world, and how to live in harmony with the rest of Creation. I'm of course not positing that the natural world without our restlessness and conflictual meddling is all peaceful enjoyment—there is angst and suffering that can't be avoided and is simply part of the fabric of incarnate life in this world—but what we've done in contemporary Western cultures is something that profoundly worsens our situation (and the situation of all other species on the planet) and brings no sense of interior balance or wholeness to our lives. We've managed somehow to convince ourselves that we're innately at odds with Nature, victims of our own inherent flaws and of the brokenness of all Creation. That position, of course, is profoundly ironic if one believes that an omniscient, all-loving, and perfect creator deity gave rise to all things. Moreover, it is alienating, crass, and immoral, and has wreaked as much havoc in our own troubled psyches as it has in the ecosystems we inhabit.

In essence, 'conscious interbeing' describes a state of awareness in which one directly experiences oneself to be in clear, totalizing, and undeniable relationship with all other beings—which requires being liberated from the conditioning of those corrosive narratives just mentioned. And I think that state of conscious interbeing is most fully experienced, and therefore best articulated, within the framework of an animistic worldview, in which all things in our perceptible reality are ensouled or at the most foundational level constituted by a real, distinct, and novel mode or expression of consciousness. To me, if we wish to preserve the dignity of human life, and of life as a whole on this planet, then that experience—and I stress 'experience' here, as opposed to mere ideation—has to be among our central aims, not just in our subjective spiritual pursuits, but in the greater project of human consciousness and development.

If we want to know what it means to be whole again, if we want to reverse the toxic ways of life we've created, if we want to find real peace, belonging, fulfillment, then we have to let go of all those backwards ideologies, those corrosive stories, which we've allowed ourselves to be relentlessly conditioned by. That's the first step. But it's a difficult and complicated project. Unfortunately, we don't just decide to let it go and magically wake up the next morning to find ourselves completely freed of it. What's required is real de-conditioning, and then re-conditioning to a more holistic and life giving way of thinking, perceiving, and being in the world. That can be summarized (again, in very broad terms) as radically changing the kinds of stories we hold and propagate.

Q: So what do we do to facilitate that de-conditioning and reconditioning?
A: It's a process that requires communal structure and support, as well as a fairly intrepid psychological orientation. To some extent, the process of shedding the old, toxic narratives is already underway—though perhaps not rapidly enough. But one of the great problems we face now, as I see it, is that we have nothing more desirable and more fitting at hand in the broader culture to replace those corrosive stories. So the first part is the shedding, the necessary grieving, the coming-to-terms. The second part, the reconditioning, is the formation in new and more life giving narratives, in a more healthful and resonant worldview, and in more naturally connected lifeways. Ideally, these two stages unfold simultaneously, so that the amount of time folks are left out in 'existential winter' is minimized. But that's not, unfortunately, how things are unfolding for most people right now. Folks are 'losing their religion,' so to speak, but receiving nothing of equivalent ideational weight—nothing of greater depth and quality—to replace it.

So we have to also do the necessary work to reclaim these deeper, more archaic, and more holistic cultural inheritances, and really embrace them so they once more take on an integrative and organic quality within our hearts and minds and communal settings—which means, in part, establishing legitimate and authentic socio-cultural structures to support them: in ideology, in discourse, in education, in ritual, in communal organization, in spiritual care and support, in artistic endeavor, in habit, and in daily practice. And it has to be a process of shared discovery.

Q: You critique some of the core Judaeo-Christian themes and narratives— or at least the normative Western use and understanding of them. It's been suggested that one of the chief problems with our adoption of Christianity in the West is that we are essentially still living in an Homeric paradigm, unconsciously reading Biblical narrative through that lens, which can never yield the intended efficacy of Biblical revelation. I'd be curious to hear what you think of that idea, and also if you feel the primary invitations of Biblical tradition—for example, to take the suffering that human error brings and channel it toward personal and communal transformation—are being lost or ignored by Westerners, and if that might be the primary reason that contemporary Christianity seems denuded of its transformative capacity.

A: Normative Christianity has been denuded of its transformative capacity because it's completely lost its potential as a legitimate Mystery Tradition: lost the dimension of metaphoric truth, lost the efficacy of its sacramental and initiatory processes, and forgotten the essence of its own mythology. It's become more a social club, a pastime, and a political platform than anything resembling a serious spiritual endeavor aimed at foundational change in the human person.

But what I've seen in looking closely at—and trying to embody—European myth and folktale (which includes the Hellenistic tradition, though that hasn't been my specific cultural focus), as well as Biblical narrative, is that the old European traditions in fact contain a more poignant and less convoluted rendering of the needful models for human transformation than do the Abrahamic ones. And, unlike the Biblical stories, the ancient European stories are generally not embedded in textual contexts of legalism and mass genocidal violence; nor do they carry the baggage of centuries of lethal political appropriation, absurd hermeneutics, and imagined infallibility. So I'd say that in actuality it's the hermeneutical approaches that are more native to Abrahamic thought that have gotten the West into trouble: it's the tendency to embed mythic narrative in a literal-historical context to prove its factual 'truth', while effectively ignoring symbolic truth, attendant to the notion that an omniscient God has spoken once for all in a set of immovable textual objects, that constitute the central problem. Apologists love to claim that it's precisely all this bizarre and aberrant confusion that proves the unique value or 'miraculousness' of the Judaeo-Christian witness, but to me it looks rather like the opposite: it's in fact these aberrations that have made Abrahamic religion such a dangerous—and, in many cases, outright poisonous—force in the world.

Granted, there was a period in Hellenistic culture where influential philosophers (often today called the Greek rationalists) responded skeptically to an apparently popular reading of Homer and Hesiod as 'history'. So the problem of historicization is not exclusive to Judaic thinking, but it seems to have come to us in the West largely attached to Biblical tradition. The European context as a whole, until the arrival of Christianity, was still steeped in myth, traditionally framed and understood—: in the Hellenistic Mystery Schools, in the tribal cultures of the Celts, the Norse, the Balts, the Sámi, et al.

Ironically, the Greek rationalist critique, while sound in its rejection of myth as literal history, also betrayed a total misunderstanding and devaluation of myth in its essence. And maybe this is where we see the first major showing of the errors of rationalism: in the emergence of a worldview that equates myth with mere 'fiction' and incorrectly imagines its aim as literal and historical. In some way the mythic imagination and its attendant ritual actions seem to be innate to the human person, and therefore to all traditional cultures. They repeat continuously in cyclical or spiral time. So the division between what we today call 'history' (apprehended rationally, in linear or 'mundane' time) and myth (apprehended non-rationally, in cyclical or 'sacral' time) is in fact incoherent. I suppose we could say that mythology and the study of history are in this sense like 'non-overlapping magisteria'.

It's worth noting, too, as Eliade and others have done, that it was primarily a moral critique of the symbolic portrayals of the gods in the old myths (which did not fit the mold of the new philosophical ethic) that gave way to the critique of myth itself, in favor of a more rationalistic outlook. And, again, that critique in itself fails to grasp the symbolic dimensionality and purpose of myth, and shows the fundamental unclarity of the argument. This division offers one angle on the psycho-cultural split in Western experience that's been referred to as the *mythos-logos* binary. We're left, then, with a rather convoluted milieu in later, Christianized Western thinking, where native myths have been 'disproved' as history (a category fundamentally foreign to their nature), while at the same time misunderstood and denuded of their true power and purpose, and Biblical narrative is accepted (or misapprehended) as history in a climate in which myth is no longer valued or effectively applied; the tangible text-object, with all its attendant superstitions and potential for control, supersedes the inherently more open and dynamic oral traditions.

You'll recall, I'm sure, that the Homeric texts were originally oral: lyric poetry, orally transmitted in chant by Greek poets—essentially the Hellenistic equivalent of the Bards of Celtic cultures. Things break down, lose their original nuance, dynamism, and purpose when they're concretized in text. I'll speak again here for the wisdom of my Celtic Ancestors, who deemed it right that nothing truly sacred from the ancient oral tradition should ever be thusly concretized, knowing the material would thereby be effectively killed, made vulnerable to endless abuses, misperceptions, misappropriations, and misuses.

In my assessment, the world-denying, anti-natural myths that Western cultures eventually took on—and the hermeneutic of literalism generally applied to them—came principally from the remote deserts of Palestine: poisonous memes that arose from Middle Eastern cultures and geographies, and came into Europe largely by way of the Roman Empire and its vestiges. And they came clinging to the structures and assumptions of the Judaeo-Christian literatures. Those memes were used as sharp instruments by a dominator empire to control its subjects—a violent game that still goes on to this day, though now often played in subtler ways. I'm reminded of a sign I once saw in Mexico, which read, 'They put us to sleep with the Bible, and when we woke up they had the Land and the wealth'. (*Nos dormicron con la Biblia, y cuando despertamos ellos tenian la Tierra y la riqueza.*) That saying speaks for any native culture where the colonialist, dominator agendas of the Church and its conveniently world-negating, anti-human ideologies—along with its greatest tool of manipulation: the imposition of infallible and divinely wrought texts, interpreted by and for those who stand in the position of power—have reigned. This very much includes European cultures. Indeed, the dominator powers have always aimed to take not only the Land and the wealth, but the language, the myth, the folklore, the customs, and the sovereignty—to replace the ways of Life with the ways of death; to replace the freedom in Nature with enslavement to a social, spiritual, and ideational tyranny.

Q: So you think putting all these ancient narratives into textual form and elevating the texts to some kind of exalted cultural status is really where the problem begins? In both the Hellenistic and the Abrahamic contexts?

A: Well, I wouldn't say it's necessarily where the problem begins, because you can have problematic elements that are endemic to mythic structures themselves, which could, at least theoretically, exist apart from the text—as evinced by Judaic and Gnostic cosmogonies, for example, which render Nature in its nonhuman realms incidental or evil: something to be exploited at will. But locking that kind of ideology into textual form is where the problem becomes intractable. I might put it this way: Without the textualizing process, it's very difficult to get religious fundamentalism, because mythic narratives are generally too dynamic in the oral mode to sustain it. The stories subtly change and evolve, depending on time, location or landscape, according to the needs of the age and the inclinations of the individual tellers. And anciently these stories were often told in an environment of ritual ambience and/or ritual action, intended to symbolically recreate the mythic unfoldment implied in the narrative. Those cultural factors, combined with the foundational mythic images they reinforce, situate the human psyche in a framework already primed for symbolic thinking—for example, 'I see (consciously or unconsciously) that by doing this ritual to invoke a certain dimension of the cultural mythos, to produce a certain change in me or in us as a community, I am symbolically participating in these stories that reveal perennial truths about Life and the human experience.'

By contrast, there's something about concretizing the stories in text, pinning them down to one location in time and form, making them 'indelible', that inclines the human psyche toward historicization, literalism, and, where dominator ideology breeds it, absolutism. And I should also say that I don't intend to reduce myth only to metaphor—and certainly not to 'mere' metaphor. As Campbell says: Mythology cannot be rationally grasped. Myth is inherently inscrutable to literal, mechanistic, and categorical modes of thought and discourse. It resists that sort of rational tidiness. I think Campbell once said something like, 'theology renders myth ridiculous, and literary criticism renders it simply a metaphor', and that's quite true. He was interested particularly in structural, biological, and bio-psychological explanations for the perennial nature and functionality of myth. I do agree that in some way image, myth, and the narrative impulse are part of the deep structures not only of human reality, but of Life itself.

There's another dimension implied here that's important to touch on, and that's the matter of mythically framed and reinforced transformational processes. Many of the old European stories show a characteristic focus on initiatory models, and therefore on the deep-rooted human idea that only through meaningful trial can we be fundamentally transformed. I see this in some of the Biblical narratives, too, of course; in particular, the symbolic core of the entire Christian mythos, the Christ story, is an expression of that much more ancient and perennial idea. But I actually see this core motif expressed in greater abundance in Western ancestral traditions; and I would argue that our denial of that reality, or our inability to see it, is part of a pathology that has for many centuries unconsciously negated and suppressed something hugely valuable in native (i.e., pre-Christian) Western cultures and religious expressions.

The self-sacrificial, initiatory model is actually found in nearly every indigenous culture, so far as I know. Mircea Eliade did some fantastic work on this topic. His principal study of initiation rites and concepts of self-sacrifice, *Rites and Symbols of Initiation,* provides a very thorough treatment of that material. I argue that it is primarily we in the Christianized West who have lost a real sense of that foundational life-model: less because we're 'Hellenized' and more because we're 'Judaeo-Christianized'—because we've rejected our own indigenous wisdoms. We adopted Christianity in a profoundly unhelpful way, as literal-historical truth and special revelation for the world for all time, when it would have been best received as a Mystery Cult, a symbolic framework to be applied metaphorically in one's journey of initiatory transformation. And, as a result of that mistaken adoption, we came to see our own roots as 'evil' or contrary to the Judaic God's agenda. And I don't think it's hard to see, just applying basic psychological principles, how damaging that kind of self-hatred and ancestral trauma would inevitably be. And indeed it has been.

Q: You suggest that folktale and traditional storytelling are critical in the journey to what you refer to as 'atonement' and 'restoration to wholeness'. Could you express in summary how and why that's the case? You've already mentioned how narrative in general—and myth, more specifically—is crucial to the religious endeavor, but how and why are folktale and oral forms of storytelling so central to the necessary journey of transformation?

A: Firstly, because we are narratively oriented creatures. Symbol—and narrative symbol in particular—has the power to frame, and to some degree determine, our worldview and perception. Human beings have, since the advent of language, always told stories to one another, in part to attempt to make sense symbolically of a world that can so often seem harsh and alienating. I think folktale, along with its symbol systems, represents one expression of what Alan Grossman called (referring to poetic speech) 'the language of necessity'. In other words, just as there are things in the expanse of human experience that can only be described or accessed with poetic language, there are also things that can only be described or accessed with the symbol, imagery, and structure of myth and folktale. The folk and mythic narrative both possess certain qualities in their structures, in their origins, and in how they unfold when told in traditional ways, that speak uniquely to our largely dormant spiritual imaginations. And we need to awaken that imaginal capacity if we want to move toward a way of seeing and being in the world that really honors its spiritual depth and diversity.

Folktale helps to reawaken in us the ancient ancestral knowing that the world is awake with spirit, that Nature is ensouled, that the world is much more mysterious than we're ordinarily inclined to think. And reclaiming or reawakening in us that worldview and experience is absolutely crucial for the individual and cultural transformation we must now undergo. The traditional telling in an oral setting, with its archaic ritual ambience, is like a supernal tool for kindling the imaginal capacity in the human heart and mind, which makes the hearer more vulnerable to the insights and impact of the worldview preserved in the tales and their motifs.

On some level, most of us intuitively know all this, and some of us feel the pull to reclaim our own depth of ancestral wisdom, so in the West, lacking common access to that wisdom, we have often appropriated the myths, folktales, and lifeways of other cultures, being hungry for that depth, trying unconsciously to scratch the archaic itch, yet so far removed from those resources in our own ancestral transmissions. We have colonized, abused, and in some cases outright destroyed so many non-Western streams of indigenous wisdom, which might contain the knowledge of how to live wholly and truly, to walk in Beauty on the Earth. It's time for us to re-member our own indigenous roots, and to reclaim those roots as our most sacred inheritance—and that process must necessarily include, in a place of centrality, our own ancient myths and folktales, whatever those happen to be.

Q: Given the radical nature of your ideas, it seems to be a somewhat confrontational—or at least controversial—stance you're in with relation to normative Western religion, though I don't feel totally clear about all the specific dimensions of Judaeo-Christian thought you deny, and which ones you affirm. I wonder if you could state here concisely some of the major Christian premises and religious norms you're rejecting. And I'm also curious where you think this mode of deconstructive discourse is headed, realistically—in terms of your work, but also in terms of the Western religious landscape, such as it is.

A: Sure, I can give at least a cursory enumeration here of some of the primary worldview premises from that milieu that I reject. And I'll also give some alternative views that I embrace in lieu of those Abrahamic norms—or rather, views I *reclaim*, since the reality as I see it is that most of the premises I would affirm as valuable and useful for the human quest have long been foolishly abandoned or rejected by Western religious institutions, and in many cases they were from the start mutually exclusive to Judaeo-Christian assumptions.

I think it's also important to mention here my underlying premises for rejecting these things. It's of course nothing new or novel to point out that normative Christian doctrine is rationally incoherent. In fact, in the face of this obvious embarrassment, certain Christian theologians throughout the centuries have claimed that it is precisely *because* Christianity's doctrines are self-evidently absurd that one should adopt them. Tertullian is probably the most famous of those voices, with his *Prorsus credibile est, quia ineptum est...certum est, quia impossibile* ('It is credible because it is unfitting...it is certain because it is impossible'), but there's also Justin Martyr's rather amazing statement, 'The word of truth is free and carries its own authority, disdaining to be subject to any skillful argument, or to endure the logical scrutiny of its hearers'. That sort of statement should be offensive to all free-thinking people, particularly when it's used to justify ideological systems of debasement and control—and when it arises from a system like orthodox Christianity that attempts to make literal, historical, or factual claims for mythic truths, and foolishly confuses or conflates those categories.

I want to point out here that this anti-rational approach is not in any way akin to embracing the *non*-rational mythic core of the Christian tradition. It's important to distinguish the irrational (as we understand that term colloquially) from the *trans*-rational. Had these theologians embraced the mythos of the tradition in its fullness, and chosen to emphasize that, instead of trying to forcibly contrive a literal-historical sense of that which is native to the realm of the mythic, then the results would have been very different. The dissonance comes with attempting to make something mythically true into a rationally comprehensible and historically cogent 'fact', when the reality is that these two modes of knowledge are mutually exclusive. So Christian theology backs itself into a corner intellectually, becomes frustrated, and then has effectively no choice but to (a) abandon its premises and give up the argument, or (b) make silly claims like those of Justin and Tertullian, in appeal to 'mystery': the great 'get out of jail free card' of Abrahamic theology. Had they simply accepted the mythic insights of the narratives in their natural form, and not engaged in the absurd charade of trying to historicize them; had they maintained Christianity as a Mystery Tradition; had they eschewed the Judaic inclinations toward textual obsession and imagined inerrancy, historical apocalypticism, and all the other ideological rubbish, then Christianity would have been much less problematic for the world, and much easier to defend. But argumentation over whether or not normative Christian doctrine—or any Abrahamic doctrine for that matter—is rationally coherent or demonstrable as factually and historically true seems to me moot at this juncture: what has already been made clearly evident needs no further conversation. So the basis of my critique doesn't really come from that direction.

Instead, I contend that the doctrines of normative Christianity—chained as they are to a literal-historical set of assumptions—are also metaphysically incoherent, and, perhaps especially where experiencers lack deep-rooted Christian conditioning, do not stand up to the phenomenology of legitimately deep, transformative religious experience. By the latter I mean to indicate such shattering and psychologically reorienting experiences as those engendered by, for example, truly committed, long-term, expansive, and ideologically neutral contemplative practice in solitude; prolonged wilderness fasting; or the sufficiently serious use of entheogenic Sacraments. In other words, radically altered states of perception, which might afford (and generally *do* afford) a glimpse behind the proverbial veil, through what Huxley called the cleansed 'doors of perception', into a more lucid plane of awareness. The assumptions of normative Christianity, in my observation and experience, simply don't hold up under the light of such occurrences. And I submit that these are crucial indicators—perhaps the most crucial indicators we have, because they are referent to the realm of immediate experience. So it's primarily from the metaphysical and phenomenological perspectives that I'll be speaking here. (I do think the moral cogency of widely represented Christian teaching is likewise a very important point for continuing critical discourse, and there are thankfully sound voices speaking now in that realm.)

To begin with, I reject all 'belief', per se—as an impulse or interior orientation, and as a personal or communal tool for organization and meaning-making.

I reject the notion that dogma, creed, and enforced ideology have any value whatsoever for the journey of human transformation—which is to say, for the authentically religious or spiritual life.

I reject the notion that the Judaic war god, *Yahweh*—a violent, Bronze Age tribal deity of the ancient Israelites, likely a patron deity of metallurgic arts, originally considered to be one among many gods—is actually the one and only true God and fashioner of the cosmos.

I reject the concept of a singular, omniscient, personal divinity who created the world and then saw fit to punish those souls born into it for the circumstances this god himself had created—a god who also determined, after two hundred thousand years or so of human history, that interventional salvation by way of blood sacrifice in the remote wasteland of a Palestinian desert was suddenly right, needful, and effectual.

I reject the corrosive, sadistic, and non-evidentiary doctrines of original sin, substitutionary or penal atonement, 'hell' as an afterlife state, and the possibility of eternal divine judgment (or an eternity confined to any one state or cosmic locality).

I reject the narrow and limiting doctrine of determinism, in all its forms.

I reject the hermeneutic of literalism in the reading of mythic text; and to the extent that such texts in themselves claim historical veracity, or an authority to demand literal obeisance to culturally constituted legalisms, I reject those texts, categorize them as having failed in the proper form and function of mythic expression, and therefore count them as unfit for serious reference or reflection.

I reject the concept that sacred text (of any cultural origin) is divinely authored, should be imbued with total authority, is inerrant, wholly good, free of human agency, or 'perfect', either as a measure of truth or as a communication of authentic divine will; and, similarly, I reject the indefensible notion that any textual object—including the collection of texts known commonly as 'The Bible'—holds in itself some form of absolute or compelling authority and should be considered immune from correction and revision.

I reject all Gnostic and crypto-Gnostic or world-denying ideological tendencies, which do not honor and privilege the sanctity of incarnate or material life, and do not make their core aim a perpetual increase of the freedom, peace, joy, and wholeness of all beings.

I reject the epistemologically naive and totalitarian tendencies of dominator religious institutions and their hierarchies, along with the claimed wisdom and authority of all such institutions, particularly as relates to their ability to adequately speak to the human pursuit of authentic spiritual depth and transformation.

Those are a few—and certainly not all—of the common premises I denounce and eschew within the context of Abrahamic religious thought and practice, or dominant religious thought in the West more broadly.

To perhaps balance this out, I'll also offer a few things I've decisively set out to reclaim in place of the corrosive worldview elements aforementioned:

I reclaim, as the only proper focus, goal, and organizing principle of religion in any form, an unyielding commitment to the pursuit of direct, personal experience—: experience of those beauties, insights, and depths of human beingness that are ordinarily hidden from our ill-conditioned perception; and I reclaim this in light of the need for a serious, devoted, and integrous cultivation of expansive altered states of consciousness.

I reclaim the primacy of the Ancestors.

I reclaim 'God' as the ineffable and impersonal but dynamic Ground of Being, symbolically expressed in the eternal movement of three primary qualities: Creation, Preservation, and Dissolution.

I reclaim a feminine vision, expression, and experience of the sacred.

I reclaim the ancient technologies of oral tradition, and affirm their unique value—in storytelling, in mythopoesy, in the handing on of sacred wisdom, in healing, and in sacral leadership—as appropriate instruments for guiding and supporting the life of the soul.

I reclaim the perennial, ancestral worldview and experience of animism, a knowing of the cosmos as immeasurably vast, inherently sacred, and ensouled: an endless landscape of eternal consciousnesses in pursuit of ever deeper and more novel forms of Beauty.

I reclaim a nuanced, deep-rooted, ancestral understanding and application of myth and metaphor in the process of spiritual transformation.

I reclaim the ancient—and, in the Christianized West, long forgotten—knowledge of efficacious Sacraments, along with the spiritual technologies required to honorably, safely, and meaningfully employ them.

I reclaim the perennial indigenous wisdom which knows the necessity for—and the way to adequately support—the ancient ritual technology of foundationally transformative initiation.

I reclaim the wisdom that direct, personal experience is ultimately the only adequate test and measure of metaphysical truth claims, checked against the ancient, shared framework of mystical witness, and particularly the archaic witness of shamanic exploration.

In terms of how I see the future of this mode of discourse, and of these ideas: As I've stated in the book, it seems to me that if we don't intelligently reclaim the kinds of archaic values and worldview components I just gave some examples of, then we'll simply continue unabated down a pathway of dissipation, and ultimately self-destruction. So those are the real stakes here, as I see them. Technology alone won't save us, and nor will the ideals of reason; we have to transform the very foundations of our worldviews, our mythologies, our narratives. And it is definitely possible to do so. Whether or not I think it's realistic to imagine this coming to practical fruition on any notable scale in the foreseeable future is another matter. I have to say I'm not optimistic. But I am hopeful, which is a very different thing.

You asked, too, where I think this might all be headed for me personally or for my work. Regardless of the reactions to what I'm offering, I see my chief mandate as the clear communication of these ideas and their attendant experiential dimensions—and perhaps the creation of an authentic communal framework to support those who feel called to seriously pursue their practical application. But I'm continuously mindful of the fact that none of this really belongs to me; it belongs to the Ancestors. My job at present is to share the knowledge, and, where relevant, my own subjective experience, and to offer the essential fruits of both as constituting one possible way forward through the thicket of our rather desperate planetary circumstances. And, in the meanwhile, to bring as much healing and spiritual nourishment as I possibly can to those in the contexts I inhabit.

Q: You mentioned 'the ideals of reason'. How would you respond to claims that rationality—which you challenge, at least in its most determined or self-assured forms—is in fact the answer to how we as a species move forward soundly and ethically into the future?

A: Reason is obviously crucial, as I've stated in the book; we have to embrace, cultivate, and utilize the tools of rationality to deconstruct or disassemble the frames of dominant culture and religion that have led us so desperately astray. In some instances I've perhaps overstated or deliberately exaggerated the case *against* reason in order to make a largely unexamined point, which is that reason alone is insufficient to guide the human person. This is because the human person is not merely a bundle of material components, or a disembodied set of rational mental faculties floating around in the world. The soul or element of consciousness that animates and is reified by the material form, along with our evolved self-reflective capacities, make us animals of meaning, animals of metaphor, animals of art, image, language, abstraction, narrative, myth, and poesy. These are absolutely fundamental to who and what we are. So if we reject or marginalize these dimensions of ourselves, as philosophical materialism, rationalism, and scientism have done in the West, then we are cutting ourselves off from at least half of the content and potential of what it is to be human. That's called, 'not playing with a full deck', and I see it as a kind of naivety.

In fact, it seems not only naive but also arrogant to imagine that our rational faculties alone will carry us forward, and, consequently, that our egoic minds are powerful enough in their scope and capacity to 'go it alone': we don't need the rest of Creation; we certainly don't need the 'primitive' wisdom of the Ancestors; we don't even need our own depth of humanness. It's an incredibly bifurcated and isolating worldview, and it's therefore in my estimation a disastrous starting point for trying to solve the problems of the world.

It's not as if our problems are merely technological—though many people like to think in this way: 'Once we make enough technological progress, we'll finally save the sinking ship.' To me that's a fallacy. It doesn't matter what we do rationally, technologically, or outwardly in the world in general if we're still being fueled by bankrupt and corrosive ideologies, whether consciously embraced by us as individuals or not. (These could be toxic religious ideologies, or, equally, reductionistic material ideologies.) Then we'll only repeat the same absurd tragedies over and over. And the reconditioning of ideology and worldview cannot be thoroughly done on the basis of reason alone; that simply won't cut it. The transformation must include dimensions of the unseen, the soul, the poetic, the creative, the symbolic; it must be totalizing and encompass the whole of the human person, not merely our rational faculties of mind; and it will have to bring us back into the great family of Being, with full, conscious awareness.

I sometimes think of this in terms of a kind of 'Tolstoyan wager'—a reference to Tolstoy's realization that reason in isolation leads to internal contradiction and despair, and, pursued to its fullest logical extent, most likely to suicide. So he essentially made the wager to seek meaning from those who seemed to actually possess it, rather than from those who had lost it. And he realized that it was the millions of 'common folk' who from ancient times had lived and labored with a seemingly natural knowledge and acceptance of what lies beyond the scope of our rational faculties, with a certain tranquil understanding of the natural dynamics of life and death, who were most likely to possess a real grasp on meaning and purpose. In a way, this is the same sort of faith commitment I made in going back to the ancient oral traditions and fragmentary literary survivals of the cultures of my ancient Ancestors. And, in so doing, I discovered that the old stories, songs, and poems carried a profound store of wisdom. That kind of wisdom is simply not to be found among reductionistic rationalists or materialists.

Having sought the light of deep insight in a number of formalized religious and philosophical contexts, I ultimately returned to the indigenous wisdom of the 'folk', of the Ancestors, and discovered that there seemed to be much more richness and illumination in their 'simple' tales, in their intimacy with root and soil, with the animal soul, with poetic symbol, metaphor, and ancient mysticism rooted in the living Earth. There was much more wisdom, value, and Beauty, I found, in the present moment of felt experience, in intimate relationship with the Land, the Ancestors, and the unseen dimensions of Nature. Where to place one's trust or where to stake one's claim of knowledge is a critical human question, and I've personally concluded that the ancient Ancestors and their wisdom simply hold the most weight, have the best track-record, and offer the most resonant counsel for us, particularly given the dire mistakes and challenges of our time.

As Tolstoy likewise discovered, if one wishes to live, one must invest one's faith in someone or something—and I say *faith* here in contradistinction to 'belief': two very different things, in my view. Faith is searching and dynamic, and has nothing to do with the acceptance of dogmas or unverified concepts; belief is static and confining, and essentially means placing your confidence in ideas for which you have no evidence. The human person has to make a wager of confidence in some particular source of knowledge. One could certainly place one's bet on a purely rationalistic source of knowledge (internal or otherwise), but that bet doesn't seem to return the most desirable results.

Q: You suggest that 'direct, personal experience' is the only way to move forward into lasting individual—and, by extension, communal—transformation, and that it's perhaps the only valid arbiter of truth. Could you offer up one or two examples of what 'direct experience' might look like in a revival of the ancient cultural practices you're advocating for?

A: I think all the most significant dimensions of a revival of ancient ancestral traditions would in fact be experiential by nature—and *immersively* experiential. For example, participation in traditional storytelling (particularly as a hearer thereof); a long, demanding process of legitimate initiation; a wilderness quest; communal ritual actualized in an authentic, nontrivial fashion. All of these things are oriented toward participants experiencing the transformative capacity of ancestral lifeways, imagery, and narrative, in a largely non-prescriptive way. In other words, they facilitate and anchor to the 'felt presence of immediate experience' (as Terence McKenna was fond of saying)—to a space of freedom in which their own direct experiences and discoveries are aided and supported to unfold—rather than to some sort of ideational construct, dogma, or agenda of control. This stands in pretty stark contrast to any model of culture and religion that's oriented toward texts or beliefs, and rooted in histories of domination, wherein the primary aim or expectation is the fervent adoption of a certain set of concepts and creeds. In itself, the adoption of ideas—or worse, beliefs—is ultimately trivial, often dangerous, and incapable of bringing foundational, life giving transformation. This is, of course, one of the chief mistakes or wrong aims of dominant Western religion. Hence, when Nietzsche proclaims, 'God is dead', my response is, 'At last! Perhaps now we can finally get back to the real depth of felt experience.'

Q: So felt experience, interior vision, imagination, mythic image, ritual, and oral story all hold special keys to unlock human potential, which rational thought and the realm of ideas do not possess?

A: Yes, exactly. I've personally never experienced a sudden, foundational shift or transformation in myself based solely on an idea—and certainly not on the hearing or repetition of any creed or dogma. And I've never seen that in anyone else, either—in spite of what many religious people wish or will or attempt to convince themselves of. The other side of that coin, however, is that deeply conditioned ideology, reinforced over long periods of time, can be determinative with relation to human life and action in an incredibly toxic way. So by itself ideation can't really bring us any foundational, life giving transformation, but through long-term conditioning it can pretty easily create destructive patterns of human behavior. Not to mention the fact that belief and dogma, held stringently enough, shut down our intuitive and subtle capacities for numinous experience, and serve to cut us off from the possibility of real, transmutative revelation—which is *direct* revelation, had through ecstatic and initiatory experience. This is why I continuously counsel people to throw out ideology and belief. They're not just worthless, they're actually quite corrosive. It's much better to approach the human journey of transformation, the true quest for the Grail, in a spirit of freedom, openness, and discovery, with a hunger for Beauty and depth of experience. In fact, you can't really embark on that journey in any other way. Like Gawain, who recklessly and without resorting to rationalization or falling back on prior conditioning agrees to engage in the dangerous quest that the spirit of Nature has offered: a quest that looks to the normative, uninitiated human world surrounding him like madness. But it is, in fact, the gateway to real initiation, to transmutation of self, to at-one-ment, to the Grail Castle, to the Waste Land healed and Logres renewed.

Clement of Alexandria once said, 'Those who are overly focused on words, and who devote their time to them, miss the point of the whole picture.' Ironic that this comes from a father of the Church, an institution which has built its whole ethos precisely on the supposed supremacy of the 'Word' (and the written word in particular), but Clement was part of that early Alexandrian milieu where there was still close proximity to the realms of Hellenistic philosophy and Mystery Tradition, and still therefore a good dose of wisdom and sanity. The term 'picture' at the end of that statement is very poignant, I think. Perhaps if we spent more time with one another and with the rest of the natural world in silence, just listening deeply, and with more exposure to life giving image rather than text, we'd be in a much better position to perceive clearly and to come upon a real sense of meaning and connection, to re-member who we really are and our rightful place in familial relationship with the rest of Nature.

Q: With all the resistances to normative Christian doctrine you've offered here, the question can't help but arise: Why operate within the context of the Church? Your previous answer about what you foresee on that path is duly noted, and I can see the prophetic dimension of your role in that context, but why become an Episcopal priest to begin with? What made you decide that was the right direction for you, given your particular religious and philosophical proclivities, which seem to stand pretty clearly at odds with most of the Church and what it represents?

A: The short answer to this is that my intention has always been to effectively subvert Christian norms, to do my own small part to reform Western religious thinking in general from the *inside*, rather than from the outside. The impact of the external critic has its place, and can be powerful, but in my personal experience it also leaves a lot of wreckage by failing to offer viable alternatives in place of the worldview one is dismantling. And the chances that 'insiders' will actually heed the voice of an outside critic are small. I vowed at one point in my younger life that I would no longer take the approach of the 'drive-by critic', and that, if I was going to deconstruct someone's framework of religious assumptions, I would always have a more meaningful and life giving alternative to offer in its stead. One of the gifts of being in a role of spiritual leadership within the Church is that I've been able to help people who are ready to disassemble these toxic assumptions and conditionings, while at the same time supporting them to pursue their own interior experience of the sacred, empowering and equipping them to discover and integrate something far more meaningful into their lives in place of all that Life-negating nonsense. That's an opportunity that can only come from being within the context of the Church. Had I pursued this particular dimension of my work as a complete outsider, there's no way it could have had the same impact, and there's no way I would have been able to play the kind of supportive role I wanted to play in guiding folks through that mode of transformation. So, in spite of the inevitable frustrations, it's been very beneficial.

You mention the so-called 'prophetic' role—in practice, that's nothing more than the vocation of one who is called to speak out against the ossified norms of the institution he or she inhabits. Which naturally makes one an alien within one's own environment. There has always been a discomfort for me in operating within the framework of the Church—and of Christianity more generally—but the tension has been fruitful, and the circumstances of that particular aspect of my vocation have provided a platform from which to do the subversive work of my particular kind of teaching and spiritual direction, as well as spiritual care-giving, which, again, would have otherwise not been possible. There are plenty of examples of folks who have made themselves 'anathema' in the institutional structures of Christian religiosity by speaking boldly and honestly about what they see as right and true, over and against the accepted norms of the institution—who have unintentionally rendered themselves *personae non grata* for calling out the problematical dynamics and unexamined errors or dysfunctions within the Church—and that's essentially the path I'm on, which is something I'm willing to accept as a necessary consequence of authentically living out the vocation to which I've been called.

Like so many things one is likely to encounter in life, involvement in the Church is a mixed bag of blessings and hardships. Given the generally expansive and non-dogmatic nature of the Episcopal Church in particular, my alliance with that institution has felt to some degree like the 'lesser of necessary evils'. That's not to say, of course, that the Episcopal Church is evil—though it certainly has its problems, and there is much work to be done if the Church (in any form or expression) wishes to become truly relevant to the world; which can only be done, I think, by aligning with the values of Life, rather than with corrosive, superstitious doctrines and a misplaced emphasis on texts and creeds. That being said, the Episcopal Church has, within the larger context of Catholic Christian traditions, acted somewhat like a macrocosmic expression of the 'prophetic' vocation you referenced a moment ago: a productively subversive seed that gradually reforms the soil-bed of the larger religious context in which it's situated.

Q: It seems that in what you've outlined as your foundational premises related to Christian doctrine—what you reject of it, and what you reclaim in its stead—there's virtually nothing left of normative Christianity. Do you feel there's something there in the formal, institutional structures of the Church that's actually viable for the future and worth preserving?

A: I can answer that simply by saying that the dominant memes of normative Western religious thinking, along with the institutions that have propagated them all these centuries, *must* be transformed—because they're not going to disappear. These ideas are in the substrate of conditioning that unconsciously affects even the most self-assured secular humanist among us. And though the institutional Church (inclusively speaking) is declining at an unbelievably rapid rate throughout the postindustrial Western world, it isn't going to disappear completely. Something will have to be done with the shadow and the footprint that remain. The time for determining what that looks like is now.

Q: What about the Episcopal doctrine that 'Scripture contains all things necessary for salvation'? It seems like that can't be compatible with your ethos. Is that an instance of something you think should be abolished, or somehow reframed? And do you think there's a danger in merely reinterpreting old (and perhaps destructive) language, or treating it metaphorically, rather than throwing it out and replacing it with something more beneficial?

A: I'm willing to say that *narratively* the New Testament specifically might contain most—though certainly not all—of what's needed for salvation (i.e., atonement), because it preserves renditions of the solar rebirth, self-sacrifice, and initiation motifs. So, properly received (i.e., through a mythic lens), it might point one toward a legitimately atoning interior process. But Grimm's Fairy Tales can more realistically be said to contain 'all things necessary for salvation'.

What the New Testament (indeed, the Bible as a whole) most significantly lacks is a meaningful pathway toward a state of conscious interbeing with the whole of Nature; it lacks (or refuses) the deep and needful memory of our oneness with the rest of Life outside the human framework. And ultimately there can be no true 'salvation' or redemption of the human person barring that re-membrance. With Christian text, one of the major problems is failing to understand it as mythology, and failing to understand what mythology is for, what its real power and its most beneficial functions actually are. It's the demythicizing accretions, along with the albatross of belief in the Bible as a magical text-object, that desperately need to be shed.

If we returned to oral storytelling as a regular practice in our religious and other cultural contexts, in lieu of idolizing and repeating bits of text over and over, then most of the problems with Scripture would be solved (in any of the Abrahamic traditions, all of which have the same problematical historicizing and literalizing tendencies), because we would organically—without even having to contrive it—let loose of much of the toxic freight we've been saddled with for centuries, having inherited this superstitious view of the Bible as a kind of magical and immutable object, sacred in itself because the words it contains are at some level transcendent of the realm of human affairs.

Regarding your second question: I think there can be danger in simply reinterpreting inherited language, particularly where that language is deeply engrained and deeply associated with toxic ideas, either straightforwardly or through interpretation. There has to be a dynamic, realtime discernment process surrounding all this. Sometimes we need to simply throw things out, and folks in the Church need to begin practicing the courage required to do that without superstitious fear and inhibition. Again, once the notion of false sanctity and magical 'divine origin' appended to both text and institutional dogma are shed, then the rest will begin to sort itself out organically, because most of us already know intuitively, or sense at some level, what's right and what's needed. It's the liberation of heart, mind, body, and soul from dominator ideologies that will catalyze the necessary transformations—or at least open the landscape to make them possible.

Q: Do you envision a future scenario in which the particular approach to religious pursuit you're outlining here might actually be made to merge harmoniously with whatever remains of the institutional Church?

A: I don't have much confidence that such radical restructuring and reconditioning is possible within the institutional framework as it presently stands. With regard to the older generations in the Church particularly, the percentage of folks who are actually willing and able to make those kinds of changes to their worldview and lifestyle is, I'm sorry to say, extremely small. To put it in a direct (and I hope not overly coarse) way: a lot of folks will have to die before any measurable institutional change is possible. I say this without a trace of callousness; it's simply the reality, so far as I can tell. And even another generation or two down the line, it seems likely that movements to redeem and preserve the spiritually valuable vestiges of Christianity will be largely non-centralized, and will take place outside the institutional remains.

When the structures of the Church break down from lack of resources, lack of adherents, and lack of leadership, as they most certainly will, there will probably be a lot of very small, locally led groups that take things in their own directions, and there won't be the kind of central authority there has traditionally been to monitor those developments. Some of what that decentralized landscape produces will probably horrify me (there will no doubt be propagation of the absolute worst of Judaeo-Christian speculation: apocalypticism, fundamentalism, and the like), but I suspect there will also be small groups of folks who set out to really understand and preserve the mystical and symbolic underpinnings of the Christian tradition. In a context like that, I could imagine groups of people who wanted to root those laudable pursuits in one or more streams of pre-Christian, indigenous cultural inheritance, as I've advocated for in the book, and that would be a very fruitful thing.

Q: How do you see your own role in all that, and your future in the institutional Church? And do you have any alternative models of religious community you're presently working on?

A: My aim is really to do as much as I can to facilitate a productive transformation of religious thought, discourse, orientation, and experience, in my own small context, wherever that happens to be—: to help change worldviews, to help change conditioned approaches to myth and religious practice, and to help guide people into deeper experience, both individually and communally. So much of what I do at this point unfolds outside the institutional boundaries of the Church, for reasons that I'm sure will be obvious. The Mystery School of ancestral Celtic wisdom I recently founded, along with some discussion and spiritual practice groups I've been leading the past several years, show promise of a possible sacred context for learning and living that exists outside the perimeters of institutional religion, and isn't at risk of becoming in itself a limiting ideological structure. Perhaps those two models—the Mystery School on the one hand, and the spiritual practice and discussion group on the other—indicate the beginnings of one viable approach to formational, initiatory, and self-sustaining spiritual community for the future. The school brings folks through an initiatory process of deep formation and reorientation, away from the dominant narratives, and helps shape them into spiritual adults; the community of practice receives them simultaneous and subsequent to that process, and gives them a social and vocational context in which to thrive, as well as a supportive structure to help them honor the commitments they've made, to follow out their own quest of transformation and wisdom. Together these two things seem to create a fruitful framework in a culturally rich and nourishing communal setting, free of dogmatism and bureaucracy. But of course it's not the whole picture; the supportive social structure and lifeways have to follow eventually, to make it a viable context of deep-rooted and effective ancestral reclamation. These are experiments to explore ways of authentically and adequately reclaiming traditional models of spiritual formation, initiation, and community, which can function in our present social context and bear transformative fruit. All of us who are concerned with these matters have to be willing, in our own environments, to get together and try on new and ancient models. If we aren't willing to try things, we'll never learn what actually works and what doesn't.

One thing I feel very keenly is that we need to discover together how to rebuild a localized, village-oriented way of life that's sensible and sustainable, not anachronistic or twee, but serious and well considered, structured around an old-world, integrative vision of human life wherein the spiritual and the mundane are seamlessly merged, and the society is soundly framed in all its dimensions with effective, life giving ritual, with rooted sacrality. A socio-cultural framework in which our shamanic functionaries could naturally return, and in which the sanctity of all Life could again become intuitive, organically expressed in our actions, our stories, our ceremonies, our art, our internal and external discourse.

Q: Throughout the book you allude in different ways to the potential presence and use of entheogenic plants or fungi as Sacraments and initiatory tools in ancient cultures—including Celtic cultures. But, in reading it, it felt to me like this was almost a ghost in the darkened halls of the text, left only to vaguely haunt the material—it's never something you come out and talk about at length, or with much reference to specifics, either historically or as something potentially applicable in our own time and place. I'm wondering why that is, and what we should make of it, both with reference to the book itself and also to what you seem to be advocating for in terms of practical reclamation of the archaic technologies you outline.

A: That approach was very intentional, and there are several reasons for it. Firstly, there is still a lot of comparative analysis that needs to be done, in an interdisciplinary fashion, surrounding the possible usage of such Sacraments in ancient Celtic cultures. This is research and writing I've already begun to do, and in fact that will likely form the basis of my next major project.

Secondly, I'm wary (with good evidence, I think) about the potential abuse of sacramental plant medicines in our current cultural context. I feel very strongly that any authentic reclamation of a partnership with those kinds of allies must be done with the utmost care and respect, and in a way that reflects a grounding in deep natural values like reciprocity, acknowledgement of the reality of Otherworld landscapes, and an appropriate seriousness in approaching our potential partners in the unseen realms. Without that foundation—without the narrative, ritual, and symbolic underpinnings that must necessarily frame those relationships and sacramental techniques—an appropriation of such relational gifts could be destructive. I worry about this on multiple levels: physical, psychological, spiritual, and socio-cultural. For instance, the clinical research that's being done now with Psilocybin—: if pharmaceutical companies get a hold of these kinds of medicines, commodify them and sell them as cures for whatever human ills, totally divorced from their naturally occurring forms and contexts, and from the traditional relationships human beings have had with those allies, then troubles will inevitably abound. We must tread very, very lightly with regard to this kind of thing. There is also the highly problematical appropriation of plant or fungal Sacraments with no history of Western usage, and the unwitting colonization that accompanies it—e.g., in South American countries, with the recent craze over Ayahuasca, which has become so rampant. I could probably write a whole book on this alone, but suffice it to say there are many profound problems with it.

Thirdly, all indications from the extant historical and folkloric material show that, in ancient Celtic cultures, the exact identity and usage of these kinds of Sacraments constituted a secret body of knowledge held close by the sacral class, the druids and poet-seers (and possibly the bards as well). And I think there probably was and is good reason for that secrecy, just like there was and is good reason for refusing to codify any sacred teachings in textual form. Trusting the wisdom of the Ancestors, and the guidance I receive from them, I feel bound to honor and uphold these sorts of cultural conventions.

We might reflect here on Pliny's account of the druids ceremonially gathering Mistletoe from the high boughs of sacred Oak trees. That sort of ceremonial gathering of plants with whom the human community has a deep and crucial relationship was clearly performed with loving intentionality, with great care and sensitivity to timing, appropriate ritual gesture, sacrifice, and reciprocal offering. This is true for similar traditions in many ancient cultures. That's the spirit in which we should approach these sorts of questions; it's the only proper, honorable, and respectful way. In fact, I would argue that it's the same spirit in which we must learn again to approach the whole of life. Then we might begin to redeem the project of human cultural endeavor on this planet, and walk once more in Beauty on the living Earth, in harmony with the souls of all our non-human brothers and sisters.

Q: Speaking of ancient religious functionaries, you mention throughout the book the role of the poet-seer (*fili*), and I gather from your website and other materials that this feels to you like a helpful way to identify your own vocation. I'm wondering how that relates to or maybe overlaps with the various aspects of your healing and teaching work. I know you have done shamanic healing work for many years, and also practice now as a Western herbalist, counselor, spiritual director, and teacher. Are those dimensions of the traditional vocation of the poet-seer? And is the poet-seer essentially equivalent to the 'shaman' in other cultures?

A: Historically, the role of the poet-seer does seem to have been a type of shamanic role. The *filidh* were ritualists, seers and diviners, storytellers, poets, healers, and made regular use of trance states, probably often induced by entheogenic plants, by fasting, isolation and other ordeals, as well as by rhythmic chant and possibly bronze bells or other ancient rhythmic instruments. They were also associated with a variety of common shamanic symbols and ritual actions: feathered cloaks, shapeshifting, journeying to other worlds, allying with totem spirits, ancestral communication, magic, and initiatory trials. And surviving in medieval Welsh tradition we find the seer (*awenydd*) as trance-medium, functioning in a manner very similar to shamanic figures from other parts of the world, including shamans of the Siberian milieu still practicing today. This is a very brief summary, but all these things indicate that the poet-seer fits at least broadly into the framework of the perennial shamanic typology.

As far as how this relates to my own vocation: I've discovered over the years that the traditional role of the *fili* provides the most accurate descriptor for who I am and what I've been called to do in this life. I experience it as a very specific ancestral calling. And I certainly don't self-apply this kind of term lightly, or without a continuous sense of the weight and responsibility it brings; though I suppose I do *hold* it lightly, in the sense that I am very cautious about claiming this kind of vocational designation in a socio-cultural environment that completely lacks the traditional understanding and support which would contextualize the role and make it optimally effectual. This is something I'm constantly (and often painfully) aware of. And, as I've said both here and in the book, I do feel that we in the West need our shamanic functionaries back—whatever the cultural specificity of those roles happens to look like, in each cultural tradition. We need to create again the cultural frameworks that give full life and purpose to those roles, because the shamanic witness—which is the archaic ancestral and animistic witness—is the witness we now most desperately need in our world.

There's of course a great deal that needs to be considered—and an appropriate caution applied—when utilizing the word 'shaman' outside its native cultural context, which is Siberian (the term is likely *Tungusic* in origin, though a number of Siberian cultures use it). I use the term in a technical sense, as a pan-cultural descriptor, in the way it's become commonly used in anthropology. But there's been so much cultural insensitivity and appropriation (over the past forty years or so especially), and I am critical of Euro-American folks announcing themselves to be 'shamans' because they've taken a workshop on 'core shamanism' or the like, while having absolutely no connection to—and certainly no vocational call or appropriate initiation within—a traditional culture where those roles are still living and understood. I think it's a much healthier and more effectual approach for European and European-descended peoples who might genuinely feel this kind of calling—that is to say, those who have received a direct calling from the spirits, from the Ancestors, which is the universal requisite—to apply themselves to the difficult work of finding out how their own Ancestors viewed and treated that vocation, and help co-create a new and ancient cultural context in which such a calling could once again make natural sense. Appropriating the cultural traditions of others only damages the culture in question, as well as the one who is doing the appropriating—and it dishonors the Ancestors of both. Reconstructing and reclaiming one's own deep ancestral roots, however, is a work both sacred and fruitful, which, so long as it isn't tied up with political, racial, or nationalistic agendas, can only bring life and healing. And that's a healing that is deeply needed in the West.

Q: In closing, I'd like to ask you about how animism—a worldview you clearly hold and advocate strongly for—relates to the insights of contemplative practice. Many folks who practice meditation or some form of contemplative technique seem to testify to—or at least aspire to—a kind of monistic intuition or experience of reality, in which they are part of one ultimately undivided expanse of consciousness. But an animistic worldview implies a multiplicity or diversity of consciousnesses, rather than one ultimately undifferentiated consciousness. I know you have practiced and taught meditation and other contemplative practices over a long period of time, and I'm wondering how the results of those experiences and ideas align or don't align with the notion, intuition, or experience of an animistic cosmos.

A: The seemingly paradoxical reality in my own experience has been that, in pursuing what has so often been framed as the core aim of 'unitary' experience or consciousness, I was brought back to what feels like a deeper or truer reality of multiplicity. It's almost as if through pursuing the conditioned aim of unified consciousness, over many years of contemplative practice, I was eventually made ready to fully accept and integrate a deeper truth, which I'd always known and experienced. Of course, I can only speak for myself in this, and I would certainly never suggest that anyone else's deep spiritual experiences were in any way lesser or provisional, but for me personally that has been the journey. And while the unitary mode of experience remains as true and resonant as ever for me, those experiences are felt and processed within a larger context of diversity: a vast ecology of souls, and of vibrant relationships with many of those souls.

Q: Was there a particular practice or tool, or some kind of change in your interior orientation, that brought this full integration about? Is there a traceable genesis of that shift in your experience?

A: It feels to me like something that was always there, but which required a deeper clarity, an interior expansiveness, and probably the dying-and-re-birth process of some deep initiations to be fully grasped and integrated. As far as spiritual practices: a majority of the core tools of my personal practice were already in place in my late teens. By about nineteen years old, the overall shape of the toolkit was pretty much established. Perhaps gradually, in the immeasurable sort of way such things take place in the human person, my perception and approach to the spiritual life changed shape, until finally the walls were eroded enough, and the dam broke loose, and the whole thing shifted and opened out into this fully dwelt-in landscape of animistic experience and relationship. But it wasn't really a singular, decisive event where this happened, so it's diffi-cult to trace out in that way. At least from age twelve the intuition of an ensouled cosmos was alive in me, and the experiences I had at that age, and throughout my teens—being visited and 'called' by the Ancestors and other spirits—were foundational; then at age sixteen I had my first training in shamanic techniques of trance induction and healing, and there was some real relational interaction with the spirits in that context; and then there was this long journey of spiritual practice and seeking— with a number of shattering initiations interspersed throughout—where on some level I tried to set the multiplicity and the whole archaic wit-ness of animism aside, to pursue what seemed like the 'deeper' truths of unitary experience, of *theosis*, of *samadhi*, or what have you. The irony, I suppose, is that it turned out that the latter mode of experience didn't reflect a deeper truth, and in pursuing it I was eventually returned to what was there all along: the perception and full embrace of the eternal multiplicity, the call to relationship, to the unending pursuit of wisdom in an endless stream of rebirth. Granted, I returned to all that with new eyes, with a fresh readiness of internal clarity to really receive and fully integrate it into my everyday perception, my personal lifeways, and my work—and also with a lot more knowledge about its place in my ancestral inheritance, about the 'how' and the 'why'.

All that being said, though, I think it's also important to look at the ways in which the experiences of meditation (e.g., Vipassanā, as taught and practiced in Theravada Buddhism) are phenomenologically different from experiences that come, for example, with intensive initiatory crises or with the sacramental usage of entheogenic plants or fungi. These two broad categories of consciousness-expanding tools represent different modes of spiritual technology, different approaches that elicit differing phenomena. They're certainly not mutually exclusive by any stretch—and I've personally employed both approaches for many years—but they do reveal different landscapes, different aspects of ontology and of our subjective experience as human beings. They can inform each other, as my own journey indicates, but we might say they each provide an angle on different facets of reality. And it seems to me that both are needed in some form if we want to make real progress on the path toward legitimate transformation of perception and personhood.

Praxis, at any rate, is the bottom line. When we're talking about spiritual development, existential transformation, the pursuit of wisdom or illumination, we're necessarily talking about altered states of consciousness, because it is only through fundamentally altering our ordinary state of perception, coming to see things through a radically different lens, that we can open the passages that lead to true atonement.